"A marvelous way to enter into the Sunday r[...]
on what a preacher or a Bible commentary [...]
Both are important of course. But just as im[...]
us. The Bible is the Living Word, through wh[...] the Holy Spirit is powerfully
at work. *Ponder* will help both groups and individuals encounter God more
deeply and more fully through the riches of Scripture."

—James Martin, SJ
Author of *Learning to Pray*

"Mahri Leonard-Fleckman has written a beautiful resource for those
seeking contemplative, lectionary-based spirituality grounded in excellent
biblical scholarship. Each unit includes the lectionary texts, along with brief
commentary setting the material within its historical and literary context,
followed by a guided opportunity for reflection, all within a Catholic context.
I recommend this book to parish Bible studies as well as to individuals seeking
quality spiritual approaches to Scripture."

—Corrine Carvalho
Professor of Theology, University of St. Thomas

"*Ponder* is both practical and profound. Mahri Leonard-Fleckman has created
a resource that leads individuals and groups in praying with Scripture. With
a mix of commentary and 'ponder' sections, Leonard-Fleckman shows
attentiveness to biblical scholarship and faith-based biblical study, inspiring
readers to pray with and contemplate Scripture throughout the liturgical year."

—Jaime L. Waters
Associate Professor of Old Testament, Boston College School
of Theology and Ministry

"Strongly rooted in *Lectio Divina* and Ignatian Contemplation, *Ponder* opens
readers to the best of contemporary biblical scholarship and some of the best
Christian meditative practices for a deeper reading of Sacred Scripture. Leonard-
Fleckman's attention to the text's key words offers her audience profound insight
into the readings, and her highlighting of both Catholic and Jewish tradition
brings today's readers into dialogue with the richness of the past. I highly
recommend this most fruitful tool for a richer reading of God's Word."

—Garrett Galvin, OFM
President and Associate Professor of Sacred Scripture, Franciscan
School of Theology

"In *Ponder: Contemplative Bible Study for Year A*, Mahri Leonard-Fleckman draws on Ignatian spirituality and *Lectio Divina* to create an engaging model for the study of the Sunday readings, attending to the important details of the passages and encouraging personal engagement with Scripture."

—Laurie Brink, OP
Professor of New Testament Studies and Director of the Certificate in Biblical Spirituality, Catholic Theological Union

"Our Small Church Community selected *Ponder* because of its flexibility for reflecting together on the Sunday readings. The 'ponder' section at the end of each Sunday's material allows us to move from meditation to action with the question: *How will we live differently after meditating on the readings?* The commentary providing the historical and theological context of the readings is another important feature, allowing us to look at the world behind the text in addition to how we personally respond to Scripture passages. *Ponder* is a rich, practical, and easy-to-use resource for building small communities of fellowship and faith."

—Sandra Rueb
St. Thomas More Small Church Community at Yale University

Ponder

CONTEMPLATIVE BIBLE STUDY
FOR YEAR A

MAHRI LEONARD-FLECKMAN

Little Rock
Scripture Study

LITURGICAL PRESS
Collegeville, Minnesota

www.littlerockscripture.org

Nihil Obstat: Reverend Robert Harren, J.C.L., *Censor deputatus.*

Imprimatur: ✠ Most Reverend Donald J. Kettler, J.C.L., Bishop of Saint Cloud, March 3, 2022.

Cover design by Amy Marc. Cover art courtesy of Getty Images.

1	2	3	4	5	6	7	8	9

Library of Congress Cataloging-in-Publication Data

Names: Leonard-Fleckman, Mahri, author.
Title: Ponder : contemplative Bible study / Mahri Leonard-Fleckman.
Description: Collegeville, Minnesota : Liturgical Press, 2020- | Contents: Year A | Summary: "Ponder: Contemplative Bible Study for Year A is the third book in a three-volume series designed to accompany hearers and preachers of the Word as they pray with and ponder the Sunday readings throughout the liturgical year. The Sunday readings are provided, along with brief commentary, reflections, and guidance on how to use this resource alone or with a group"— Provided by publisher.
Identifiers: LCCN 2020015109 (print) | LCCN 2020015110 (ebook) | ISBN 9780814665824 (Year A : epub) | ISBN 9780814665008 (Year B : paperback) | ISBN 9780814665572 (Year A : paperback) | ISBN 9780814665824 (Year A : mobi) | ISBN 9780814665824 (Year A : pdf) | ISBN 9780814665251 (Year B : epub) | ISBN 9780814665251 (Year B : mobi) | ISBN 9780814665251 (Year B : pdf) | ISBN 9780814665589 (Year C : paperback) | ISBN 9780814665831 (Year C : epub) | ISBN 9780814665831 (Year C : mobi) | ISBN 9780814665831 (Year C : pdf)
Subjects: LCSH: Church year meditations. | Bible—Meditations. | Catholic Church—Prayers and devotions. | Catholic Church. Lectionary for Mass (U.S.)
Classification: LCC BX2170.C55 L46 2020 (print) | LCC BX2170.C55 (ebook) | DDC 242/.3—dc23
LC record available at https://lccn.loc.gov/2020015109
LC ebook record available at https://lccn.loc.gov/2020015110

To Amy Ekeh,
editor extraordinaire,
with gratitude for her care and devotion
in transforming *Ponder* from prayer to book.

*"Were not our hearts burning within us while he spoke to us
on the way and opened the Scriptures to us?"*

Luke 24:32

Contents

Season of Easter

Ordinary Time

Acknowledgments

In the summer of 2012, I attended my first international meeting of the Catholic Biblical Association of America. I was overwhelmed. The conference was held at Notre Dame—which seemed a formidable place at the time—and I was an introverted graduate student. I remember escaping down to the book exhibit one afternoon for a moment of quiet. As chance (or providence) would have it, I met Mary Stommes, the editor of *Give Us This Day.* She was kind and gracious, and after talking for a while, she invited me to write for the publication. That moment marked the beginning of my relationship with Liturgical Press, for which I am deeply grateful.

I wish to thank all the wonderful editors at Lit Press who have made this project possible. Peter Dwyer believed in the idea of *Ponder* at an early stage and worked hard with me to craft the proposal. I must also express my thanks to Hans Christoffersen, whose presence through the years has been important in so many other ways, especially in his dedication to the Wisdom Commentary series. And to Mary Stommes, who first brought me into the fold: thank you. Liturgical Press feels like a family to me; I am honored to be part of it.

Outside of Liturgical Press, I also wish to thank the Rev. William Campbell, SJ, who read the Introduction to the manuscript when it was still in the beginning stages and whose insights and suggestions have been invaluable.

Above all, my deepest thanks go to the members of the Bible study at St. John's parish in Worcester, Massachusetts, for praying *Ponder* into being with me. We began our Bible study in the fall of 2014, and it continues to live on in these pages.

As I draw this project to a close, I dedicate this third and final volume of *Ponder* to my editor Amy Ekeh, whom I have come to trust completely and to whom I am indebted for giving shape and texture to this project over the years. For her wisdom and discernment, her sharp editorial eye, her incredible care for this project, and above all, her friendship, I express my heartfelt appreciation.

Introduction

Our Roots: St. John's Bible Study or "Neighborhood"

To explain the goals and format of this Bible study, let me first describe its roots, the community from which it emerged. It began at St. John's Catholic Church, a mid-nineteenth-century parish that is known historically as the "mother church" of Worcester in central Massachusetts. It is a flourishing, gritty, downtown parish that draws a rich and diverse mix of people. Its mission is to serve the poor, and it hosts the largest daily soup kitchen in the city. St. John's also hosts thriving devotions, including its yearly Novena of Grace in Honor of Saint Francis Xavier, also called "The Lenten Retreat of the City of Worcester."

The rectory next door is a sprawling building that once housed priests in the diocese and now provides transitional sober housing for men. The setting for our weekly Bible study is the rectory dining room, a tired but dignified space. We gather at a well-worn table with old, wide, high-backed armchairs. The dining room sits just behind the Worcester train station, close enough that in summer evenings with the windows open, we have to shout to hear ourselves above the sound of trains pulling in and out. In the winter, the old furnace pumps out enough heat directly into the dining room to give us heat stroke, while the rest of the house remains drafty.

We gather after Mass on Tuesday evenings for one hour. Ours is a simple, drop-in, lectionary-based study that regularly gathers five to fifteen people. I provide a handout with the readings for the upcoming Sunday and some corresponding notes. Together, we pray with and then discuss one of the readings, sometimes two, then offer up communal prayers and go on our way.

The group that has been meeting for the past five years, in shifting forms and combinations, is a ragtag community, a mismatch of members. What unites us is our faith. Generally, we are Roman Catholic. Many of us would not rub shoulders outside the Bible study, excepting perhaps sporadic handshakes in the pews. One member (Matthew) called our Bible study a "neighborhood" of bracing experiences and ideals, as distinguished from the "mutual admiration and unchallenged agreement" that so often marks the sameness of the people we choose to socialize with. "As it is with the neighborhood," said Matthew, "so it is with the Bible study."[1]

And so it is. When gathering each week, one never knows who will show up or what the discussion dynamics will be. Lord knows, sometimes the results aren't pretty! Yet we come back and try again. We are conservative, liberal, and moderate. We range in age from our twenties to our eighties. We are blue collar and white collar, jobless, retired, and working. Over the years, some of our participants have had homes to live in and others have not. Some of us come with mental or physical illnesses or histories of addiction. Our pastor attends regularly to prepare for Sunday's homily. And I, the Bible scholar, "lead" the group, but the term is loose. When I am unable to make it (which once lasted a full year while I was teaching out of state), other members step in and guide the group with only the aid of the weekly handout.

Over the years, some members of the St. John's Bible Study have carefully collected these handouts in order to have a full, three-year set. Returning to earlier handouts years later, I find myself surprised by how much I gain from these notes and reflections, as if they were written by someone else. They have become a rich, ongoing treasure in my own personal prayer life. Now that these handouts have been gathered together into this series of books, I hope they may become a valuable resource in your prayer life too.

The Format

To truly understand this study and the flexibility it offers to individuals or groups, I invite you to use your liturgical imagination. The format on the following pages is simple. Some would perhaps even

---

1. Matthew was reflecting on and quoting from Christopher Lasch's *Revolt of the Elites and the Betrayal of Democracy* (New York; London: W.W. Norton & Company, 1996), in particular Lasch's discussion of "communities" of like-minded people versus "neighborhoods" in which people meet as equals, without regard to race, class, or national origins (Lasch, 117, 119–21).

consider it simplistic, though this perception would be misguided. Most importantly, the simplicity of the format allows for freedom and independence of prayer and study. First, I provide the entirety of Sunday's readings so that participants have easy access to the texts without having to consult additional Bibles or missalettes. Only the psalm is missing, not because it is less important, but for issues of space. Having the readings easily accessible has proven invaluable in our own slightly chaotic parish, where the notion of ordering extra Bibles and somehow keeping them together in one space is daunting.

Under each reading are my commentary notes. These notes provide some basic background and information about the readings. The goal is not to lead readers into viewing the texts a certain way (in other words, my way), but to invite readers into their own deep knowledge of the texts, a kind of full-bodied understanding that I like to call "bone knowledge." Therefore, these notes are streamlined to create minimal mental clutter. They include historical and literary context, discussions of translation choices from the Hebrew or Greek (sometimes Aramaic), the broader contexts from the surrounding passages and books, and references to other Sunday readings. In these short summaries, I have distilled my own ideas, in consultation with commentaries and study Bibles, into what I consider to be the most pertinent information for a wide-ranging audience.

Finally, I include a section called "Ponder" that provides possible connections, essential ideas, or ongoing questions to consider from the texts. I have placed these last so as not to overly influence participants at the outset of the study; the goal is to refrain from reading them as long as necessary. This section, connected with the commentary notes below each reading, may be particularly helpful for those who lead the Bible study or are preparing to preach.

Together, the readings, notes, and "ponderings" provide a valuable yet simple tool for ongoing prayer and study. They also create a sort of Sunday missalette that some of our Bible study members take into the pews on Sunday for continued prayer and thoughtful preparation.

Union of Heart and Mind

As for the core principle of this Bible study, it is simple: union of heart and mind. The study takes the words of Vatican II's *Dei Verbum* seriously: Scripture, "the force and power of the word of God," is so great that it stands as "the church's support and strength, imparting robustness to the faith of its daughters and sons and providing food for their souls. It is a pure and unfailing fount of spiritual life."[2] This Bible study is, first and foremost, a practice in gaining intimacy with God through intimacy with our sacred texts. It is to learn to trust our ability to hear God speak to us with great love through Scripture, and to become increasingly comfortable opening our hearts and minds to hear God's word. We gain this intimacy by full-bodied attention to the text, just as love of God calls for the full-bodied union of heart, spirit, mind, and strength (Mark 12:30).[3] Through prayer and study of Scripture, then, the goal of this study is that each of us knows, deeply and profoundly, that the Scriptures are "nourishment" which "enlightens" our minds, "strengthens" our wills, and "fires [our] hearts . . . with the love of God."[4]

As a Hebrew Bible scholar,[5] I must admit that I find this distinction between "mind" and "heart" woolly. There is no word for "mind" in the Hebrew Bible, and in the ancient world there was little use for that messy jumble inside our heads. Rather, the ancient Israelites were an embodied people. Everything was rooted in felt experience, including thinking. When we read the term "mind" in our translated Hebrew Bibles, the literal term in Hebrew is most often "heart" or "spirit." Sometimes it is even liver, intestines or "kidneys," as in Psalm 26:2, which translates literally, "Examine me, LORD, and test me, search my kidneys and my heart." According to this ancient people, the heart was the seat of all knowledge. Our intentionality and thinking, our

2. Dogmatic Constitution on Divine Revelation, *Dei Verbum* (November 18, 1965) 21, in Austin Flannery, ed., *Vatican Council II: Constitutions, Decrees, Declarations; The Basic Sixteen Documents* (Collegeville, MN: Liturgical Press, 2014).

3. The word for "mind" in Mark 12:30, *dianoia*, also translates as "intention" or "purpose." Mark's Gospel draws from Deut 6:5, which translates literally from the Hebrew as: "You shall love YHWH your God with all your heart, with all your life force, and with all your muchness." The Gospel adds "mind" to the list of faculties.

4. *Dei Verbum* 23.

5. I use the phrase "Hebrew Bible" rather than "Old Testament" intentionally. Though an imperfect expression, for me it reflects the reality that this inspired corpus of texts is considered holy for both Jews and Christians. As Christians, we use the expression "Old Testament" to reflect our commitment to both the Old and New Testaments. For Jews, we simply refer to "the Bible" or, more specifically, the Tanakh (the Torah or "teaching," the Prophets, and the Writings).

ability to follow God's teachings comes from within our "inmost being," as knowledge "inscribed upon the heart" (cf. Jer 31:33).

In our contemporary world, saturated as it is with studies of the mind, mindfulness, and mental training, I find myself leaning back into this ancient worldview of the heart as the seat of knowledge (don't tell my neuroscientist husband!). Particularly in a Bible study focused on genuine connection to and understanding of the text, personal experience and prayer are crucial starting points. This heart-centered practice then leads to more careful, authentic reading and attention. In this Bible study, the movement from heart to mind often happens organically, the most thoughtful ideas and challenging questions emerging from a strong grounding in prayer. And this is not a practice that I subscribe to only with Bible study. I have found that even in my own more cerebral, scholarly work, some of the best intellectual questions and insights bubble up organically while marinating in heart-centered reflection.

The Heart

That said, we begin our Bible study by praying with a Scripture text. This period sometimes takes twenty minutes; sometimes it leads to reflections that take up the majority of the hour. We choose one of the Sunday readings and, without introduction, read and pray with it together. Further below, you'll find the specific instructions that we use to guide our Bible study sessions. Here, I'll describe the two key forms of prayer that our group uses: *Lectio Divina* and Ignatian Contemplation.

Lectio Divina

This ancient form of Christian prayer translates imperfectly as "Divine Reading." It is a tool for recollection, contemplation, and, ultimately, resting in God. In group *Lectio Divina*, we begin by having a participant read one of the Sunday texts aloud, slowly and prayerfully. (If done as personal prayer outside of a group, the person reads the text on their own in the same way, though with greater freedom to stop, linger, and contemplate or "chew" on any words, phrases, or images that come to mind.) As we listen for the first time in the group, we open our hearts to the text, listening as if we have never heard it before, entering into it with curiosity and imagination. Trusting that the Holy Spirit guides us, we allow it to break open and speak to us. After the first read-through of the text and a moment of silence, we go around the room and share a word or phrase that especially struck us (we say *only* the word or phrase, without further explanation). Participants can always simply say "pass" when their turn comes. One of the gems that comes from this group practice is the creation of a prayer or litany in the repetition of certain words or phrases as we move around the room (again, without any additional commentary).

After this first read-through and response, we repeat, this time with a different voice. (It's important to have distinct and diverse voices throughout the process.) This second person reads the same passage again, slowly and meditatively. As they do so, we continue to sink into the text, digesting it. Perhaps we linger on the word or phrase we heard in the first read-through of the text. Perhaps another insight presents itself to us. After another moment of silence following the reading, we may go around the room again and take turns offering heart-based reflections on how the text spoke to us, or we may simply open up the space for these reflections in a less-structured way, as participants feel pulled to speak.

Another way of describing "heart-based" here is "experience-based." In other words, people speak from their *personal experience* of the text, saving the intellectual questions and ideas for later. Examples of experience-based reflections include what thoughts or feelings arose in the person while praying with the text, how the text spoke to them personally, how a particular phrase struck them, etc.

This process is a shortened form of group *Lectio Divina*, the full practice of which often includes three repetitions of the same passage: the first for hearing a word or a phrase, the second for listening for how God speaks to us, and the third for hearing an invitation, or how God calls or invites us to live and act. Sometimes, our group chooses to do a third reading of the same passage, but I have found that in a one-hour period, reading the selected passage twice is enough to ground us firmly enough in our hearts and personal experiences before moving on.

Further Resources

Casey, Michael. *Sacred Reading: The Ancient Art of Lectio Divina*. Liguori: Liguori/Triumph, 1995.

Hall, Thelma, r.c. *Too Deep for Words: Rediscovering Lectio Divina.* New York: Paulist Press, 1998.

Pennington, M. Basil. *Lectio Divina: Renewing the Ancient Practice of Praying the Scriptures.* New York: Crossroads, 1998.

Ignatian Contemplation

Some of the passages that we read, especially Gospel passages as well as some stories in the Hebrew Bible, are conducive to Ignatian Contemplation. According to Ignatian spirituality, one of many ways that God speaks to us is through the imagination. The imagination becomes a tool to tap into our natural curiosity, to enter into a text and experience it in a fresh way, and to pay attention to the sometimes subtle ways that God meets us and invites us through this practice. Ignatian spirituality is not disconnected from *Lectio Divina*, which similarly invites us to curiosity, imagination, and contemplation. Both assume cooperation with and guidance by the Holy Spirit, whom we invite into the practice. Yet the tools in Ignatian spirituality are more precise and particular in terms of active engagement in and through a passage.

In our Bible study, then, when a text is particularly promising for engaging the imagination, I offer this tool to participants in our second reading of a text. I invite the group to enter into a scene and to notice every detail. I tell them to notice the sights, the smells, the sounds, the feel of the scene. I invite them to linger on the people, those described in the text as well as those who go unseen, unnoticed. I invite them to lose themselves in the scene and perhaps to become part of it. Perhaps they become an observer, an anonymous member of a crowd, a disciple, or a prophet. As they use their imaginations, I invite them to consider how God is speaking to them and calling to them through the text. My friend and spiritual director uses the expression "daydream as prayer" to describe how the imagination can become prayer when we are open to and trust the Spirit's guidance.[6]

After the second read-through, we open up the space as usual for sharing around the table. Reflections on this Ignatian practice will often arise naturally. At times, after the reflection period is over, I will ask further questions of the group, such as where they found

6. My thanks to Rev. William Campbell, SJ, for this insight.

themselves in the scene, and what insights or questions this vantage point gave to them.

Further Resources

Barry, William, SJ. *Letting God Come Close: An Approach to the Ignatian Spiritual Exercises.* Chicago: Loyola, 2011.

Martin, James, SJ. *The Jesuit Guide to (Almost) Everything: A Spirituality for Real Life.* New York: HarperCollins, 2012.

O'Brien, Kevin, SJ. *The Ignatian Adventure: Experiencing the Spiritual Exercises of St. Ignatius in Daily Life.* Chicago: Loyola, 2011.

The Mind

At some natural transition point, our group moves from sharing our reflections after the second reading (a time when we allow one another to speak, but without responding or entering into discussion) to open, more intellectual discussion about the text. At this point, the commentary notes can be helpful as an aid for context and meaning. I would suggest waiting until the very end of your time together to explore the notes in the "Ponder" section as a group, or even refraining from reading them altogether. These final "ponderings" can be useful for ongoing personal reflection and exploration during the week. Yet each Bible study group should feel the freedom to follow its own format as needed.

As for leaders or group facilitators, you may consider reading over the commentary notes and even the final "Ponder" section in preparation for the Bible study. Some of the Bible study leaders at St. John's have told me that they like to go into the Bible study unprepared and learn alongside the group (and these are leaders without any formal training in Scripture). The most important task for the leader in this second half of the Bible study is to keep people focused on the text; I have found that when we shift from prayer to "study," a common tendency is to move away from the text altogether and begin to speak in theological generalities or platitudes rather than remaining grounded in the passage. As a Bible study leader, I often find that my role is less "leader" and more "nagger," whose main task is to remind people to allow the text to guide their thinking, rather than to place their thinking on the text. My most common comments at this stage are: "Let's remember to stay focused on the text"; "Where do you see that in the text?"; or, "That's an interesting theological statement, but what does the text say?" For example, we may like to talk about God as "all-knowing," but in the creation stories of Genesis 1–11, God seems to be constantly surprised by the outcome of creation (particularly the messiness of humans) and slowly figuring out what to do as a result. Remember that theology cleans up what the Bible often leaves untidy. Our goal is to give the text its space to speak, even to the "untidiness" of God's word and our lives.

In closing, I hope that you will find this Bible study life-giving. Personally, as a scholar, I don't often have the opportunity to bridge serious scholarship with personal prayer and a community of faith. In writing this Bible study, I have been grateful for the opportunity to do just this sort of bridging between scholarship, prayer, and practice. I have done my very best to sink into the weekly readings, to pray with the texts and present them as authentically as I possibly can. I pray that you enjoy this pondering, and that our great God draws you closer through the words on the following pages.

Mahri Leonard-Fleckman, PhD
College of the Holy Cross
Worcester, MA

How to Use this Study—Groups

A basic "how-to guide" can be found on the inside front cover of this book, but the following description will provide more detailed guidance. Of course, you should feel free to adapt the following approach as needed to suit the needs, time constraints, and temperament of your group.

Silence. The group leader may invite everyone to settle into silence and come home to God if they've been "away" for a while. Remind the group that God is always present. Allow silence to take root for several long moments.

Opening Prayer. You will find an Opening Prayer on the inside front cover of this book.[1] You may wish to say this together, or your group may choose an alternative Opening Prayer.

Lectio Divina **(20–30 min.).** Choose one of the Sunday readings (the first reading, the second reading, or the Gospel) and two people from your group to read. At this point, the group leader may wish to offer an invitation such as the following: "In this reading of our text, I invite us to open our hearts to this passage, to be curious, and to listen as if we've never heard this passage before. I invite us to listen, in particular, for a word or phrase that speaks to us today. At the end of the reading, we'll go around the room and simply speak our words or phrases out loud, without any explanation. As always, when your turn comes, you can simply pass."

Read the text slowly. One of the readers reads the selected text slowly and meditatively. The group listens for a word or phrase that especially speaks to them.

Share a word or phrase. After a moment of silence, group members speak their words or phrases out loud with no elaboration or discussion (or they may "pass"). Savor this litany of shared words.

---

1. The opening prayer is my translation of Psalm 19:15 (v. 14 in some English translations).

Read the text a second time. The second reader now reads the same text slowly and meditatively. The group continues to sink into the text and ponder the word or phrase they have heard, listening for how God might be speaking to or calling them.

Engage in Ignatian Contemplation if desired. At this point, if the text is conducive to an imaginative exercise, your group may engage in Ignatian Contemplation. Using the method for Ignatian Contemplation described above, the group leader may invite participants into the scene.

Share experience-based reflections. After a moment of silence, participants can share their thoughts and reflections on the text. Allow everyone to speak as prompted by the Spirit. At times, it may be helpful for the group leader to remind participants to stay in their hearts and leave any intellectual questions aside for the moment. The leader may also need to steer the sharing away from discussion and debate, keeping everyone focused on the text. Allow this sharing to continue until a natural stopping point.

Bible Study (20–30 min.). At this point, your group can move into the Bible "study" portion of your time together. Invite participants to move from "heart" to "mind." Begin with discussing the reading you selected for *Lectio Divina,* but feel free to explore other readings if you exhaust your discussion of the originally selected text. Your group may wish to read the commentary notes together and discuss any lingering questions or insights. Along the way, you may need to remind the group to stay rooted in the text (see notes above on "The Mind").

Ponder. Hold off on this section for as long as possible—or even avoid it altogether—so that participants can use this material for further pondering of the Sunday readings throughout the week.

Closing Prayer. At the end of the hour, draw the discussion to a natural close. Invite the group to join in prayer with an invitation such as: "For what shall we pray tonight?" After prayers are offered, you may offer a conclusion such as: "For these prayers that we speak out loud, and for those that we hold in the silence of our hearts, we pray together in the words that Jesus taught us." Join together in praying the "Our Father."

How to Use this Study—Individuals

For those using this study as individuals, you may find the group guide helpful, but the flow will be much freer and up to the movement of the Spirit. You will essentially follow the steps for individual practice of *Lectio Divina*. There are four parts to this practice: *lectio* (reading), *meditatio* (meditation), *oratio* (prayer), and *contemplatio* (contemplation). For further resources and explanation, see the above descriptions for *Lectio Divina* and Ignatian Contemplation.

Begin by finding a quiet and comfortable space. Often, people find that committing to a specific place for daily prayer, whether a particular chair or room, or perhaps even a specific church pew, can be conducive to regular practice. You may want to set a timer for your prayer period. I used to pray in the pews for twenty minutes before Mass, so the beginning of the Mass became my natural "timer."

I would suggest picking one text (or a part of a text) for your prayer period. Don't attempt to go beyond that reading, unless you are strongly pulled to do so. Before beginning, open with a prayer or an intention for your prayer period. Then begin by reading the text slowly and meditatively. Do not try to get through the entire reading! Allow yourself to stop on any word, phrase, or image that strikes you. Rather than trying to move on quickly, stop and "sit" with this word or phrase. Marinate in it. Ingest it as a cow might chew its cud, chewing and swallowing, regurgitating and re-chewing to swallow again. This is the practice of *meditatio* or meditating on Scripture. If the imagery is particularly vivid, you might also find yourself drawn to Ignatian Contemplation, allowing your imagination to draw you into the scene and play with the word or image.

As you see fit, allow this practice of *meditatio* to open you to pray with God (*oratio*). You might reflect on why you were drawn to a particular word, phrase, or imagery. You might reflect on how God is speaking to you through the text. You may find yourself praying aloud or silently to God. You may experience God calling you to a particular form of action or "being" through the word. You may simply feel God's presence.

The ultimate aim of this practice is to lead you to *contemplatio,* the practice of stillness or resting in God. Prayer is a winding ladder that we ascend and descend regularly, and this last stage is up to God's grace that helps draw you further and further into the quiet and stillness. This sense of interior stillness is what we call "recollection," when the mind and the senses become quiet and focused on listening to God. *Contemplatio* does not always happen. Yet praying with Scripture is ultimately about intimacy with God, and this stillness before God, this practice of *listening* rather than speaking to God, is the deepest form of intimacy.

During this period of prayer, you may end up praying through the entire passage. Or, you may never make it through the first verse. Just remember that there are no set "rules," and there is nothing to accomplish! You may spend the entire time meditating on a particular word. You may end up speaking to God about something on your heart and mind. You may never make it to *contemplatio.* You may even end up feeling like the whole time was a waste. Don't worry; this is all part of the practice! Even if the prayer period felt difficult or dry, like nothing was happening, trust that God was present. The fact that you made time for prayer reveals your desire and God's desire working through you. That is enough.

As you finish your period of prayer, take a few moments to re-orient yourself slowly. You might take a few moments simply to sit silently, and to express gratitude for the time. Whatever you do, be sure to close with a prayer. In group *Lectio Divina,* we pray the "Our Father" together. On your own, you may be drawn toward another prayer that feels more authentically yours.

As you shift from this heart-centered practice, you may be drawn to integrate the heart with the mind by reading the commentary notes under your passage. I would suggest waiting on these notes until you are finished with your period of prayer, though some may find that beginning with the commentary notes are helpful for sinking into prayer. You may also be drawn to peruse the other readings and consider how the readings are meant to fit together. Or perhaps you wish to remain in the heart and ponder further, in which case I would suggest reading the "Ponder" sections, which are created for deeper reflection on the readings.

Above all, remember that the format of this Bible study is open and flexible. How you use it is entirely up to you and the movement of the Spirit.

About the Sunday Readings

As you engage in this lectionary-based study, it may be useful to review the types of readings we hear proclaimed each Sunday and to have a sense of how these readings are selected.

As you probably know, the Sunday readings are on a three-year cycle: Years A, B, and C. You can easily orient yourself to the current liturgical year with some simple math. Year C is always divisible by three. So, for example, the year 2022 is divisible by three and is therefore Year C. (You can quickly determine this by adding the digits of the year together and dividing by three. No need to do long division!) Once you locate Year C, you can determine that the previous year is Year B, and the following year is Year A. Note that the liturgical year begins with the First Sunday of Advent of the prior year. So, in our example above, Year C (2022) actually begins with Advent of 2021.

You will find a volume of *Ponder: Contemplative Bible Study* published for each liturgical year: A, B, and C.

Now let's turn to the structure of each Sunday. During the Liturgy of the Word at each Sunday Mass, we hear a series of four readings:

1. **The first reading** is taken from the Hebrew Bible (the Christian Old Testament). This reading is selected to correspond with the Gospel reading for the day, so it may come from anywhere in the Hebrew Bible. We have no "semi-continuous" readings of a single book in the Hebrew Bible on Sundays (semi-continuous means that a reading continues from what was read the previous Sunday, though often skipping over verses or even chapters to do so). This lack of continuity is one reason why Christians lack familiarity with the Hebrew Bible. (Note that during the Easter season, the first reading comes from a New Testament book: The Acts of the Apostles.)

2. **The responsorial psalm.** The psalm, which is often sung, is intended to be a *response* to the first reading. Its theme may tie directly into a theme of the first reading. For space purposes (not for lack of importance!), we have not included the full text of the Sunday psalm, but you will find the reference if you wish to look it up.

3. **The second reading** is taken from the New Testament, usually from one of Paul's letters. Unlike the first reading, this reading is semi-continuous. While we do not typically read an entire New Testament letter, we may read large sections of one letter over the course of multiple weeks. This also means that, unlike the first reading, the second reading may or may not clearly correspond with the Gospel reading.

4. **The Gospel.** The Sunday Gospel readings in Year A feature the Gospel of Matthew; Year B features Mark; and Year C features Luke. The Gospel of John is sprinkled throughout the three years, mostly during the Lent and Easter seasons (except in the case of Year B, in which we have more readings from John's Gospel because Mark's Gospel is relatively short and doesn't fill the entire year). The Gospel readings are fairly continuous, but we do not read the entire Gospel from beginning to end.

Navigating the Church Year

It may be helpful to have a basic understanding of the church's liturgical calendar as you navigate this book from Sunday to Sunday.

We begin the liturgical year with Advent and Christmas, followed by a period of Ordinary Time (I). Next come Lent and Easter, followed by another period of Ordinary Time (II). Because the number of Sundays in Ordinary Time I and II differs from year to year (due to variation in the dating of Easter), Ordinary Time is organized in a single section in this book.

The following guide will help you navigate your way through the year.

Season of Advent	Four Sundays of Advent
Season of Christmas	From Christmas Day through The Baptism of the Lord
Ordinary Time I	**4-8 WEEKS** From the Second Sunday in Ordinary Time through the Sunday in Ordinary Time that falls before Ash Wednesday
Season of Lent	Five Sundays of Lent and Palm Sunday
Season of Easter	From Easter Day through Pentecost Sunday
Ordinary Time II	**APPROXIMATELY 6 MONTHS** Begins with Most Holy Trinity and Most Holy Body and Blood of Christ (Corpus Christi).

Ordinary Time II picks up
where Ordinary Time I leaves off
(though often skipping a few Sundays
in Ordinary Time
due to variation in the calendar).
The season concludes with Our Lord Jesus
Christ, King of the Universe.

Here's another useful tip: if you aren't sure how to locate the current Sunday in the liturgical year, you can consult the daily readings calendar at usccb.org. Each day of the church year is clearly identified, and the lectionary readings are provided.

First Sunday of Advent

This is what Isaiah, son of Amoz,
    saw concerning Judah and Jerusalem.
      In days to come,
    the mountain of the LORD's house
      shall be established as the highest mountain
      and raised above the hills.
    All nations shall stream toward it;
      many peoples shall come and say:
    "Come, let us climb the LORD's mountain,
      to the house of the God of Jacob,
    that he may instruct us in his ways,
      and we may walk in his paths."
    For from Zion shall go forth instruction,
      and the word of the LORD from Jerusalem.
    He shall judge between the nations,
      and impose terms on many peoples.
    They shall beat their swords into plowshares
      and their spears into pruning hooks;
    one nation shall not raise the sword against another,
      nor shall they train for war again.
    O house of Jacob, come,
      let us walk in the light of the LORD!

During the Advent season, our first readings draw largely from Israel's prophets. This year, Isaiah will guide us through all four Sundays of Advent. Isaiah is the longest prophetic book of the Hebrew Bible (66 chaps.), and scholars widely agree that it was composed during two or three historical periods. The prophet Isaiah wrote the first half, or "First Isaiah" (chaps. 1–39), during the latter half of the eighth century BCE in Judah. The second part, or "Second Isaiah" (chaps. 40–55), is the work of an anonymous prophet or community of prophets living in Babylon toward the end of Judah's exile to Babylon (the late sixth century BCE). The final eleven chapters, or "Third Isaiah" (chaps. 56–66), were perhaps written even later, during the Persian Period in Jerusalem (late sixth to early fourth centuries BCE). Our reading comes from Isaiah's staggering vision of peace and justice in the beginning of the book. Isaiah prophesies that one day, Israel's God will be recognized as the one true God of all the nations. From the ends of the known world, people will stream to the "mountain" of God's "house" (temple), Jerusalem (also called "Zion"). From Zion will go forth "instruction" or "teachings" (Hebrew *tôrâ* or Torah). All people will follow the Torah, the laws and teachings that originally marked the unique and sacred relationship between God and Israel alone (see Exod 19:1-6).

RESPONSORIAL PSALM   PSALM 122:1-2, 3-4, 4-5, 6-7, 8-9

Let us go rejoicing to the house of the Lord.

SECOND READING   ROMANS 13:11-14

Brothers and sisters:
You know the time;
    it is the hour now for you to awake from sleep.
For our salvation is nearer now than when we first believed;
    the night is advanced, the day is at hand.
Let us then throw off the works of darkness
    and put on the armor of light;
    let us conduct ourselves properly as in the day,
    not in orgies and drunkenness,
    not in promiscuity and lust,
    not in rivalry and jealousy.
But put on the Lord Jesus Christ,
    and make no provision for the desires of the flesh.

Paul's letter to the Romans is a key text this liturgical year, as we will read from it during Advent, Lent, and throughout Ordinary Time (from the Ninth through the Twenty-Fourth Weeks in Ordinary Time). Likely Paul's last (existing) letter before his death, it is named for the community of believers in Rome, a community that Paul himself did not establish. Scholars often refer to this letter as Paul's magnum opus, his theological masterpiece on the gospel message of salvation through Jesus Christ. The letter reflects Paul's deep concern for his people, the Jews, as well as the tension created in Rome in the late 50s CE by the various dynamics between Jewish-Christians, Gentile believers, and Jews who did not believe in Christ. In this portion of the letter, Paul describes how believers are already living into the end times. Paul envisions the present reality and the coming future age collapsing into each other, for the end times have already begun through Christ's death and resurrection. Light and darkness symbolize good and evil, and the "armor of light" is Jesus Christ. Elsewhere in the New Testament, armor is a symbol of salvation, faith, and love (e.g., Eph 6:13; 1 Thess 5:8). Through baptism, believers have already "put on" or clothed themselves in Christ, yet this reality must be lived into and borne out in one's actions. Like our Gospel passage, Paul uses the metaphor of waking versus sleeping as part of his instructions for preparing for Christ.

GOSPEL   MATTHEW 24:37-44

Jesus said to his disciples:
"As it was in the days of Noah,
    so it will be at the coming of the Son of Man.
In those days before the flood,
    they were eating and drinking,
    marrying and giving in marriage,
    up to the day that Noah entered the ark.
They did not know until the flood came and carried them all away.
So will it be also at the coming of the Son of Man.
Two men will be out in the field;
    one will be taken, and one will be left.
Two women will be grinding at the mill;
    one will be taken, and one will be left.
Therefore, stay awake!
For you do not know on which day your Lord will come.
Be sure of this: if the master of the house
    had known the hour of night when the thief was coming,
    he would have stayed awake
    and not let his house be broken into.
So too, you also must be prepared,
    for at an hour you do not expect, the Son of Man will come."

This Sunday, we begin our journey through the Gospel of Matthew, which was likely written in the 80s CE. Matthew was a Jewish believer, and his Gospel draws extensively from the Hebrew Bible (his Scriptures) to make his claims about Jesus. Matthew's Gospel has also frequently been used for Christian catechesis, in large part because it contains many of Jesus's most prominent teachings, not least of which is the Sermon on the Mount (Matt 5–7). Matthew's Gospel also contains a unique account of Jesus's birth that begins with a long and important genealogy linking Jesus back to Abraham (see the readings for the Christmas Vigil Mass). It is perhaps for this reason that the Gospel of Matthew is the first book of the New Testament, for more than any other Gospel, it acts as a bridge from the Hebrew Bible. This Sunday, however, we focus not on the beginning of the Gospel but on the end. Jesus is in the midst of instructing his disciples to stay vigilant in preparation for his return (the return of the "Son of Man"). Like the flood (Gen 6–8), this return will take people by surprise while they are absorbed in other tasks and will expose their interior characters. Jesus illustrates this with examples of two people who seem alike externally, yet only one is prepared internally. As we enter the Advent season, the message is simple: we are to live mindfully and alertly, always preparing for Christ's return.

Ponder

Outside the United Nations Headquarters in New York City stands the sculpture "Let Us Beat Swords into Plowshares" (see Isa 2:4), a gift from the former Soviet Union. The sculpture depicts a muscular man holding a hammer aloft in one hand and a sword that he is crafting into a plowshare in the other. Drawing from our Isaiah reading, the sculpture symbolizes the human yearning for peace and an end to war. For Isaiah, this yearning is bound up with our yearning for God's kingdom. Isaiah promises that this vision of peace will become a reality, that God is slowly leading us into the fullness and wholeness of the kingdom. As you pray with the first reading, do you believe that Isaiah's vision is possible? What helps or hinders you from trusting and living into this promise?

Advent is a season of introspection and preparation. Shortened days invite stillness as we enter a new liturgical year and prepare for Christ's coming at Christmas. It is also a time of the "already" and "not yet": our Messiah has already come into this world, yet now we wait for the fulfillment of the Messiah's return. Our readings from Romans and Matthew call us to a state of wakeful waiting, to "put on" Christ, the "armor of light," in our thoughts and our actions. They also call us to remember that Christ's return is not just symbolic or a pie-in-the-sky story. It is real, and it is happening through God's presence and intervention in human history. Advent is therefore not just a season but a state of mind and heart. We are to be Advent people, living in hope, wakeful and working toward the coming of God's kingdom.

Second Sunday of Advent

On that day, a shoot shall sprout from the stump of Jesse,
    and from his roots a bud shall blossom.
The spirit of the LORD shall rest upon him:
    a spirit of wisdom and of understanding,
a spirit of counsel and of strength,
    a spirit of knowledge and of fear of the LORD,
    and his delight shall be the fear of the LORD.
Not by appearance shall he judge,
    nor by hearsay shall he decide,
but he shall judge the poor with justice,
    and decide aright for the land's afflicted.
He shall strike the ruthless with the rod of his mouth,
    and with the breath of his lips he shall slay the wicked.
Justice shall be the band around his waist,
    and faithfulness a belt upon his hips.
Then the wolf shall be a guest of the lamb,
    and the leopard shall lie down with the kid;
the calf and the young lion shall browse together,
    with a little child to guide them.
The cow and the bear shall be neighbors,
    together their young shall rest;
    the lion shall eat hay like the ox.
The baby shall play by the cobra's den,
    and the child lay his hand on the adder's lair.
There shall be no harm or ruin on all my holy mountain;
    for the earth shall be filled with knowledge of the LORD,
    as water covers the sea.
On that day, the root of Jesse,
    set up as a signal for the nations,
the Gentiles shall seek out,
    for his dwelling shall be glorious.

Isaiah's oracle (prophecy) is set within the looming threat of the
Assyrian Empire in the eighth century BCE. Watching the Assyrian

conquest of northern Israel, Isaiah anticipates a similar conquering of Judah to the south (though in reality, Judah would be spared). He draws imagery of "scorched earth" tactics of warfare (which involved the razing of forests) into his concern for the razing or dismantling of Judah's monarchy, envisioning the Assyrians transforming the Davidic monarchy into a "stump" like the land itself. Yet Isaiah promises that the stump will remain alive and will one day produce a new sprout, the future king or "anointed one" (Hebrew *māšîaḥ*) of Judah from David's line. Isaiah describes God's spirit or breath (Hebrew *rûaḥ*) endowing this ruler with extraordinary power, insight, wisdom, and other qualities rooted in "fear" (meaning "awe" or "reverence") of God. In Catholic tradition, the seven gifts of the Holy Spirit draw upon this description (and add one additional gift: piety). The ruler's most intimate qualities will be justice and faithfulness, worn as close to him as the loincloth ("band" or "belt") next to the body. Perfect justice brings perfect peace, including a utopian vision of harmony in the animal kingdom and "knowledge" of God even among Gentiles. The "holy mountain" is Mount Zion, the home of the temple in Jerusalem.

RESPONSORIAL PSALM   PSALM 72:1-2, 7-8, 12-13, 17

Justice shall flourish in his time, and fullness of peace for ever.

SECOND READING   ROMANS 15:4-9

Brothers and sisters:
Whatever was written previously was written for our instruction,
    that by endurance and by the encouragement of the Scriptures
    we might have hope.
May the God of endurance and encouragement
    grant you to think in harmony with one another,
    in keeping with Christ Jesus,
    that with one accord you may with one voice
    glorify the God and Father of our Lord Jesus Christ.

Welcome one another, then, as Christ welcomed you,
    for the glory of God.

For I say that Christ became a minister of the circumcised
   to show God's truthfulness,
   to confirm the promises to the patriarchs,
   but so that the Gentiles might glorify God for his mercy.
As it is written:
   Therefore, I will praise you among the Gentiles
      and sing praises to your name.

Our reading is part of a longer exhortation to unity and harmony among Gentile and Jewish believers (14:1–15:13). Directly preceding our reading, Paul calls those who are "strong" in faith to help build up weaker members of the community (15:1), and he describes Christ's selfless example as the pattern by which believers should welcome and encourage each other (15:2-3). He then affirms the meaning and purpose of his holy Scriptures, the Hebrew Bible, and the scriptural promises given to the ancestors of Israel. According to Paul, Jesus came primarily to minister to the Jews in fulfillment of these promises and secondarily to minister to the Gentiles. Paul envisions a community of believers unified in belief. To "think in harmony" (Greek *phroneō*) does not mean rigid conformity of thought but thoughtful consideration of others' views, to "think harmoniously" with one another. He calls the whole community of believers to "glorify" God together "with one voice," building each other up in hope and endurance (see also Phil 2:1-11). The final verse is a quote from 2 Samuel 22:50 (see also Ps 22:23).

GOSPEL   MATTHEW 3:1-12

John the Baptist appeared, preaching in the desert of Judea
   and saying, "Repent, for the kingdom of heaven is at hand!"
It was of him that the prophet Isaiah had spoken when he said:
      A voice of one crying out in the desert,
      Prepare the way of the Lord,
         make straight his paths.
John wore clothing made of camel's hair
   and had a leather belt around his waist.
His food was locusts and wild honey.
At that time Jerusalem, all Judea,
   and the whole region around the Jordan

were going out to him
and were being baptized by him in the Jordan River
  as they acknowledged their sins.

When he saw many of the Pharisees and Sadducees
  coming to his baptism, he said to them, "You brood of vipers!
Who warned you to flee from the coming wrath?
Produce good fruit as evidence of your repentance.
And do not presume to say to yourselves,
  'We have Abraham as our father.'
For I tell you,
  God can raise up children to Abraham from these stones.
Even now the ax lies at the root of the trees.
Therefore every tree that does not bear good fruit
  will be cut down and thrown into the fire.
I am baptizing you with water, for repentance,
  but the one who is coming after me is mightier than I.
I am not worthy to carry his sandals.
He will baptize you with the Holy Spirit and fire.
His winnowing fan is in his hand.
He will clear his threshing floor
  and gather his wheat into his barn,
  but the chaff he will burn with unquenchable fire."

Each year on the Second Sunday of Advent, we are introduced to John the Baptist, the prophetic precursor to Jesus. His is a fitting message of self-emptying and preparation for the coming of the messiah. John is also a discomforting figure. He preaches in the steep slopes of the eastern Judean Desert, facing the Dead Sea, near the Jordan River, a liminal space of entry and departure from Israel. His clothing mirrors that of the prophet Elijah (see 2 Kgs 1:8), and he eats ritually pure food designated for the poor (see Lev 11:22). To prefigure Jesus's coming, he quotes the prophetic message of comfort and hope originally given to the people in the midst of the Babylonian exile (Isa 40:3). He pronounces the coming of God's kingdom, or the "kingdom of heaven," God's authority over human history. Yet his words are as biting as they are hopeful. He condemns the Jewish elite (Pharisees and Sadducees, two main religious sects in early Judaism) using inflammatory language ("brood of vipers"; see also Matt 12:34; 23:33). He foretells the inclusion of the Gentiles and focuses on the need for repentance or a radical reorientation of one's relationship with God. A "winnowing fan" was a forked shovel used to separate wheat kernels from the husks and straw (the "chaff"). Most importantly, John shifts the focus from himself to "the one who is coming" (Jesus). On the Third Sunday of Advent, we will hear more about John the Baptist's witness to Christ (Matt 11:2-11). John is an enigmatic figure in Christianity. In the early church, he had his own following of people who considered him to be the messiah. The Gospels reflect this historical reality and intentionally deflect attention to Jesus.

Ponder

Our readings call us to the barren, desert spaces of our hearts. They invite us to repentance, which in Hebrew means a literal turning back or return to God (*šûb*) and in Greek means a transformation of thought and action (*metanoia*). In many ways, genuine repentance means returning to who we really are; it means becoming *real*. This return, this becoming, can only happen in the internal, quiet space of self-emptying that allows us to receive God. This Advent season, follow the call into the desert. No matter the noise around you, the responsibilities and commitments, allow John the Baptist to guide you to your internal desert, to make space for inner quiet, to be transformed or re-grounded into who you really are.

The world around us is also filled with desert places—places of loneliness and grief, broken relationships, inequity, and injustice. Into these places Isaiah offers a radical promise of transformation and a vision of justice and peace, what the psalmist calls "profound peace" (72:7). Paul echoes this vision in calling for a community that lives and thinks "in harmony." As these readings once inspired a suffering people living in their own desert places, allow them to inspire you. Do you believe there is room for grace in the desert places around you? How is God calling you to live into these scriptural promises, to become one who acts justly and inspires others to hope?

Third Sunday of Advent (Gaudete Sunday)

FIRST READING   ISAIAH 35:1-6a, 10

The desert and the parched land will exult;
   the steppe will rejoice and bloom.
They will bloom with abundant flowers,
   and rejoice with joyful song.
The glory of Lebanon will be given to them,
   the splendor of Carmel and Sharon;
they will see the glory of the LORD,
   the splendor of our God.
Strengthen the hands that are feeble,
   make firm the knees that are weak,
say to those whose hearts are frightened:
   Be strong, fear not!
Here is your God,
   he comes with vindication;
with divine recompense
   he comes to save you.
Then will the eyes of the blind be opened,
   the ears of the deaf be cleared;
then will the lame leap like a stag,
   then the tongue of the mute will sing.

Those whom the LORD has ransomed will return
   and enter Zion singing,
   crowned with everlasting joy;
they will meet with joy and gladness,
   sorrow and mourning will flee.

This prophetic oracle of Judah's renewal and return from exile comes toward the end of First Isaiah. In the preceding chapter, the land becomes a desert; here, the imagery reverses when God transforms the desert into a fertile landscape. Normally, travelers from Babylon to Israel would skirt the desert by heading northwest along the Euphrates and then southwest through Syria, yet here the people journey

through the desert, nourished along the way. The oracle is filled with
rejoicing, and the first two verses alone contain five Hebrew terms for
joy and exultation that our English translation does not fully preserve.
Lebanon is a mountain range north of Israel, Carmel is a mountain
range that stretches from the Mediterranean coast toward the south-
east in northern Israel, and Sharon is the coastal plain west of Carmel.
Judah's return also evokes imagery from the Israelites' exodus from
Egypt in describing this second exodus out of Babylon. Our passage
shares language and imagery with the book of Jeremiah (e.g., 31:7-9)
and other passages in First Isaiah (e.g., 7:4; 32:1-6; 37:6). The open-
ing of eyes and ears reverses the prophecy in Isaiah 6:9-10, in which
God renders people blind and deaf so they are unable to repent. Here,
God liberates the people into rejoicing. Jesus's message to John in our
Gospel reading echoes the language we read here.

RESPONSORIAL PSALM   PSALM 146:6-7, 8-9, 9-10

Lord, come and save us.
or: Alleluia.

SECOND READING   JAMES 5:7-10

Be patient, brothers and sisters,
    until the coming of the Lord.
See how the farmer waits for the precious fruit of the earth,
    being patient with it
until it receives the early and the late rains.
You too must be patient.
Make your hearts firm,
    because the coming of the Lord is at hand.
Do not complain, brothers and sisters, about one another,
    that you may not be judged.
Behold, the Judge is standing before the gates.
Take as an example of hardship and patience, brothers and sisters,
    the prophets who spoke in the name of the Lord.

The inclusion of the letter of James in the Christian canon was de-
bated until the late fourth century CE. Martin Luther later called it

an "epistle of straw."[1] Yet the early church used the letter frequently, and Roman Catholics read segments of it in our lectionary cycle. The author James (Jacob in Hebrew) was likely a Jewish follower of Jesus; his knowledge of Torah is clear throughout the letter. The text of the letter seems to indicate that James was conversant with Paul's theology and letters (e.g., Jas 2:14-17), and for this reason scholars often date the letter to about 60 CE, in relation to Paul's writings. While Paul stresses faith and James stresses its resultant actions, both view faith as trust in God that results in outward transformation. The letter of James focuses on ethical themes regarding how one is to act as a result of faith, including proper speech and right relationships. Our reading, from the last chapter of James, describes Christ's return and coming judgment. The chapter opens with judgments toward those who grow rich at the expense of others (vv. 1-6). The focus then moves to consoling those who wait for Christ's return. They are to be patient through life's daily trials, looking to the example of the prophets who faced outrageous injustice (vv. 7-11). The author employs the image of the farmer in Israel, who waits for the early (October–November) and late (April–May) rains. He also incorporates a distinctly Christian view of the "Judge" standing before the gates of heaven.

GOSPEL   MATTHEW 11:2-11

When John the Baptist heard in prison of the works of the Christ,
    he sent his disciples to Jesus with this question,
    "Are you the one who is to come,
    or should we look for another?"
Jesus said to them in reply,
    "Go and tell John what you hear and see:
    the blind regain their sight,
    the lame walk,
    lepers are cleansed,
    the deaf hear,
    the dead are raised,
    and the poor have the good news proclaimed to them.
And blessed is the one who takes no offense at me."

1. "Luther's Preface to the New Testament," in *Works of Martin Luther*, vol. 6, trans. C. M. Jacobs (Philadelphia: Muhlenberg Press, 1932 [1522, rev. 1545]), 443–44.

As they were going off,
    Jesus began to speak to the crowds about John,
    "What did you go out to the desert to see?
A reed swayed by the wind?
Then what did you go out to see?
Someone dressed in fine clothing?
Those who wear fine clothing are in royal palaces.
Then why did you go out? To see a prophet?
Yes, I tell you, and more than a prophet.
This is the one about whom it is written:
    Behold, I am sending my messenger ahead of you;
        he will prepare your way before you.
Amen, I say to you,
    among those born of women
    there has been none greater than John the Baptist;
    yet the least in the kingdom of heaven is greater than he."

This Sunday reintroduces us to John the Baptist, who is now impris-
oned (see Matt 4:12; 14:1-12). The "works of the Christ" are Jesus's
deeds throughout Matthew 8–9. The linchpin of the passage is John's
question: Is Jesus the messiah, the one "to come," or should the people
keep waiting? The question is striking in light of John's recognition
of Jesus directly following last Sunday's Gospel (see Matt 3:13-17).
Perhaps John expected the messiah to emphasize the urgency of
repentance and the end times, as John himself did. Jesus responds
to John by conflating multiple prophecies from Isaiah (26:19; 29:18;
35:5-6; 42:7, 18; 61:1) to describe how his deeds fulfill these prophecies. When Jesus says, "And blessed is the one who takes no offense
at me," he may be warning people not to get hung up or stumble
over him ("offense," Greek *scandalizō*, also translates as "obstacle" or
"stumbling block") but instead to look toward the kingdom of God.
Jesus then declares John to be the last and greatest of the prophets,
and he quotes from Malachi 3:1 to identify John with the prophet
Elijah. The final line is a great paradox and may reflect the Gospel
writer's attempt to minimize John's importance in early Christianity;
John is the greatest among those on earth, yet the least in the kingdom of heaven will be greater than John.

Ponder

The call to "rejoice" (Latin *gaudete*) at the heart of Advent high-lights the importance of joy in our faith lives. But what is joy? For the believer, it is not a superficial feeling of happiness dependent on life's circumstances, but a deep wellspring of hope and trust in God. Isaiah's prophetic oracle imagines the joy of a people who trust that God will bring them home while restoring and healing all life. Our Gospel applies Isaiah's imagery to the messianic pe-riod and to Jesus's acts of healing. Both readings are set within historical periods of great suffering and social inequity, yet they call readers to take the longer view, trusting in God's ultimate salvation, as echoed in today's responsorial psalm. As you pray with the readings this week, ponder and savor this message of joy. How do you experience this wellspring in your life?

John's question to Jesus is an honest one: "Are you the one who is to come?" Jews of Jesus's time believed the messiah's arrival would mimic the imagery from Isaiah: the messiah would swoop down in glory and power, righting the world and saving the people from corrupt social systems. Yet Jesus did not come (and will not return!) according to these literal expectations. Thousands of years later, we join first-century believers in awaiting the Mes-siah's return. Our readings describe key qualities to cultivate in the meantime: joy, patience, ethical behavior, the ability to be prophetic witnesses in our world. But how real does this return seem to us? John lived in expectation of a "yes" to his question. Do we?

Fourth Sunday of Advent

FIRST READING   ISAIAH 7:10-14

The LORD spoke to Ahaz, saying:
　Ask for a sign from the LORD, your God;
　let it be deep as the netherworld, or high as the sky!
But Ahaz answered,
　"I will not ask! I will not tempt the LORD!"
Then Isaiah said:
　Listen, O house of David!
Is it not enough for you to weary people,
　must you also weary my God?
Therefore the Lord himself will give you this sign:
　the virgin shall conceive, and bear a son,
　and shall name him Emmanuel.

A national crisis in Judah underlies this prophecy, the Syro-Ephraimite War of 735–732 BCE. During this time, Jerusalem was threatened by a coalition comprised of Israel (the northern kingdom, also known as Ephraim) and Aram further north (present-day Syria). The coalition sought to depose Ahaz of Judah and replace him with a new leader who would be more open to their anti-Assyrian cause. In the verses preceding our reading, Isaiah tries to assure Ahaz that the coalition will not succeed, that he should trust in God and stand firm in faith (vv. 4-9). Ahaz is skeptical, and Isaiah prompts him to ask for a sign of divine assurance, but Ahaz refuses. His refusal to test God is a pious act, but Isaiah views it negatively and responds with the divine sign nonetheless: the promise of the continuation of the Jerusalem monarchy and God's steadfast presence among the people through the birth of "Emmanuel" (meaning "God is with us" in Hebrew). The final line of this reading is cited in Matthew 1:23 as corroboration of the virgin birth of Jesus, but the Hebrew ʿalmâ (translated as "the virgin" here and in Matthew's Greek translation) simply means a young woman of marriageable age.

RESPONSORIAL PSALM   PSALM 24:1-2, 3-4, 5-6

Let the Lord enter; he is king of glory.

SECOND READING   ROMANS 1:1-7

Paul, a slave of Christ Jesus,
    called to be an apostle and set apart for the gospel of God,
    which he promised previously through his prophets in the holy
        Scriptures,
the gospel about his Son, descended from David according to
    the flesh,
    but established as Son of God in power
    according to the Spirit of holiness
    through resurrection from the dead, Jesus Christ our Lord.
Through him we have received the grace of apostleship,
    to bring about the obedience of faith,
    for the sake of his name, among all the Gentiles,
    among whom are you also, who are called to belong to
        Jesus Christ;
    to all the beloved of God in Rome, called to be holy.
Grace to you and peace from God our Father
    and the Lord Jesus Christ.

This Sunday, we turn to Paul's opening greeting in his letter to the Romans, the most formal greeting of any of his letters. Writing to a community that does not know him personally, Paul introduces himself and his relationship to Jesus Christ carefully, employing words that are rich in significance. Paul calls himself a "slave" (or "servant," Greek *doulos*), a term that also describes great figures in the Hebrew Bible like Moses and Joshua, who participated actively in God's plan for Israel (see Judg 2:8; Dan 9:11). Paul emphasizes the divine origin of his mission; like the prophets, he is called to be an "apostle" (literally one who is "sent forth") and he is "set apart" (see Jer 1:5; Amos 7:15). The word for "set apart" (Greek *aphorizō*) also underlies the term "Pharisee," and Paul may be stressing the importance or holiness of his Jewish, Pharisaic background (see Phil 3:5). Paul also emphasizes that the gospel (literally "good news") of salvation is an ancient, divine plan alluded to throughout the

Hebrew Bible. Paul affirms that Jesus is physically son of David and spiritually Son of God through his resurrection. "Spirit of holiness" in Greek corresponds with the phrase "holy spirit" in Hebrew. For Paul, "obedience" begins with hearing, and in fact, the Greek term for "obedience" (*hypakoē*) comes from the same root as the word for "hear" (*akouein*). As Paul writes in Romans 10:17, "[F]aith comes from what is heard, and what is heard comes through the word of Christ." Hearing then leads to personal commitment and service to God. When Paul states that the people are "called to be holy," he is referring to those who are loved and designated to be set apart by the God of Israel. Paul addresses his hearers as Gentiles, yet his audience clearly includes Jewish believers, and much of his language is addressed to those who are intimate with the Hebrew Scriptures.

GOSPEL   MATTHEW 1:18-24

This is how the birth of Jesus Christ came about.
When his mother Mary was betrothed to Joseph,
    but before they lived together,
    she was found with child through the Holy Spirit.
Joseph her husband, since he was a righteous man,
    yet unwilling to expose her to shame,
    decided to divorce her quietly.
Such was his intention when, behold,
    the angel of the Lord appeared to him in a dream and said,
    "Joseph, son of David,
    do not be afraid to take Mary your wife into your home.
For it is through the Holy Spirit
    that this child has been conceived in her.
She will bear a son and you are to name him Jesus,
    because he will save his people from their sins."
All this took place to fulfill what the Lord had said through the
        prophet:
    Behold, the virgin shall conceive and bear a son,
    and they shall name him Emmanuel,
    which means "God is with us."
When Joseph awoke,
    he did as the angel of the Lord had commanded him
    and took his wife into his home.

Each year on the Fourth Sunday of Advent, our Gospel focuses on the birth of Jesus. This year, our reading draws from Matthew, the only Gospel where Joseph plays a central role in the birth narrative. We enter the story at the point after the marriage contract has been written up between Joseph's and Mary's parents, yet before Joseph has taken Mary into his home. His repudiation of the contract would therefore not constitute "divorce" in the full sense of the word. Joseph is called a righteous man both because of his desire to follow the Jewish law and because of his unwillingness to expose Mary in a public way (in Judaism, "righteousness" is linked with Torah observance, ethics, and justice). Joseph then becomes the recipient of divine revelation, in contrast to Luke 1:26-38, where the angel appears to Mary. The dream evokes the story of Joseph in Genesis 39–50, a righteous ancestor of Israel who loves his family selflessly despite their injustices toward him. The motif of divine beings revealing messages of miraculous births or prophecies involving the futures of unborn children is common throughout the Hebrew Bible, yet many of these messages come first and foremost to women (e.g., Rebekah in Gen 25; Samson's mother in Judg 13). Often when they include men (e.g., Samson's father in Judg 13; Zechariah in Luke 1), the men either question or fail to understand the message. Not so with Joseph. When the angel appears, Joseph is told that the child's name will be Jesus (*Yehoshua*, or Joshua, in Hebrew), meaning "Yahweh is salvation." The idea that this story "fulfills" Isaiah's prophecies means that it gives Isaiah's divine revelation a new dimension of reality through Jesus. When Joseph awakes, he follows the angel's bidding without question.

Ponder

Isaiah dares Ahaz to ask for a sign. It could be anything, as "deep as the netherworld, or high as the sky." Ahaz refuses, saying he does not want to "tempt" God. Perhaps this is a faithful response, or perhaps Ahaz is afraid of what the sign will be. God sends the sign anyway. Ahaz is the foil to Joseph, our example of pure openness and attention to God's revelation even in a dream. When Joseph wakes up, he does exactly what the angel commands. As Ahaz's situation proves, we cannot stop God's revelations, which are happening all the time in and through our daily lives. To see, we need only be attentive and open, like Joseph. Do we dare?

Only through faith do we see God, and through faith God is revealed to us. Our readings describe certain attributes of faith that help us maintain a stance of readiness in our lives. In the responsorial psalm, it is the one "whose hands are sinless" and "whose heart is clean" who can seek and stand confidently before God. For Paul, the cornerstone of faith is obedience, which begins with the openness to hear God's call and then respond. Joseph's selflessness and mercy beyond any sense of personal injustice give him the freedom to hear and respond to God's voice. Soon, Christmas will be here, God-with-us. As we continue to ready ourselves, how is our faith? How free are we to see, hear, and respond?

The Nativity of the Lord (Christmas) (Vigil Mass)[1]

FIRST READING   ISAIAH 62:1-5

For Zion's sake I will not be silent,
   for Jerusalem's sake I will not be quiet,
until her vindication[2] shines forth like the dawn
   and her victory[3] like a burning torch.

Nations shall behold your vindication,
   and all the kings your glory;
you shall be called by a new name
   pronounced by the mouth of the LORD.
You shall be a glorious crown in the hand of the LORD,
   a royal diadem held by your God.
No more shall people call you "Forsaken,"
   or your land "Desolate,"
but you shall be called "My Delight,"
   and your land "Espoused."
For the LORD delights in you
   and makes your land his spouse.
As a young man marries a virgin,
   your Builder shall marry you;
and as a bridegroom rejoices in his bride
   so shall your God rejoice in you.

Our reading comes from the last portion of Isaiah ("Third Isaiah"; consult the notes on Isaiah from the First Sunday of Advent). The setting is postexilic Judah, after 536 BCE. The tone is one of renewal and hope with a twofold focus: God's love for the holy city of Jerusalem

---

1. Christmas Mass readings are the same each year throughout the three-year lectionary cycle. See *Ponder: Year B* for commentary on the readings for the Mass During the Day and *Ponder: Year C* for commentary on the readings for the Mass During the Night.
2. "Vindication" translates more literally as "righteousness" (Hebrew ṣedeq).
3. "Victory" translates more literally as "salvation" (Hebrew yĕšû'ā).

(Zion) and the ultimate inclusion of all people into the divine covenant with Israel. Our passage lies at the center of this message of hope. The prophet speaks on behalf of God to prophesy Jerusalem's renewal, a time in which the Holy City will become the physical manifestation of God's glory. In the passage, Jerusalem is a city as well as a people in whom God will delight. The relationship and love between God and Jerusalem is expressed as a marriage. In our English translations, we miss the sound play in Hebrew between the terms "forsaken" (*'ăzûbâ*) and "my delight" (*ḥefṣî-bâ*), "desolate" (*šĕmāmâ*) and "espoused" (*bĕ'ûlâ*).

RESPONSORIAL PSALM   PSALM 89:4-5, 16-17, 27, 29

For ever I will sing the goodness of the Lord.

SECOND READING   ACTS 13:16-17, 22-25

When Paul reached Antioch in Pisidia and entered the
      synagogue,
   he stood up, motioned with his hand, and said,
   "Fellow Israelites and you others who are God-fearing, listen.
The God of this people Israel chose our ancestors
   and exalted the people during their sojourn in the land of Egypt.
With uplifted arm he led them out of it.
Then he removed Saul and raised up David as king;
   of him he testified,
   'I have found David, son of Jesse, a man after my own heart;
   he will carry out my every wish.'
From this man's descendants God, according to his promise,
   has brought to Israel a savior, Jesus.
John heralded his coming by proclaiming a baptism of
      repentance
   to all the people of Israel;
   and as John was completing his course, he would say,
   'What do you suppose that I am? I am not he.
Behold, one is coming after me;
   I am not worthy to unfasten the sandals of his feet.'"

Acts tells the story of the spread of the early church after Jesus's resurrection, focusing on the disciples' missions to both Jews and Gentiles. Paul's mission to the Gentiles begins during his first trip to Antioch in Syria, narrated in Acts 13:1–15:35. Our reading takes place early in this mission. On the Sabbath, Paul and his companions go to the synagogue as usual. After the customary readings, the synagogue officials invite Paul to preach, and he uses the occasion to recount all of salvation history leading up to Christ (13:15-41). Our reading includes only specific verses from this long sermon that describe the exodus story, the establishment of David's monarchic line in Judah, and the coming of John the Baptist. When Paul finishes his sermon, the people urge Paul and Barnabas to preach again the following Sabbath. The following week, the same people become enraged when they see that the disciples include the Gentiles in their message of salvation through Jesus (vv. 44-45).

GOSPEL   MATTHEW 1:1-25 [OR 1:18-25]

The book of the genealogy of Jesus Christ,
    the son of David, the son of Abraham.

Abraham became the father of Isaac,
    Isaac the father of Jacob,
    Jacob the father of Judah and his brothers.
Judah became the father of Perez and Zerah,
    whose mother was Tamar.
Perez became the father of Hezron,
    Hezron the father of Ram,
    Ram the father of Amminadab.
Amminadab became the father of Nahshon,
    Nahshon the father of Salmon,
    Salmon the father of Boaz,
    whose mother was Rahab.
Boaz became the father of Obed,
    whose mother was Ruth.
Obed became the father of Jesse,
    Jesse the father of David the king.

David became the father of Solomon,
    whose mother had been the wife of Uriah.

Solomon became the father of Rehoboam,
   Rehoboam the father of Abijah,
   Abijah the father of Asaph.
Asaph became the father of Jehoshaphat,
   Jehoshaphat the father of Joram,
   Joram the father of Uzziah.
Uzziah became the father of Jotham,
   Jotham the father of Ahaz,
   Ahaz the father of Hezekiah.
Hezekiah became the father of Manasseh,
   Manasseh the father of Amos,
   Amos the father of Josiah.
Josiah became the father of Jechoniah and his brothers
   at the time of the Babylonian exile.

After the Babylonian exile,
   Jechoniah became the father of Shealtiel,
   Shealtiel the father of Zerubbabel,
   Zerubbabel the father of Abiud.
Abiud became the father of Eliakim,
   Eliakim the father of Azor,
   Azor the father of Zadok.
Zadok became the father of Achim,
   Achim the father of Eliud,
   Eliud the father of Eleazar.
Eleazar became the father of Matthan,
   Matthan the father of Jacob,
   Jacob the father of Joseph, the husband of Mary.
Of her was born Jesus who is called the Christ.

Thus the total number of generations
   from Abraham to David
   is fourteen generations;
   from David to the Babylonian exile,
   fourteen generations;
   from the Babylonian exile to the Christ,
   fourteen generations.

Now this is how the birth of Jesus Christ came about.
When his mother Mary was betrothed to Joseph,
   but before they lived together,
   she was found with child through the Holy Spirit.

Joseph her husband, since he was a righteous man,
> yet unwilling to expose her to shame,
> decided to divorce her quietly.
Such was his intention when, behold,
> the angel of the Lord appeared to him in a dream and said,
> "Joseph, son of David,
> do not be afraid to take Mary your wife into your home.
For it is through the Holy Spirit
> that this child has been conceived in her.
She will bear a son and you are to name him Jesus,
> because he will save his people from their sins."
All this took place to fulfill
> what the Lord had said through the prophet:
>> *Behold, the virgin shall conceive and bear a son,*
>> *and they shall name him Emmanuel,*
> which means "God is with us."
When Joseph awoke,
> he did as the angel of the Lord had commanded him
> and took his wife into his home.
He had no relations with her until she bore a son,
> and he named him Jesus.

For notes to the second half of this Gospel reading (beginning "Now this is how the birth of Jesus Christ came about"), consult the Fourth Sunday of Advent. Genealogies were essential to the ancient world; they underscored the importance of particular figures by establishing their patriarchal lines. Genealogies also make strong ideological and theological statements, and the Hebrew Bible is therefore full of them (e.g., Gen 4:17-22). Matthew's genealogy of Jesus is no different. It is perhaps the most important text in the Gospel, for it explains Matthew's theological stance about Jesus as Messiah. According to Matthew, Jesus descends not only from David but from Abraham, linking Jesus back to the original patriarch of Israel. Matthew creates his genealogy with three sets of fourteen generations (though curiously, he lists only thirteen generations in the last set). Fourteen is the sum of the numerical value of the Hebrew letters *dalet* (four), *vav* (six), and *dalet* (four), which spell "David." Most importantly, Matthew includes four women in this otherwise male-focused genealogy. Not all of these women are Israelites; instead, they are mostly foreign women. All four had messy backstories and reputations and helped perpetuate the line of Israel through their grit and determination. Tamar was a Canaanite woman who arguably tricked her father-in-law Judah into sleeping with her to perpetuate his line (Gen 38); Rahab was a Canaanite prostitute faithful to Israelite spies (Josh 2); Ruth was a Moabite woman and proselyte (the book of Ruth); and Bathsheba, or the "wife of Uriah," was a woman with whom David committed adultery (2 Sam 11) and who eventually bore Solomon. Matthew elevates all of these women to underscore Jesus's own messy, thoroughly human (and therefore imperfect) background. His genealogy then leads to Mary, another seemingly scandalous woman (pregnant while "betrothed") who nonetheless continues the line of Israel through her courage and faith.

Ponder

Salvation is a daring vision. It is rooted in human history, God-with-us here and now, and simultaneously breaks forward into future horizons of hope. Our vigil readings call us to believe and live into the fullness of this vision. The prophetic voice imagines the future restoration of Jerusalem, when the Holy City will become the manifestation of God's glory and salvation. The prophet refuses to "be silent" until his daring vision becomes a reality: Judah will be transformed from its current desolate and forsaken state into a bride who shines with righteousness and is God's "delight." In the post-resurrection world of Acts, Paul tells the story of salvation history, declaring that every historical event has culminated in the saving events of Jesus's birth, life, death, and resurrection. Finally, Matthew describes salvation history not through historical events but through historical figures. He links Jesus all the way back to Abraham, the father of many nations. The Christmas mystery that we celebrate this week is rooted in the real events of our lives. The Messiah has come and lives with us through human history and human relationships. Yet this mystery also moves forward beyond the confines of our present reality to an expansive future hope. May we dare to embrace this Christmas message with imagination and boldness, proclaiming the future promise tirelessly like the prophets while trusting that God is present with us and for us, here and now.

The Holy Family
of Jesus, Mary, and Joseph

FIRST READING   SIRACH 3:2-6, 12-14

God sets a father in honor over his children;
    a mother's authority he confirms over her sons.
Whoever honors his father atones for sins,
    and preserves himself from them.
When he prays, he is heard;
    he stores up riches who reveres his mother.
Whoever honors his father is gladdened by children,
    and, when he prays, is heard.
Whoever reveres his father will live a long life;
    he who obeys his father brings comfort to his mother.

My son, take care of your father when he is old;
    grieve him not as long as he lives.
Even if his mind fail, be considerate of him;
    revile him not all the days of his life;
kindness to a father will not be forgotten,
    firmly planted against the debt of your sins
    —a house raised in justice to you.

The book of Sirach dates to the second century BCE. Though written in Hebrew by a certain Ben Sira, it was the Greek translation by the author's grandson that became part of the Greek Septuagint (LXX), the canon of Jewish texts composed and translated from the Hebrew in Alexandria, Egypt. Sirach is part of the canon of Scripture for Roman Catholics and Orthodox Christians, but not for Jews or Protestants. The book is a summary or collection of Wisdom teachings, likely used as an educational tool for scribes and sages in training. Ben Sira was conservative, a traditional Jew of his time, and his worldview was hierarchical, a glimpse of which we see in the above text. The household (women, children, slaves) was under the ultimate authority of the man. Such a perspective reflects a patriarchal household code that originated in the time of Aristotle. Yet the above reading stresses a child's honor for both parents, and it is framed within a broader section (3:1-16) that roots proper family relationships in wisdom and "fear" (reverence) of God.

RESPONSORIAL PSALM　　　　　　　　　　PSALM 128:1-2, 3, 4-5

Blessed are those who fear the Lord and walk in his ways.

SECOND READING　　　　　　　COLOSSIANS 3:12-21 [OR 3:12-17]

Brothers and sisters:
Put on, as God's chosen ones, holy and beloved,
　　heartfelt compassion, kindness, humility, gentleness, and
　　　　patience,
　　bearing with one another and forgiving one another,
　　if one has a grievance against another;
　　as the Lord has forgiven you, so must you also do.
And over all these put on love,
　　that is, the bond of perfection.
And let the peace of Christ control your hearts,
　　the peace into which you were also called in one body.
And be thankful.
Let the word of Christ dwell in you richly,
　　as in all wisdom you teach and admonish one another,
　　singing psalms, hymns, and spiritual songs
　　with gratitude in your hearts to God.
And whatever you do, in word or in deed,
　　do everything in the name of the Lord Jesus,
　　giving thanks to God the Father through him.

Wives, be subordinate to your husbands,
　　as is proper in the Lord.
Husbands, love your wives,
　　and avoid any bitterness toward them.[1]
Children, obey your parents in everything,
　　for this is pleasing to the Lord.
Fathers, do not provoke your children,
　　so they may not become discouraged.

---

1. An alternative translation for "avoid any bitterness toward them" is "never treat them harshly."

The city of Colossae was located in Asia Minor (contemporary Turkey), about 110 miles east of Ephesus. Though the author purports to have been Paul, most likely the letter was composed by one of Paul's followers after his death (ca. 60s CE). It was written for this early community of believers to deal with a controversy surrounding the liberating power of Christ's death and resurrection. The author reaffirms that, through Christ, believers have been liberated once and for all, and there are no necessary requirements beyond baptism and new life in Christ (or "Christ in you"; see 1:27). In chapter 3, the author describes the ethical and moral standards of a new life in Christ that calls believers to "[p]ut to death" (v. 5) negative habits ("anger, fury, malice, slander, and obscene language"; v. 8) and to clothe themselves or "put on" the virtues of a new life in the image of God (v. 10). These virtues include compassion, kindness, humility, gentleness, patience, forgiveness, peace, gratitude, and love, and they provide the framework for the household codes described in the latter half of our reading (see also Eph 5:21–6:9; 1 Pet 2:18–3:7; and our first reading from Sirach). Christian household codes are rooted in oneness in the Body of Christ and extend from the family out to the community. The point is that the family is the powerful nucleus for the transformative values of a life in Christ.

GOSPEL	MATTHEW 2:13-15, 19-23

When the magi had departed, behold,
   the angel of the Lord appeared to Joseph in a dream and said,
   "Rise, take the child and his mother, flee to Egypt,
   and stay there until I tell you.
Herod is going to search for the child to destroy him."
Joseph rose and took the child and his mother by night
   and departed for Egypt.
He stayed there until the death of Herod,
   that what the Lord had said through the prophet might be
      fulfilled,
Out of Egypt I called my son.

When Herod had died, behold,
   the angel of the Lord appeared in a dream
   to Joseph in Egypt and said,

"Rise, take the child and his mother and go to the land of Israel,
    for those who sought the child's life are dead."
He rose, took the child and his mother,
    and went to the land of Israel.
But when he heard that Archelaus was ruling over Judea
    in place of his father Herod,
        he was afraid to go back there.
And because he had been warned in a dream,
    he departed for the region of Galilee.
He went and dwelt in a town called Nazareth,
    so that what had been spoken through the prophets might be
        fulfilled,
    He shall be called a Nazorean.

Matthew depicts the Holy Family as a refugee family and Jesus as a new Moses. To make these connections, our passage is steeped in allusions to the exodus narrative. Just as the baby Moses escaped Pharaoh's order for all Hebrew male infants to be killed (Exod 1:16; 2:1-10), here Jesus escapes Herod's order for all boys aged two and under in Bethlehem and its vicinity to be slaughtered (see Matt 2:16-18, which we skip over in our reading). Both rulers felt their power threatened by children; both infants became saviors of their people. The Holy Family's return to Israel then recalls God's deliverance of Israel from oppression in Egypt through Moses, quoting a prophetic reference to the exodus story: "When Israel was a child, I loved him, / out of Egypt I called my son" (Hos 11:1). In Hosea, "son" refers to the Israelites; here, it refers to Jesus. In terms of the political situation of Israel at the time, King Herod died around 4 BCE, after which his son Archelaus ruled for ten years (until 6 CE). Simultaneously, Archelaus's brother Herod Antipas controlled Galilee (see Matt 14:1). The area was no less dangerous under these rulers, yet Joseph obediently follows the angel's command to return to Israel, and the family settles in the small and insignificant town of Nazareth. Matthew's final quote regarding the fulfillment of what "had been spoken through the prophets" is not in the Hebrew Bible, though there may be vague links to Nazareth in Judges 13:5 and 7 (regarding the birth of Samson as a "nazirite" or holy one of God) and in Isaiah 11:1 (in which a royal "shoot," Hebrew *nēṣer*, comes from "the stump of Jesse," the father of King David).

Ponder

Our first and second readings promote patriarchal models for the household that can be challenging in light of contemporary values. These teachings, situated in a time and culture very different from our own, are not to be taken wholesale as timeless truths (e.g., Col 3:22 continues with an exhortation to slaves to obey their masters). While their historical contexts are different from today, our readings do contain valuable ideas about what it means to love one another as family and community. Sirach roots family life in wisdom and reverence for God, and Colossians emphasizes the importance of ethical virtues and, especially, love in family and community structure. Ultimately, Colossians emphasizes mutuality in the Body of Christ over status and hierarchy. As we pray discerningly with these readings, what are the timeless elements that challenge us to growth today?

While Sirach and Colossians focus on the *internal* dimensions of family life, Matthew focuses on *external* challenges. The Gospel makes two powerful points: First, the ancient world was marked by immense insecurity, and the family (not the government or social programming) was the nucleus that provided social security, stability, and support. Second, Jesus was born into a poor refugee family. The Holy Family also disrupts the nuclear family structure: Joseph was a foster father; Mary conceived a child outside of marriage. Today's feast day is a reminder that families take many forms and can be spaces of struggle—physical, emotional, and spiritual. Yet it is precisely in these struggling spaces where Jesus dwells. This reality is a comfort when we are struggling and a call to love and care for all people as family, especially those most in need of our support.

Solemnity of Mary,
the Holy Mother of God

The LORD said to Moses:
  "Speak to Aaron and his sons and tell them:
  This is how you shall bless the Israelites.
Say to them:
  The LORD bless you and keep you!
  The LORD let his face shine upon
    you, and be gracious to you!
  The LORD look upon you kindly and
    give you peace!
So shall they invoke my name upon the Israelites,
  and I will bless them."

The book of Numbers is the fourth book of the Torah or Pentateuch (the first five books of the Hebrew Bible). It continues the
story of wilderness wandering that begins in Exodus and continues
through Leviticus, a story in which God liberates the Israelites from
Egypt, makes a covenant with them, and reveals the commandments
through Moses at Sinai. The Israelites then build a portable tabernacle as God's holy place as they journey toward the Promised Land.
Numbers is a compilation of sources that includes old stories, folk
traditions, and legal material. The above text is an ancient priestly
blessing that all priests were required to bestow upon the people (see
also Lev 9:22-23). It is a three-part blessing, each part slightly longer than the previous, to evoke God's overflowing mercy and favor.
The Hebrew words in each blessing contain a wealth of meanings.
For example, in the first blessing, "keep you" literally means "guard
you" (*šāmar*, often translated as "protect"). This is the same word
used in God's admonitions to the people to "guard" or "keep" the
commandments (e.g., Exod 19:5), and it is the command given to
Adam to "keep" the Garden of Eden (Gen 2:15; NRSV). In the second
blessing, to "let [one's] face shine" upon another is to deal kindly

or with compassion toward them. In the last of the three blessings, the literal translation of "The LORD look upon you kindly" is "The LORD lift up his face upon you." Finally, "peace" (Hebrew *šālôm*) means wholeness and completeness. Old amulets (small ornaments or pieces of jewelry worn for protection) inscribed with this blessing have been discovered in Israel dating as far back as the First Temple period (sixth century BCE or earlier). People wore these amulets as a way of continually invoking God's name.

RESPONSORIAL PSALM   PSALM 67:2-3, 5, 6, 8

May God bless us in his mercy.

SECOND READING   GALATIANS 4:4-7

Brothers and sisters:
When the fullness of time had come, God sent his Son,
    born of a woman, born under the law,
    to ransom those under the law,
    so that we might receive adoption as sons.
As proof that you are sons,
    God sent the Spirit of his Son into our hearts,
    crying out, "Abba, Father!"
So you are no longer a slave but a son,
    and if a son then also an heir, through God.

Likely written in the mid-50s CE, Paul's letter to the Galatians highlights a critical moment in the identity and mission of the early Christian movement. In this historical period, the movement was still very much connected to Judaism, yet an increasing number of its members were Gentiles (thanks in large part to Paul). As a result, the question arose regarding the extent to which converts should be circumcised and adhere to Jewish law and tradition. In the book of Acts, Paul's position is that the demands of the Jewish law place an unnecessary burden upon Gentile Christians. In Galatians, he pushes his point further to argue that "righteousness," understood in this context as a covenant relationship with God through faith in Christ, sets one free from observance to Jewish law. To require Gentile believers to adhere to the law would render Christ's death meaningless. In this section of his letter, Paul compares the giving of the Jewish law with Christ's coming and the Gentiles' adoption as children of God through faith (3:1–4:31). His argument includes the analogies of slavery (to the cosmic forces of evil) and adoption (into the household of faith; see 4:1-11). In our reading, Paul stresses that Jesus was both human ("born of a woman") and Jewish ("born under the law"), sent as God's Son to liberate his own people (those under the law) and adopt the Gentiles into God's family. Through faith, Jews and Gentiles become equal heirs and children of God. A key to understanding Paul is to remember that he was a devout Jew who kept the commandments and did not believe that the law in itself was "bad." Elsewhere, he reminds his readers that "the law is holy, and the commandment is holy and righteous and good" (Rom 7:12). However, in Paul's view, the human person is subject to sin and is ultimately incapable of holding to the standards of the law. True liberation from these standards comes through faith in Christ.

GOSPEL   LUKE 2:16-21

The shepherds went in haste to Bethlehem and found Mary and
    Joseph,
    and the infant lying in the manger.
When they saw this,
    they made known the message
    that had been told them about this child.
All who heard it were amazed
    by what had been told them by the shepherds.
And Mary kept all these things,
    reflecting on them in her heart.
Then the shepherds returned,
    glorifying and praising God
    for all they had heard and seen,
    just as it had been told to them.

When eight days were completed for his circumcision,
    he was named Jesus, the name given him by the angel
    before he was conceived in the womb.

This is the same Gospel story that is read at the Christmas Mass at Dawn. The newborn Jesus lies in a manger in Bethlehem. An angel of God comes to a group of shepherds and reveals that the Messiah has been born. The shepherds hurry to find Mary and Joseph and relay the information to others. We read this text today because it conveys the relationship between Jesus and his mother, Mary. She is known as the "God-bearer" (Greek *theotokos*), a term given to her at the Council of Ephesus in 431 CE. Our passage also describes Mary as the first true disciple, the one who hears the shepherds' words and keeps (or treasures) these things quietly in her heart. Luke uses the Greek term *symballō* to describe Mary's pondering, a word that literally means "to throw together." In other words, Mary holds together the entire story of Christ within herself. She will again "[keep] all these things in her heart" after she and Joseph lose Jesus in the temple after the Passover (Luke 2:41-52).

Ponder

In 1968, Pope Paul VI asked that the church observe January 1 as a World Day of Peace. His request connects with our first reading, a famous priestly blessing and prayer for peace: "The LORD bless you and keep you! / The LORD let his face shine upon you, and be gracious to you! / The LORD look upon you kindly and give you peace!" This prayer is rich in meaning. To be "kept" by God is to be guarded, protected, and lovingly tended. To experience God's face shining upon us is to know God's overflowing compassion and care. The prayer further invokes God's grace, kindness, and "peace," meaning a wholeness and completeness rooted in God. This week offers an invitation to meditate with this blessing, praying that all people throughout the world can experience this deep and holy peace that only God can give.

The World Day of Peace is also intimately linked with today's veneration of the divine motherhood of Mary. Pope Paul VI prayed that Mary and Jesus would "shed their light of goodness, wisdom and hope" upon our prayer for "the gift of Peace, of which the world has so much need."[1] Mary is our model for this deep inner peace rooted in God, even though she lived in a time of immense conflict and suffering. Hers was a peace that helped her to say "yes" to God, to become "God-bearer" and mother to us all as adopted children. She lived an inwardly contemplative life, pondering and treasuring God's great mystery through Jesus. Allow yourself to lean on Mary, praying for her help to cultivate an inner quiet and readiness so that you, too, may be a God-bearer who brings peace to this world.

1. Pope Paul VI, Message of His Holiness Pope Paul VI for the Observance of a Day of Peace, January 1, 1968.

The Epiphany of the Lord

Rise up in splendor, Jerusalem! Your light has come,
    the glory of the Lord shines upon you.
See, darkness covers the earth,
    and thick clouds cover the peoples;
but upon you the LORD shines,
    and over you appears his glory.
Nations shall walk by your light,
    and kings by your shining radiance.
Raise your eyes and look about;
    they all gather and come to you:
your sons come from afar,
    and your daughters in the arms of their nurses.

Then you shall be radiant at what you see,
    your heart shall throb and overflow,
for the riches of the sea shall be emptied out before you,
    the wealth of nations shall be brought to you.
Caravans of camels shall fill you,
    dromedaries from Midian and Ephah;
all from Sheba shall come
    bearing gold and frankincense,
    and proclaiming the praises of the LORD.

This Sunday we return to the last portion of Isaiah, or "Third Isaiah" (consult the notes to the first reading for the First Sunday of Advent). Written after the Persian defeat of Babylon (ca. 538 BCE), our reading begins a long poem in Isaiah 60–62 that is addressed to Judeans returning to Jerusalem from Babylon (see also the notes for the Christmas Vigil Mass on Isa 62:1-5). In the above verses, the prophetic voice speaks directly to Jerusalem as a woman, imagining the Holy City's restoration and glory. The text is filled with light imagery, describing Jerusalem as a beacon of hope suffused by the radiance of God's glory. The righteous remnant will return by her (Jerusalem's) light, both Judeans from exile (her "sons" and "daughters") and the

Gentiles or "nations" (Hebrew *gôyim*) who now universally recognize the God of Israel. The nations approach as in procession to Jerusalem alongside the Judeans, offering their wealth in praise and reverence. In earlier chapters of Isaiah (and in other prophetic texts), God uses these nations as a tool for Israel's punishment. Here, the nations will worship the God of Israel and care lovingly for God's Holy City.

RESPONSORIAL PSALM   PSALM 72:1-2, 7-8, 10-11, 12-13

Lord, every nation on earth will adore you.

SECOND READING   EPHESIANS 3:2-3a, 5-6

Brothers and sisters:
You have heard of the stewardship[1] of God's grace
    that was given to me for your benefit,
    namely, that the mystery was made known to me by
        revelation.
It was not made known to people in other generations
    as it has now been revealed
    to his holy apostles and prophets by the Spirit:
    that the Gentiles are coheirs, members of the same body,
    and copartners in the promise in Christ Jesus through
        the gospel.

One of the key themes of Ephesians is unity between Jews and Gentiles. It is likely that one of Paul's Jewish-Christian followers (rather than Paul himself) wrote this letter in the late first century CE, perhaps during a time when Jewish-Christians and Gentiles were splitting off into separate communities. One of the letter's concerns is the continued unity of the growing church community as the Body of Christ. The "mystery" spoken of here is the union of Jewish and Gentile believers into a single community through Christ. The letter uses a variety of terms to emphasize what faith in Christ means for Gentiles: they become "coheirs" or coinheritors, co-body members,

1. The Greek *oikonomia* is often used in the sense of "stewardship" or "task." Here it refers to God's plan realized through Paul. (An alternative translation is "commission.")

and "copartners" or sharers in the promise of God's plan of salvation to the Jews through Christ.

GOSPEL   MATTHEW 2:1-12

When Jesus was born in Bethlehem of Judea,
    in the days of King Herod,
    behold, magi from the east arrived in Jerusalem, saying,
    "Where is the newborn king of the Jews?
We saw his star at its rising
    and have come to do him homage."
When King Herod heard this,
    he was greatly troubled,
    and all Jerusalem with him.
Assembling all the chief priests and the scribes of the people,
    he inquired of them where the Christ was to be born.
They said to him, "In Bethlehem of Judea,
    for thus it has been written through the prophet:
    And you, Bethlehem, land of Judah,
        are by no means least among the rulers of Judah;
    since from you shall come a ruler,
        who is to shepherd my people Israel."
Then Herod called the magi secretly
    and ascertained from them the time of the star's appearance.
He sent them to Bethlehem and said,
    "Go and search diligently for the child.
When you have found him, bring me word,
    that I too may go and do him homage."
After their audience with the king they set out.
And behold, the star that they had seen at its rising preceded
        them,
    until it came and stopped over the place where the child was.
They were overjoyed at seeing the star,
    and on entering the house
    they saw the child with Mary his mother.
They prostrated themselves and did him homage.
Then they opened their treasures
    and offered him gifts of gold, frankincense, and myrrh.
And having been warned in a dream not to return to Herod,
    they departed for their country by another way.

Historically, the word "magi" designated both a priestly Persian group and all those with supernatural knowledge or abilities (not unlike our modern word "magician"). But in Matthew's Gospel, the word "magi" refers to those with astrological knowledge and, more importantly, to Gentiles from the east (Mesopotamia) who have come to worship Jesus. This story therefore demonstrates that Gentiles are included in Jesus's mission from the very beginning. Both Matthew's and Luke's Gospels contain stories of Jesus's birth, but while Luke places the Jewish poor at the birth scene, Matthew has Gentiles visit first. (Note that Luke was a Gentile Christian, while Matthew was a Jewish-Christian, yet each of them places the other community first.) This story of the magi also affirms that Jesus is the Jewish messiah, for Bethlehem is the place of King David's birth according to 1 Samuel, and our passage includes various texts from the Hebrew Bible that affirm that Jesus descends from the line of David (see Mic 5:1-3; 2 Sam 5:2). As in the first reading, visitors from afar bring gifts of gold and frankincense; the Gospel also includes myrrh. These were valuable items and standard offerings made to a king or deity in the ancient Middle East. Frankincense is a perfume or incense, and myrrh is an anointing oil. In the verses following our reading, the Holy Family flees to Egypt to escape the massacre of infant boys as Herod seeks to destroy Jesus (vv. 13-23; see the Gospel notes for The Holy Family of Jesus, Mary, and Joseph).

Ponder

Today's feast day links revelation with light. In Isaiah, God's glory radiates over and through Jerusalem, and the Holy City becomes a manifestation of God's "shining radiance." In the Gospel, the star in the night guides the foreigners as they travel to worship Jesus. These readings use light to underscore the meaning of today's feast of the Epiphany, a word that means both "radiance" and "manifestation" (from the Greek *epiphaneia*). Today, we celebrate God's manifestation and radiance through Christ as both a historical event and a continuous act. This feast day is one of celebration, but it is also a signal to stop and pay attention to where and through whom God manifests today. It is also a reminder that today *we* are called to be God's light, God's revelation in the dark spaces.

Epiphany signifies unity through Christ. Our readings describe the expansion and inclusion of God's revelation to all people as one diverse body. In Ephesians, unity is the deepest "mystery" of God's revelation, and Jews and Gentiles are depicted as coheirs, copartners, and co-body members. In Matthew, the first people to recognize Jesus are foreigners, travelers who have come from afar to revere him. Similarly, in Isaiah, all people travel to Jerusalem to revere God. In our deeply divided world, unity is a radical concept. It is also the call and challenge of Epiphany as God's true desire for us. As we near the end of the Christmas season, are you ready to commit to this Epiphany?

The Baptism of the Lord

Thus says the LORD:
Here is my servant whom I uphold,
    my chosen one with whom I am pleased,
upon whom I have put my spirit;
    he shall bring forth justice to the nations,
not crying out, not shouting,
    not making his voice heard in the street.
A bruised reed he shall not break,
    and a smoldering wick he shall not quench,
until he establishes justice on the earth;
    the coastlands will wait for his teaching.

I, the LORD, have called you for the victory of justice,
    I have grasped you by the hand;
I formed you, and set you
    as a covenant of the people,
    a light for the nations,
to open the eyes of the blind,
    to bring out prisoners from confinement,
    and from the dungeon, those who live in darkness.

Our reading draws from the first of four "Suffering Servant" poems
in the second major section of Isaiah (chaps. 40–55, or "Second
Isaiah"). In all four poems, the servant takes on the burden of a suffering people in order to bring salvation, healing, and justice to Israel
and, by extension, to the "nations" or Gentiles. The servant's message
is one of hope to the exiled Judeans at the end of the Babylonian
exile (586–536 BCE), a promise that God's covenant is permanent
and that the return to Judah is immanent. In the above passage, the
description of the servant's relationship with God is deeply moving;
God forms and chooses the servant, holds the servant's hand, and
imparts to the servant God's "spirit" or breath. God is "pleased" with
or literally "delights" in the servant. The servant is quietly gentle and
dedicated to protecting the most fragile and vulnerable (symbolized

by the bruised reed and smoldering wick). In the account of the commissioning of the prophet Isaiah, God made the people deaf and blind (6:9-10); in our reading today, God's servant will heal and liberate, symbolizing the end of a long period of punishment. Most importantly, God entrusts the servant to bring forth justice to all people. The word "justice" (Hebrew *mišpāṭ*) repeats three times in verses 1-4 (one of these attestations is missing in our reading, which excludes the end of v. 3 and the beginning of v. 4). In verse 6, the phrase "victory of justice" translates more literally as "victory of righteousness" (Hebrew *ṣedeq*). By establishing justice on earth, the servant will be the means by which all people come to know the God of Israel. The anonymous "servant" is open to multiple interpretations. Among Jews, the servant is commonly interpreted as the collective Israel or a prophetic figure. Christians understand the servant poem as a prophecy about Jesus, the one who will suffer for the many and become a light to all people.

RESPONSORIAL PSALM   PSALM 29:1-2, 3-4, 3, 9-10

The Lord will bless his people with peace.

SECOND READING   ACTS 10:34-38

Peter proceeded to speak to those gathered
   in the house of Cornelius, saying:
   "In truth, I see that God shows no partiality.
Rather, in every nation whoever fears him and acts uprightly
   is acceptable to him.
You know the word that he sent to the Israelites
   as he proclaimed peace through Jesus Christ, who is Lord of all,
   what has happened all over Judea,
   beginning in Galilee after the baptism
   that John preached,
   how God anointed Jesus of Nazareth
   with the Holy Spirit and power.
He went about doing good
   and healing all those oppressed by the devil,
   for God was with him."

In this reading, Peter presents the theological basis for inclusion of the Gentiles in the new "Way" of Jesus, the movement that will become Christianity (see Acts 11:26). In Acts 10, Cornelius, a devout Gentile and Roman centurion, receives a vision from God to invite the apostle Peter (a Jew) into his household. Simultaneously, Peter receives a vision in which God breaks down the Jewish kashrut laws (food regulations). When Cornelius and Peter come together, Cornelius shares his vision with Peter, and Peter responds with the words of our reading. While Peter is speaking, the Holy Spirit descends upon the crowd, and Peter is astounded that "the Gentiles also" receive this Spirit (10:45). He promptly baptizes them, thus expanding the Jesus movement (originally a Jewish movement) and the message of salvation through Christ to the Gentiles. Later, Peter explains his actions to Jewish believers in Jerusalem (see Acts 11). In Acts 15, the Jerusalem Council formally decides to allow Gentiles into the movement without requiring them to convert to Judaism.

GOSPEL   MATTHEW 3:13-17

Jesus came from Galilee to John at the Jordan
   to be baptized by him.
John tried to prevent him, saying,
   "I need to be baptized by you,
   and yet you are coming to me?"
Jesus said to him in reply,
   "Allow it now, for thus it is fitting for us
   to fulfill all righteousness."
Then he allowed him.
After Jesus was baptized,
   he came up from the water and behold,
   the heavens were opened for him,
   and he saw the Spirit of God descending like a dove
   and coming upon him.
And a voice came from the heavens, saying,
   "This is my beloved Son, with whom I am well pleased."

Our Gospel reading begins where John the Baptist's preaching left off in Matthew 3:12 (see notes for the Second Sunday of Advent). The attention then shifts to Jesus's baptism, the focus of today's celebration. In the early church, Jesus's baptism was a delicate theological issue. Why would Jesus need to be baptized with a baptism of repentance (Matt 3:11; see also Mark 1:4)? According to our passage, this was done in order to "fulfill all righteousness," meaning in order to follow God's will for the sake of bringing all people into right relationship with God (righteousness is a key theme throughout Matthew's Gospel and indicates right relationship with God). However, Matthew does not go so far as to describe the actual baptism and only refers to it as an accomplished act (see also Luke 3:21). Only Mark states that John baptizes Jesus, while John's Gospel, known for its high Christology, omits the baptism of Jesus altogether. Matthew's version emphasizes John the Baptist's lower status relative to Jesus ("*I* need to be baptized by *you*"; emphasis added), likely in response to those in the first century who continued to believe that John was the messiah. The opening or ripping open of the heavens breaks the barrier between heaven and earth (see also Isa 63:19–64:1; Ezek 1:1), and the dove is a symbol of peace, hope, and new beginnings (see Gen 8:8-12). In early Jewish tradition, the dove also symbolizes Israel. God's statement ("This is my beloved Son, with whom I am well pleased.") recalls God's command to Abraham to sacrifice Isaac: "Take your son Isaac, your only one, whom you love" (Gen 22:2). Matthew is likely drawing upon the Greek (Septuagint) version of this passage ("your beloved son Isaac, whom you love"), thus applying this iconic father-son relationship to God and Jesus.

Ponder

In our readings, power is expressed through gentleness and compassion. The psalmist describes God's awesome power unleashed in nature. This is the power that flows through all prophetic witnesses, including the servant in our reading from Isaiah. We see God's power in the servant's strength of character and in his tireless pursuit of justice. Yet his actions are gentle, peaceful, and compassionate. These same qualities also come to life in Jesus. Like that of the servant, the power that courses through Jesus manifests in gentleness and compassion, symbolized by the descending dove at his baptism. His baptism sets him on a path to "fulfill all righteousness" and bring the world into right relationship with God. Through our baptisms, we also become God's servants, called to walk gently and generously with strength of character and a fierce commitment to justice. How is God calling you on this path today?

Solidarity. Connection. Love that knows no partiality. As we end the Christmas cycle, our readings invite us to remember or imagine the gift of our baptisms, which give us a new identity and call us to union with God and each other. Together, we are children of God, beloved children in whom God delights and with whom God is well pleased (Isa 42:1; Matt 3:17). Just as baptism marked Jesus for change and sent him out into the world, so we are marked for change and sent out into the world. The ongoing baptismal challenge is to say "yes" continually and to live according to this new identity. This week, ponder your baptism. Can you say "yes" again? Allow yourself to open to God's love flowing through you, reminding you that you are united with God and with all of God's children through water and the Holy Spirit.

First Sunday of Lent   *temptation*

FIRST READING   GENESIS 2:7-9; 3:1-7

The LORD God formed man out of the clay of the ground
   and blew into his nostrils the breath of life,
   and so man became a living being.

Then the LORD God planted a garden in Eden, in the east,
   and placed there the man whom he had formed.
Out of the ground the LORD God made various trees grow
   that were delightful to look at and good for food,
   with the tree of life in the middle of the garden
   and the tree of the knowledge of good and evil.

Now the serpent was the most cunning of all the animals
   that the LORD God had made.
The serpent asked the woman,
   "Did God really tell you not to eat
   from any of the trees in the garden?"
The woman answered the serpent:
   "We may eat of the fruit of the trees in the garden;
   it is only about the fruit of the tree
   in the middle of the garden that God said,
   'You shall not eat it or even touch it, lest you die.'"
But the serpent said to the woman:
   "You certainly will not die!
No, God knows well that the moment you eat of it
   your eyes will be opened and you will be like gods
   who know what is good and what is evil."
The woman saw that the tree was good for food,
   pleasing to the eyes, and desirable for gaining wisdom.
So she took some of its fruit and ate it;
   and she also gave some to her husband, who was with her,
   and he ate it.
Then the eyes of both of them were opened,
   and they realized that they were naked;
   so they sewed fig leaves together
   and made loincloths for themselves.

Eve's temptations
- wisdom
- food
- delight to the eyes

Pride ~ disordered love of self

The creation story in Genesis 2–3 contains a number of wordplays and riddles. The word for "man" (Hebrew *ʼādām* or Adam) is the root of the term for "ground" (Hebrew *ʼădāmâ*; 2:7). The tree from which Adam is not to eat is the tree of the knowledge of "good and bad" (literal translation), not "good and evil" (2:9, 17). At the root of the word "woman" (Hebrew *ʼiššâ*), whom God later creates, is a second, more common Hebrew term for "man" (*ʼîš*; 2:23). And in the beginning of chapter 3, the description of the serpent as "cunning" (*ʻărûm* in Hebrew, which translates literally as "wise") links to the word for "naked" at the end of chapter 2 (*ʻărûmmîm*; 2:25). When the serpent talks to the woman in the beginning of chapter 3, she garbles God's initial instructions to the man (note that the woman had not yet been created when God told the man not to eat from the tree of knowledge in 2:16-17). She says that "the tree in the middle of the garden" is off limits, but not explicitly the tree of good and bad (we know the tree of *life* is in the middle of the garden, but is that also the location of the tree of good and bad?). She also adds that they may not "touch" the tree, though God never spoke such a warning. The serpent then tells her that if they eat from the tree, they will be like "gods" or divine beings, knowing all things, the entirety of what is good and bad. Note that the man "was with her" (3:6) while she was talking with the serpent (centuries ago, Jerome removed the Hebrew term *ʻimmâ*, "with her," from his widely influential Latin translation of the Hebrew Bible, which is why we often think the woman was entirely to blame). When the two eat from the fruit, they gain full self-awareness for the first time and realize they are naked.

RESPONSORIAL PSALM   PSALM 51:3-4, 5-6, 12-13, 17

Be merciful, O Lord, for we have sinned.

SECOND READING   ROMANS 5:12-19 [OR 5:12, 17-19]

Brothers and sisters:
Through one man sin entered the world,
    and through sin, death,
    and thus death came to all men, inasmuch as all sinned—

for up to the time of the law, sin was in the world,
though sin is not accounted when there is no law.
But death reigned from Adam to Moses,
even over those who did not sin
after the pattern of the trespass of Adam,
who is the type of the one who was to come.
But the gift is not like the transgression.
For if by the transgression of the one, the many died,
how much more did the grace of God
and the gracious gift of the one man Jesus Christ
overflow for the many.
And the gift is not like the result of the one who sinned.
For after one sin there was the judgment that brought
condemnation;
but the gift, after many transgressions, brought acquittal.
For if, by the transgression of the one,
death came to reign through that one,
how much more will those who receive the abundance of grace
and of the gift of justification
come to reign in life through the one Jesus Christ.
In conclusion, just as through one transgression
condemnation came upon all,
so, through one righteous act,
acquittal and life came to all.
For just as through the disobedience of the one man
the many were made sinners,
so, through the obedience of the one,
the many will be made righteous.

For notes on Romans, see the First Sunday of Advent. Our reading draws from a longer discourse in Romans 5 regarding what it means to be justified by faith in Christ (for the first verses of Rom 5, see notes for the Third Sunday of Lent). In these verses, Paul describes Adam and Christ as individuals whose actions had opposing effects on humanity: Adam brought death into the world through his sin or "transgression" (Greek *paraptōma*; literally "false step" or "stumbling"), while Christ brought life through his crucifixion. These two men, therefore, represent figureheads or "types": the old creation (Adam) and the new (Christ). Paul also refers back to previous discussions of the law or Torah in Romans 2–4 to explain that before God transmitted the law or Torah through Moses, sin was "not accounted" (meaning no one could be held accountable for sin) even though Adam's actions had unleashed sin, giving it free reign in the world. For Paul, Christ's crucifixion results in the "gift" that is much more powerful and expansive than Adam's transgression: life and righteousness that will "overflow for the many" through the ultimate gift, Jesus himself. See also 1 Corinthians 15:21-23 and 45-49, where Paul draws a slightly different comparison between Adam and Jesus.

GOSPEL   MATTHEW 4:1-11

At that time Jesus was led by the Spirit into the desert
    to be tempted by the devil.
He fasted for forty days and forty nights,
    and afterwards he was hungry.
The tempter approached and said to him,
    "If you are the Son of God,
    command that these stones become loaves of bread."   *desire of flesh*
He said in reply,   *(fasting)*
    "It is written:
One does not live on bread alone,
    but on every word that comes forth
    from the mouth of God."

Then the devil took him to the holy city,
    and made him stand on the parapet of the temple,
    and said to him, "If you are the Son of God, throw
        yourself down.
For it is written:
    He will command his angels concerning you   *pride*
        and with their hands they will support you, *(prayer)*
    lest you dash your foot against a stone."
Jesus answered him,
    "Again it is written,
    You shall not put the Lord, your God, to the test."
Then the devil took him up to a very high mountain,
    and showed him all the kingdoms of the world in their
        magnificence,

and he said to him, "All these I shall give to you,
if you will prostrate yourself and worship me."
At this, Jesus said to him,
"Get away, Satan!
It is written:
The Lord, your God, shall you worship
and him alone shall you serve."

Then the devil left him and, behold,
angels came and ministered to him.

After John baptizes Jesus at the end of Matthew 3, the Spirit of God descends "like a dove" upon him, and a voice from heaven declares, "This is my beloved Son, with whom I am well pleased" (3:17). The Spirit then leads Jesus directly into the desert, where he fasts for forty days before the devil tests him. This episode is filled with allusions to the Hebrew Bible. The term "devil" (v. 1) is used interchangeably with "tempter" (v. 3) and "Satan" (v. 10; literally "the accuser," from the Hebrew *śāṭān*, first mentioned in Job 1–2). "Son of God" was a term for Davidic kings of Israel (e.g., 2 Sam 7:14) and is Matthew's preferred divine title for Jesus. The phrase "forty days and forty nights" evokes numerous episodes in the Hebrew Bible that involve the number forty, including Noah and the Flood (Gen 7:12), the Israelites' wilderness period (Exod 16:35), Moses on Mount Sinai (Exod 24:18), and Elijah's journey to the same mountain (also called Mount Horeb; 1 Kgs 19:8). Mountains are spaces of revelation and appear consistently in Matthew's Gospel (e.g., 4:8; 5:1; 17:1). Each time Jesus responds to the devil, he quotes from Deuteronomy. First, he states that humans are sustained first and foremost by God (Deut 8:3). He then professes loyalty to the commandments and refuses to test God (Deut 6:16; note that the devil quotes from Ps 91:11-12). Finally he declares loyalty to God alone (Deut 6:13). Ministering angels appear at the end of Mark's and Matthew's accounts of Jesus's temptation (see Mark 1:13), just as an angel cared for Elijah in the wilderness (1 Kgs 19:5-8).

(fast, alms, prayer) Lent

Ponder

"Against you only have I sinned," prays the psalmist (51:6). In Hebrew and Greek, "sin" can be defined in many ways: as a false step, a stumbling or slippage, a missing of the mark, or a slight turning away. These definitions suggest that sin is often subtle. Temptations to sin or "stumble" often happen by manipulating the truth slightly, as the serpent and the devil do in Genesis and in the Gospel. In its extreme, sin can also lead to "death" (Paul's term), a permanent fracturing of our relationship with God. Sin and repentance are, therefore, very personal, ultimately playing out between ourselves and God, as our psalmist understands well. Lenten disciplines can help us to understand how sin works in our lives and to grapple with its profound effects. This deeper understanding can then lead us back to God. What concrete practices this Lent will help you understand and confront your own temptations and stumbling?

Our readings draw us into the garden and the desert, beginning with the reality that we are God's beloved. In the garden, God forms the man lovingly, blowing into him the breath of life. Before Jesus is drawn into the desert, he is called God's "beloved Son." Sin is what separates us from this deep truth of who we are, while Lent is a movement back to God through remembrance of this truth. Only by being in touch with this "yes" of who we are—God's beloved—will we be able to say "no" to that which distorts it. This week, meditate upon the fact that you are God's beloved. Allow this to ground you as you head into the desert with Jesus this Lenten season.

Second Sunday of Lent

FIRST READING   GENESIS 12:1-4a

The LORD said to Abram:
"Go forth from the land of your kinsfolk
and from your father's house to a land that I will show you.

"I will make of you a great nation,
and I will bless you;
I will make your name great,
so that you will be a blessing.
I will bless those who bless you
and curse those who curse you.
All the communities of the earth
shall find blessing in you."

Abram went as the LORD directed him.

The book of Genesis is a patchwork quilt of sources. Because of this, stories often seem to repeat themselves. For example, we find two distinct creation stories back-to-back in Genesis 1 and Genesis 2–3 and two intertwined sources for the Flood narrative in Genesis 6–9. The stories of Abraham and Sarah also come from multiple sources with repeating narratives and themes. The most important of these themes is God's covenant with Abraham, which runs through the tales of Abraham and Sarah in Genesis 12–22 (a careful reader will notice that God repetitively makes a permanent covenant with Abraham and his ancestors, repeating it in almost every chapter!). Each year on the Second Sunday of Lent, we read from one of these covenant stories. This year brings us to the very beginning of the Abraham cycle, when Abraham (Abram) first encounters the God of Israel from his ancestral home in Ur of Mesopotamia (contemporary southern Iraq). In our reading, God calls Abram to take his family, leave his home, and travel to the distant, foreign land of Canaan. There Abram will become a "great nation," meaning the father of many descendants as well as the leader of a politically independent social group. This promise will stand in tension with Abraham and

Sarah's apparent inability to have children until Isaac is born (Gen 21:1-7). The notion of blessings and curses attached to a specific chosen person is a formula that repeats in the Bible (e.g., Gen 27:29; Num 24:9). Here, the literal translation of "curse those who curse you" is "curse those who treat you lightly," referring to those who disrespect or pay little regard to Abraham. The sentence beginning "All the communities of the earth" becomes especially important within early Christian theology in terms of Gentile inclusion (e.g., Gal 3:8). This is the first of many instances in which Abram/Abraham listens to God and follows without hesitation. Later, in Genesis 17, God will change Abram's name to Abraham (and Sarai's to Sarah) as a sign of their new relationship with God.

RESPONSORIAL PSALM   PSALM 33:4-5, 18-19, 20, 22

Lord, let your mercy be on us, as we place our trust in you.

SECOND READING   2 TIMOTHY 1:8b-10

Beloved:
Bear your share of hardship for the gospel
    with the strength that comes from God.

He saved us and called us to a holy life,
    not according to our works
    but according to his own design
    and the grace bestowed on us in Christ Jesus before time began,
    but now made manifest
    through the appearance of our savior Christ Jesus,
    who destroyed death and brought life and immortality
    to light through the gospel.

First and Second Timothy were likely composed late in the first century CE or early in the second century, after Paul's death. Though Pauline authorship is doubtful, some argue that these letters (often called "Pastoral Epistles") come from authentic fragments of lost Pauline letters. The epistles are named for one of Paul's beloved disciples, his "true child" Timothy (1 Tim 1:2), whom Paul designates to continue his legacy and pass down his teachings. Though addressed to a particular individual, the author has in mind a much wider community of readers. Unlike 1 Timothy, 2 Timothy assumes Paul's imprisonment (likely in Rome) and looming death. Our reading excludes the first part of verse 8, yet it is essential for understanding the context: the author tells Timothy to "not be ashamed" of his "testimony" about Christ or Paul, perhaps meaning the shame associated with what others might see as inglorious imprisonment or death. Instead, Timothy is instructed to withstand "hardship" or suffering in preaching the "gospel" (the good news or message of/about Christ). A consistent teaching in the Pauline letters is that the call to salvation is a gift, independent of the person's deeds. Here, the author refers to God's particular "design" from "before time began" (literally "before eternal times") to save people through Christ and in Christ. The "appearance" (Greek *epiphaneia*) refers to Christ's incarnation. Through his resurrection, Christ "destroyed death," both physical death and the figurative death born from sin (see Rom 5:21; 6:4; 8:2).

GOSPEL   MATTHEW 17:1-9

Jesus took Peter, James, and John his brother,
    and led them up a high mountain by themselves.
And he was transfigured[1] before them;
    his face shone like the sun
    and his clothes became white as light.
And behold, Moses and Elijah appeared to them,
    conversing with him.
Then Peter said to Jesus in reply,
    "Lord, it is good that we are here.
If you wish, I will make three tents here,
    one for you, one for Moses, and one for Elijah."
While he was still speaking, behold,
    a bright cloud cast a shadow over them,
    then from the cloud came a voice that said,
    "This is my beloved Son, with whom I am well pleased;
    listen to him."

1. "Transfigured" (Greek *metamorphoō*) means literally to "change form."

When the disciples heard this, they fell prostrate
    and were very much afraid.
But Jesus came and touched them, saying,
    "Rise, and do not be afraid."
And when the disciples raised their eyes,
    they saw no one else but Jesus alone.

As they were coming down from the mountain,
    Jesus charged them,
    "Do not tell the vision to anyone
    until the Son of Man has been raised from the dead."

Each year on the Second Sunday of Lent, we read a Gospel account of the scene of Jesus's transfiguration. Each Gospel writer tells a slightly different version, thus emphasizing a distinct theological theme. Matthew focuses on Jesus's physical radiance coupled with the awesomeness of divine presence that overcomes the disciples and makes them fall "prostrate" (literally "fall upon their faces") in fear, which indicates great reverence and awe. The scene takes place on a mountain, the biblical space of revelation and divine encounter. As we read in the notes for the First Sunday of Lent, mountains are a common theme in Matthew's Gospel. This scene, in particular, links Jesus explicitly with Moses and Elijah, the two great prophets of the Hebrew Bible, associated with the law (Moses) and the prophets (Elijah). Like Jesus, Moses climbed the mountain to receive the commandments and returned with his face shining (Exod 34:29). Elijah similarly climbed a mountain to hear the "voice of thin silence" (literal translation; 1 Kgs 19:12). Jesus's dazzling white clothes likely represent a martyr's apocalyptic glory (e.g., Rev 3:5, 18). The divine voice echoes the words spoken at Jesus's baptism (Matt 3:17), yet adds the key additional command to the disciples: "listen to him." Although the scene centers on Jesus's transfiguration, the subject is discipleship. The disciples are to listen to Jesus and recognize his special status as God's Son, which they do not yet fully comprehend.

Ponder

"Go forth," God says to Abram. The terseness of our first reading hides a well of significance. Abram does not know this God, but he responds trustingly, without hesitation. We know nothing about his emotions or those of his family. There is no reason to migrate (like war or famine), especially not to a distant, unknown land. The story is therefore unrealistic, which makes it that much more powerful and moving. Abram simply listens to the divine voice and goes. In the Gospel, God similarly calls the disciples to "listen." In opening themselves to the will of God, Abram and the disciples are promised the fullness of God's blessing. So are we. What are tangible ways that you might follow God's call right now, even if it seems daunting and even if it is beyond your understanding?

Discipleship is about experiencing, then proclaiming. We visit the mountain—the place of prayer and communion with God—then return to share our experiences. So why does Jesus tell his disciples not to "tell the vision to anyone"? Maybe because they do not yet understand. Just verses before, Jesus rebukes Peter for failing to understand, saying, "You are thinking not as God does, but as human beings do" (Matt 16:23). These first disciples have not yet experienced the revealing light of the resurrection, but we have. Like Timothy in the second reading, *we* understand and are called to proclaim. During Lent, we relive the disciples' experiences. We walk the path to crucifixion and remember the life-changing, transformative power of the resurrection. This week, imagine Jesus telling you to think "as God does," not "as human beings do." What does this mean to you, and how does it manifest in your daily life?

Third Sunday of Lent

FIRST READING   EXODUS 17:3-7

In those days, in their thirst for water,
    the people grumbled against Moses,
    saying, "Why did you ever make us leave Egypt?
Was it just to have us die here of thirst
    with our children and our livestock?"
So Moses cried out to the LORD,
    "What shall I do with this people?
A little more and they will stone me!"
The LORD answered Moses,
    "Go over there in front of the people,
    along with some of the elders of Israel,
    holding in your hand, as you go,
    the staff with which you struck the river.
I will be standing there in front of you on the rock in Horeb.
Strike the rock, and the water will flow from it
    for the people to drink."
This Moses did, in the presence of the elders of Israel.
The place was called Massah and Meribah,
    because the Israelites quarreled there
    and tested the LORD, saying,
    "Is the LORD in our midst or not?"

It is the beginning of the Israelites' long journey from Egypt to Canaan. As they cross the wilderness to Mount Sinai, where they will receive the covenant (chaps. 20–24), they encounter four crises: two water shortages (15:22-27; 17:1-7), a food shortage (16:1-36), and a military threat (17:8-16). In each case, God provides for the people's needs. In our reading, God generates flowing water through a rock and Moses's staff. This is the same staff used to work miracles against Pharaoh (4:17), including rendering water undrinkable (7:15-19) and parting the Nile so the Israelites could leave Egypt (14:15-22). The place name "Massah" derives from the Hebrew verb *nāsâ*, meaning "test" or "try," and the name "Meribah" derives from the verb *rîb*, meaning "quarrel" or "contend." Throughout these desert crises, the people are judged negatively both for complaining and for lacking trust in God's care for them despite the ongoing miracles they experience. According to our responsorial psalm, the real issue is not the complaining but the fact that the people "tempted" and "tested" God (Ps 95:9). The Hebrew verb translated as "tempted" is *bāhan*, which means to examine or scrutinize closely. It is usually God's role to examine humans (as in Ps 26:2: "Examine me, Lord, and test me; / search my heart and mind.") It is not for humans to examine and test God unless God orders them to (see Mal 3:10, 15).

RESPONSORIAL PSALM   PSALM 95:1-2, 6-7, 8-9

If today you hear his voice, harden not your hearts.

SECOND READING   ROMANS 5:1-2, 5-8

Brothers and sisters:
Since we have been justified by faith,
    we have peace with God through our Lord Jesus Christ,
    through whom we have gained access by faith
    to this grace in which we stand,
    and we boast in hope of the glory of God.

And hope does not disappoint,
    because the love of God has been poured out into our hearts
    through the Holy Spirit who has been given to us.
For Christ, while we were still helpless,
    died at the appointed time for the ungodly.
Indeed, only with difficulty does one die for a just person,
    though perhaps for a good person one might even find courage
        to die.
But God proves his love for us
    in that while we were still sinners Christ died for us.

In Romans 5, Paul builds upon his discussion in chapters 2–4 regarding the law and Gentile inclusion in the covenant with Abraham through faith. Here, he describes what it means to be "justified," or rendered righteous (Greek *dikaioō*), by faith (v. 1). According to Paul, believers (Jews and Gentiles alike) are made righteous "through" Jesus, meaning through Jesus's obedience to God in his life, death, and resurrection (vv. 1-2; see also vv. 9-10, 19, and 21). Those who are justified may "boast" (v. 2) because they have been acquitted of their sins and have been given the gift of life through Christ. We skip verses 3-4, which describe how believers also boast in their afflictions or suffering because afflictions lead to endurance, endurance leads to character, and character produces hope. Hope, or "hope of the glory of God" (v. 2), is linked with the promise of life that has not yet been fully revealed to believers (see 8:18-25). The term "helpless" (v. 6) refers to helplessness or weakness in relation to sin, and it is a reminder that God's grace through Christ precedes any human act of righteousness. In other words, no human may claim to be righteous before God outside of Christ's death and resurrection. The love of God "poured out into our hearts through the Holy Spirit" (v. 5) is what strengthens believers and gives them hope, love, and endurance (see also 8:26-27). Note the essential foundation of faith in these verses, which precedes peace, hope, and love.

GOSPEL   JOHN 4:5-42 [OR 4:5-15, 19b-26, 39a, 40-42]

Jesus came to a town of Samaria called Sychar,
    near the plot of land that Jacob had given to his son Joseph.
Jacob's well was there.
Jesus, tired from his journey, sat down there at the well.
It was about noon.

A woman of Samaria came to draw water.
Jesus said to her,
    "Give me a drink."
His disciples had gone into the town to buy food.
The Samaritan woman said to him,
    "How can you, a Jew, ask me, a Samaritan woman, for a drink?"
—For Jews use nothing in common with Samaritans.—
Jesus answered and said to her,
    "If you knew the gift of God
    and who is saying to you, 'Give me a drink,'
    you would have asked him
    and he would have given you living water."

The woman said to him,
   "Sir, you do not even have a bucket and the cistern is deep;
   where then can you get this living water?
Are you greater than our father Jacob,
   who gave us this cistern and drank from it himself
   with his children and his flocks?"
Jesus answered and said to her,
   "Everyone who drinks this water will be thirsty again;
   but whoever drinks the water I shall give will never thirst;
   the water I shall give will become in him
   a spring of water welling up to eternal life."
The woman said to him,
   "Sir, give me this water, so that I may not be thirsty
   or have to keep coming here to draw water."

Jesus said to her,
   "Go call your husband and come back."
The woman answered and said to him,
   "I do not have a husband."
Jesus answered her,
   "You are right in saying, 'I do not have a husband.'
For you have had five husbands,
   and the one you have now is not your husband.
What you have said is true."
The woman said to him,
   "Sir, I can see that you are a prophet.
Our ancestors worshiped on this mountain;
   but you people say that the place to worship is in Jerusalem."
Jesus said to her,
   "Believe me, woman, the hour is coming
   when you will worship the Father
   neither on this mountain nor in Jerusalem.
You people worship what you do not understand;
   we worship what we understand,
   because salvation is from the Jews.
But the hour is coming, and is now here,
   when true worshipers will worship the Father in Spirit
      and truth;
   and indeed the Father seeks such people to worship him.

God is Spirit, and those who worship him
   must worship in Spirit and truth."
The woman said to him,
   "I know that the Messiah is coming, the one called the Christ;
   when he comes, he will tell us everything."
Jesus said to her,
   "I am he, the one speaking with you."

At that moment his disciples returned,
   and were amazed that he was talking with a woman,
   but still no one said, "What are you looking for?"
   or "Why are you talking with her?"
The woman left her water jar
   and went into the town and said to the people,
   "Come see a man who told me everything I have done.
Could he possibly be the Christ?"
They went out of the town and came to him.
Meanwhile, the disciples urged him, "Rabbi, eat."
But he said to them,
   "I have food to eat of which you do not know."
So the disciples said to one another,
   "Could someone have brought him something to eat?"
Jesus said to them,
   "My food is to do the will of the one who sent me
   and to finish his work.
Do you not say, 'In four months the harvest will be here'?
I tell you, look up and see the fields ripe for the harvest.
The reaper is already receiving payment
   and gathering crops for eternal life,
   so that the sower and reaper can rejoice together.
For here the saying is verified that 'One sows and another reaps.'
I sent you to reap what you have not worked for;
   others have done the work,
   and you are sharing the fruits of their work."

Many of the Samaritans of that town began to believe in him
   because of the word of the woman who testified,
   "He told me everything I have done."
When the Samaritans came to him,
   they invited him to stay with them;
   and he stayed there two days.

Many more began to believe in him because of his word,
   and they said to the woman,
   "We no longer believe because of your word;
   for we have heard for ourselves,
   and we know that this is truly the savior of the world."

The story of the Samaritan woman is one of three key stories from the Gospel of John that will carry us through the remaining Sundays of Lent. It comes directly after the story of Nicodemus and takes place in the light ("It was about noon"), in contrast to Nicodemus coming to Jesus in the dark. Jesus is passing through Samaria on his way north from Judea to Galilee. This story reflects a complicated history of animosity between Judeans and Samaritans that goes back to the preexilic period. In the first century CE, Samaritans and Judeans worshiped the same God and used the same Torah, but Judeans promoted centralized worship from Jerusalem, while Samaritans worshiped farther north on Mount Gerizim. Exhausted, Jesus meets the unnamed Samaritan woman at Jacob's well, located near Shechem, close to the city of Samaria (see Gen 33:18-20). She is drawing water, perhaps for the second time that day, in the noon-day heat, when others would avoid being out. In the Hebrew Bible, numerous encounters between men and women take place at wells (e.g., Gen 24). In their dialogue, we witness a transformation in both Jesus and the woman, from mutual wariness and bias to openness and understanding. Throughout their discussion, Jesus breaks down religious and cultural boundaries in numerous ways: he states that future worship will not be relegated to a single temple; he speaks to a woman in public; he offers to draw water for *her* ("living water" that leads to "eternal life") when drawing water was considered a woman's duty; and he discloses his divine status to a Samaritan *and* a woman. The text features a litany of names for Jesus that reveal a deepening understanding of who he is: from "Jew" to "prophet," "Messiah" and "Christ" (literally "the Anointed"), and finally, "savior of the world." Jesus's "I am he" (v. 26) also translates as "I AM" (Greek *egō eimi*), drawing from God's self-designation to Moses (Exod 3:14). After she begins to believe, the woman calls others to come and see (v. 29). They listen and follow her, which suggests that she is not as much of an outcast as some commentaries would suggest. The final statement that Jesus is the "savior of the world" (v. 42) collapses the boundaries between Samaritan and Judean.

Ponder

Access to clean water is a pressing concern in today's world. Water and thirst are also key themes in our readings. Exodus and the Gospel begin with people thirsting, the desperate kind of thirst that comes from trekking through the scorching midday heat of a desert climate. In this context, clean, flowing water equates to living water, and to find it is something of a miracle. Yet our texts push these themes of thirst and water further. What would it mean to imagine this desperate thirst in terms of our desire for God? What would it mean to recognize that faith is as essential for life as access to clean, flowing water? As we come closer to renewing our baptismal promises on Easter, our readings offer a space to reflect on thirst and the essential need for water. How do we satisfy this need, for ourselves and for others?

God is with us. This promise flows throughout the Bible, though it can be difficult to believe during life's challenges. It is easy to ask, like the Israelites, "Is the LORD in our midst or not?" Their concern was not whether God existed but whether God still cared for them. The answer is yes: God's love for them—for *us*—is persistent, fierce, and enduring. This love embraces weaknesses, imperfections, and even sins. According to Paul, it is not ease of life that points to God's continual presence with us but rather the love of God "poured out into our hearts" through faith and the gift of Christ. This is the living water that satiates our deeper, inner thirst. When we experience this love, it overflows from us into our communities and families. As you pray with our readings, how do you experience God's love pouring into your heart? What are tangible ways to allow the outpouring of this love today?

Fourth Sunday of Lent
(Laetare Sunday)

FIRST READING   1 SAMUEL 16:1b, 6-7, 10-13a

The LORD said to Samuel:
    "Fill your horn with oil, and be on your way.
I am sending you to Jesse of Bethlehem,
    for I have chosen my king from among his sons."

As Jesse and his sons came to the sacrifice,
    Samuel looked at Eliab and thought,
    "Surely the LORD's anointed is here before him."
But the LORD said to Samuel:
    "Do not judge from his appearance or from his lofty stature,
    because I have rejected him.
Not as man sees does God see,
    because man sees the appearance
    but the LORD looks into the heart."
In the same way Jesse presented seven sons before Samuel,
    but Samuel said to Jesse,
    "The LORD has not chosen any one of these."
Then Samuel asked Jesse,
    "Are these all the sons you have?"
Jesse replied,
    "There is still the youngest, who is tending the sheep."
Samuel said to Jesse,
    "Send for him;
    we will not begin the sacrificial banquet until he arrives here."
Jesse sent and had the young man brought to them.
He was ruddy, a youth handsome to behold
    and making a splendid appearance.
The LORD said,
    "There—anoint him, for this is the one!"
Then Samuel, with the horn of oil in hand,
    anointed David in the presence of his brothers;
    and from that day on, the spirit of the LORD rushed upon David.

David's anointing introduces us to the future king of Israel and sets the stage for a political drama that will unfold throughout the books of Samuel and until David's death in 1 Kings 2. Kings in the ancient world were anointed or consecrated for kingship by the pouring of oil over their heads, which designated them as God's "anointed" (*māšîaḥ* or messiah). Prophets like Samuel mediated between God and king and functioned as an ancient form of checks and balances. In this story, the anointing takes place secretly while Saul, Israel's first king, is still in power but has lost God's favor (see 1 Sam 15). The "horn of oil" was a ram's horn filled with fine olive oil. Bethlehem lies about six miles south of Jerusalem, and Jesse was likely one of the town's elders or leaders (see 16:4-5). God dissuades Samuel from anointing Jesse's sons, beginning with Eliab (the oldest), until he comes to the youngest. The story contains a paradox: God tells Samuel not to regard someone's height or physical good looks as a sign of their inward ability, for humans see only "the appearance," while God sees "the heart." Still, David is very handsome or of "splendid appearance." He is "ruddy," meaning of reddish or healthy complexion, and has "beautiful eyes" according to the Hebrew (translated above as "handsome to behold"). Yet his status as eighth and "youngest" son designates his humble origins (Hebrew *qāṭān* translates as "young," "small," or "unimportant"). After "the spirit of the LORD rushed upon David," God's spirit departs from Saul (v. 14).

RESPONSORIAL PSALM   PSALM 23:1-3a, 3b-4, 5, 6

The Lord is my shepherd; there is nothing I shall want.

SECOND READING   EPHESIANS 5:8-14

Brothers and sisters:
You were once darkness,
    but now you are light in the Lord.
Live as children of light,
    for light produces every kind of goodness
    and righteousness and truth.
Try to learn what is pleasing to the Lord.

Take no part in the fruitless works of darkness;
   rather expose them, for it is shameful even to mention
   the things done by them in secret;
   but everything exposed by the light becomes visible,
   for everything that becomes visible is light.
Therefore, it says:
   "Awake, O sleeper,
   and arise from the dead,
   and Christ will give you light."

For background information on Ephesians, consult the notes for The Epiphany of the Lord. The metaphor of light and darkness comes in the midst of a broader appeal to live a changed way of life through faith in Christ (4:17–5:21). Darkness is the realm of unbelieving Gentiles and spiritual forces that are hostile to God, while light is the realm of God and believers. The author speaks to those who have come to believe in Christ, who were once "darkness" but are now "light" in and through Christ. The final quoted verse ("Awake, O sleeper. . .") may be a remnant of an early Christian hymn. The association between death and sleep draws from the Hebrew Bible and early Judaism (e.g., Isa 26:19; 60:1).

GOSPEL   JOHN 9:1-41 [OR 9:1, 6-9, 13-17, 34-38]

As Jesus passed by he saw a man blind from birth.
His disciples asked him,
   "Rabbi, who sinned, this man or his parents,
   that he was born blind?"
Jesus answered,
   "Neither he nor his parents sinned;
   it is so that the works of God might be made visible
      through him.
We have to do the works of the one who sent me while it is day.
Night is coming when no one can work.
While I am in the world, I am the light of the world."
When he had said this, he spat on the ground
   and made clay with the saliva,
   and smeared the clay on his eyes, and said to him,
   "Go wash in the Pool of Siloam"—which means Sent—.

So he went and washed, and came back able to see.

His neighbors and those who had seen him earlier as a
    beggar said,
  "Isn't this the one who used to sit and beg?"
Some said, "It is,"
  but others said, "No, he just looks like him."
He said, "I am."
So they said to him, "How were your eyes opened?"
He replied,
  "The man called Jesus made clay and anointed my eyes
  and told me, 'Go to Siloam and wash.'
So I went there and washed and was able to see."
And they said to him, "Where is he?"
He said, "I don't know."

They brought the one who was once blind to the Pharisees.
Now Jesus had made clay and opened his eyes on a sabbath.
So then the Pharisees also asked him how he was able to see.
He said to them,
  "He put clay on my eyes, and I washed, and now I can see."
So some of the Pharisees said,
  "This man is not from God,
  because he does not keep the sabbath."
But others said,
  "How can a sinful man do such signs?"
And there was a division among them.
So they said to the blind man again,
  "What do you have to say about him,
  since he opened your eyes?"
He said, "He is a prophet."

Now the Jews did not believe
  that he had been blind and gained his sight
  until they summoned the parents of the one who had gained
    his sight.
They asked them,
  "Is this your son, who you say was born blind?
How does he now see?"
His parents answered and said,
  "We know that this is our son and that he was born blind.
We do not know how he sees now,
  nor do we know who opened his eyes.

Ask him, he is of age;
    he can speak for himself."
His parents said this because they were afraid of the Jews,
    for the Jews had already agreed
    that if anyone acknowledged him as the Christ,
    he would be expelled from the synagogue.
For this reason his parents said,
    "He is of age; question him."

So a second time they called the man who had been blind
    and said to him, "Give God the praise!
We know that this man is a sinner."
He replied,
    "If he is a sinner, I do not know.
One thing I do know is that I was blind and now I see."
So they said to him,
    "What did he do to you?
    How did he open your eyes?"
He answered them,
    "I told you already and you did not listen.
Why do you want to hear it again?
Do you want to become his disciples, too?"
They ridiculed him and said,
    "You are that man's disciple;
    we are disciples of Moses!
We know that God spoke to Moses,
    but we do not know where this one is from."
The man answered and said to them,
    "This is what is so amazing,
    that you do not know where he is from, yet he opened
        my eyes.
We know that God does not listen to sinners,
    but if one is devout and does his will, he listens to him.
It is unheard of that anyone ever opened the eyes of a person
        born blind.
If this man were not from God,
    he would not be able to do anything."
They answered and said to him,
    "You were born totally in sin,
    and are you trying to teach us?"
Then they threw him out.

When Jesus heard that they had thrown him out,
　he found him and said, "Do you believe in the Son of Man?"
He answered and said,
　"Who is he, sir, that I may believe in him?"
Jesus said to him,
　"You have seen him,
　and the one speaking with you is he."
He said,
　"I do believe, Lord," and he worshiped him.
Then Jesus said,
　"I came into this world for judgment,
　so that those who do not see might see,
　and those who do see might become blind."

Some of the Pharisees who were with him heard this
　and said to him, "Surely we are not also blind, are we?"
Jesus said to them,
　"If you were blind, you would have no sin;
　but now you are saying, 'We see,' so your sin remains."

This passage juxtaposes one man's spiritual journey from darkness to light with the entrenched "darkness" or ignorance of those who interrogate him. The story has a simple beginning: Jesus heals the man in the style of a prophet, applying mud to the man's eyes. This was a common ancient remedy, for mud was thought to have curative properties. The miracle involves Jesus's physical touch and is less dramatic than other miracles (in contrast, in next Sunday's Gospel, Jesus raises Lazarus from the dead simply by calling him). However, the seemingly understated miracle in today's Gospel soon shifts into a profound account of faith seeking understanding and, simultaneously, an example of ignorance seeking further entrenchment. The story reads like a trial scene. The barrage of questions and shifting tactics from the prosecutors (the religious leaders) have the opposite effect on the witness (the man) than we would expect. He remains calm and firm in his story while slowly undergoing a process of inward transformation into true sight or understanding of who Jesus is. The man begins by not knowing Jesus (v. 12), then calls him a prophet (v. 17), then a man of God (v. 33), and finally worships Jesus as Lord (v. 38). In the end, it turns out that Jesus is both true defendant and judge, as he pronounces judgment on his own judges. The story has multiple layers. On one level, it is a simple healing story. At a deeper level, it reflects on what blindness and sight really mean. And on a third level, it is a message to us about baptism and discipleship. The eyes are opened through baptism, just as Jesus smears or literally "anoints" (Greek *epichriō*) the man's eyes as a baptismal symbol. The man then becomes a disciple (v. 28).

Ponder

Both David in 1 Samuel and the man in John's Gospel are anointed, chosen for some special purpose. Both are also of little account by society's standards; one is the youngest and least important son, the other a nameless blind man. Yet according to God, David is "the one." So is the formerly blind man, chosen so that God's works could be "made visible through him." There is metaphor, journey, and rejoicing in these passages: from nothing to everything, from ignorance to anointing and discipleship. This is our journey, too, and one to embrace on this Laetare Sunday (*laetare* means "rejoice" in Latin). Imagine God looking upon you and calling you, beckoning to you as "the one." How are you anointed, chosen to serve and make manifest God's works, in your life and community?

In the Gospel, the formerly blind man slowly transforms from ignorance to understanding. Like him, we are also in a process of slow transformation, yet for us this process never ends. There is always a deeper level of understanding and intimacy with God to reach. And unlike the man in the Gospel, our path is not straightforward. We move forward and backward, sometimes closing our eyes to the light like the man's accusers, sometimes seeing clearly. We are each on a unique journey of faith. The thing to remember is that we have already become "light in the Lord," according to Ephesians. We have only to remember to trust and live in that light. Each day, each moment, is an opportunity to begin again, trusting that God is guiding us even when the path seems dark and uncertain.

Fifth Sunday of Lent

FIRST READING   EZEKIEL 37:12-14

Thus says the Lord GOD:
  O my people, I will open your graves
  and have you rise from them,
  and bring you back to the land of Israel.
Then you shall know that I am the LORD,
    when I open your graves and have you rise from them,
  O my people!
I will put my spirit in you that you may live,
  and I will settle you upon your land;
    thus you shall know that I am the LORD.
I have promised, and I will do it, says the LORD.

Ezekiel (whose name means "God strengthens") prophesied from Babylon in the sixth century BCE (ca. 593–571). He was among the first wave of exiles from Judah, and his prophecies are directed both to the exiled community of Judeans and to those still living in Judah. Ezekiel came from a priestly lineage, as evidenced by a concern for the Jerusalem temple and by themes of ritual and purity that echo throughout the book. The first part of the book emphasizes Judah's judgment (chaps. 1–24), while the second part judges foreign nations (chaps. 25–32). The book concludes with hope for Judah's restoration (chaps. 33–48). Our reading draws from one of the most poignant texts in this long message of hope. In it, God takes Ezekiel out to the middle of a valley that is full of bones. The bones represent the entire exiled community that is dead or "dried up" as a result of God's punishment (v. 11). God brings the entire community back to life, renewing their hope and returning them to Judah. It seems that bodily resurrection was at least a theoretical possibility for Ezekiel, yet the image of Israel rising up from the grave is metaphoric and alludes to the restoration of the people in their homeland. In both Jewish and Christian tradition, this text has come to represent the promise of resurrection and, especially, the resurrection of all believers in the end times.

RESPONSORIAL PSALM   PSALM 130:1-2, 3-4, 5-6, 7-8

With the Lord there is mercy and fullness of redemption.

SECOND READING   ROMANS 8:8-11

Brothers and sisters:
Those who are in the flesh cannot please God.
But you are not in the flesh;
    on the contrary, you are in the spirit,
    if only the Spirit of God dwells in you.
Whoever does not have the Spirit of Christ does not belong
        to him.
But if Christ is in you,
    although the body is dead because of sin,
    the spirit is alive because of righteousness.
If the Spirit of the One who raised Jesus from the dead dwells
        in you,
    the One who raised Christ from the dead
    will give life to your mortal bodies also,
    through his Spirit dwelling in you.

Romans 8 concludes a long explanation of the meaning of God's righteousness (1:18–8:39). In this explanation, Paul first indicts all humanity, stating that no one is righteous (3:9-20). Yet through Christ, God's righteousness repairs the divine-human relationship and justifies all who believe, Jews and Gentiles alike (3:21–5:21). This remarkable gift of (re)unification with God crucifies the old self and sets one free of sin, to be "slaves" not of sin but of righteousness (6:1-23). To be set free from sin is to be liberated from trying to live in accordance with the law, the highest spiritual standard that no human being—or one living "in the flesh"—can successfully follow (7:1-25). For Paul, "flesh" is not the body itself, which is a "temple of the holy Spirit" (1 Cor 6:19). Rather, the "flesh" refers to the susceptibility of the human person to passions and weakness. In Romans 8:1-17, Paul juxtaposes living according to the flesh with living according to the Spirit through death and resurrection, which leads to spiritual adoption as children of God. See the Fourteenth Sunday in Ordinary Time, which picks up where this reading leaves off.

GOSPEL   JOHN 11:1-45 [OR 11:3-7, 17, 20-27, 33b-45]

Now a man was ill, Lazarus from Bethany,
　　the village of Mary and her sister Martha.
Mary was the one who had anointed the Lord with perfumed oil
　　and dried his feet with her hair;
　　it was her brother Lazarus who was ill.
So the sisters sent word to Jesus saying,
　　"Master, the one you love is ill."
When Jesus heard this he said,
　　"This illness is not to end in death,
　　but is for the glory of God,
　　that the Son of God may be glorified through it."
Now Jesus loved Martha and her sister and Lazarus.
So when he heard that he was ill,
　　he remained for two days in the place where he was.
Then after this he said to his disciples,
　　"Let us go back to Judea."
The disciples said to him,
　　"Rabbi, the Jews were just trying to stone you,
　　and you want to go back there?"
Jesus answered,
　　"Are there not twelve hours in a day?
If one walks during the day, he does not stumble,
　　because he sees the light of this world.
But if one walks at night, he stumbles,
　　because the light is not in him."
He said this, and then told them,
　　"Our friend Lazarus is asleep,
　　but I am going to awaken him."
So the disciples said to him,
　　"Master, if he is asleep, he will be saved."
But Jesus was talking about his death,
　　while they thought that he meant ordinary sleep.
So then Jesus said to them clearly,
　　"Lazarus has died.
And I am glad for you that I was not there,
　　that you may believe.
Let us go to him."

So Thomas, called Didymus, said to his fellow disciples,
   "Let us also go to die with him."

When Jesus arrived, he found that Lazarus
   had already been in the tomb for four days.
Now Bethany was near Jerusalem, only about two miles away.
And many of the Jews had come to Martha and Mary
   to comfort them about their brother.
When Martha heard that Jesus was coming,
   she went to meet him;
   but Mary sat at home.
Martha said to Jesus,
   "Lord, if you had been here,
   my brother would not have died.
But even now I know that whatever you ask of God,
   God will give you."
Jesus said to her,
   "Your brother will rise."
Martha said to him,
   "I know he will rise,
   in the resurrection on the last day."
Jesus told her,
   "I am the resurrection and the life;
   whoever believes in me, even if he dies, will live,
   and everyone who lives and believes in me will never die.
Do you believe this?"
She said to him, "Yes, Lord.
I have come to believe that you are the Christ, the Son of God,
   the one who is coming into the world."

When she had said this,
   she went and called her sister Mary secretly, saying,
   "The teacher is here and is asking for you."
As soon as she heard this,
   she rose quickly and went to him.
For Jesus had not yet come into the village,
   but was still where Martha had met him.
So when the Jews who were with her in the house comforting her
   saw Mary get up quickly and go out,
   they followed her,
   presuming that she was going to the tomb to weep there.

When Mary came to where Jesus was and saw him,
  she fell at his feet and said to him,
  "Lord, if you had been here,
  my brother would not have died."
When Jesus saw her weeping and the Jews who had come with
    her weeping,
  he became perturbed and deeply troubled, and said,
  "Where have you laid him?"
They said to him, "Sir, come and see."
And Jesus wept.
So the Jews said, "See how he loved him."
But some of them said,
  "Could not the one who opened the eyes of the blind man
  have done something so that this man would not have died?"

So Jesus, perturbed again, came to the tomb.
It was a cave, and a stone lay across it.
Jesus said, "Take away the stone."
Martha, the dead man's sister, said to him,
  "Lord, by now there will be a stench;
  he has been dead for four days."
Jesus said to her,
  "Did I not tell you that if you believe
  you will see the glory of God?"
So they took away the stone.
And Jesus raised his eyes and said,
  "Father, I thank you for hearing me.
I know that you always hear me;
  but because of the crowd here I have said this,
  that they may believe that you sent me."
And when he had said this,
  he cried out in a loud voice,
  "Lazarus, come out!"
The dead man came out,
  tied hand and foot with burial bands,
  and his face was wrapped in a cloth.
So Jesus said to them,
  "Untie him and let him go."

Now many of the Jews who had come to Mary
  and seen what he had done began to believe in him.

The raising of Lazarus takes place in Bethany, just two miles east of Jerusalem. It is the last and culminating sign or miracle in John's Gospel before Jesus reaches Jerusalem, the site of his own death and resurrection. The text is about God's help for the afflicted, as demonstrated by the names in the first verse: Lazarus (Eleazar in Hebrew) means "God helps," and Bethany means "house of the afflicted." Mary and Martha are key figures in Luke 10:38-42, and Mary of Bethany will anoint Jesus in John 12:1-8. As in the Gospel accounts from the last two Sundays, the miracle becomes an opportunity to demonstrate Jesus's true identity. Yet unlike the last two accounts, a primary focus is Jesus's ability to enter into and share in the suffering of others, as demonstrated by the remarkable description of his emotions. This miracle therefore alludes to Jesus's crucifixion—his call to suffer for the many—and foreshadows his resurrection. In addition, Lazarus is not a stranger whom Jesus encounters on the way to Jerusalem; instead, the narrator tells us that Jesus "loved" Mary and Martha and Lazarus. Yet Jesus does not rush to Mary and Martha when he learns that Lazarus is ill. Instead, he waits until Lazarus is *really* dead (according to rabbinic sources, the spirit stays near the body for three days before departing). Note, too, that in contrast to the parents of the man born blind (see the Gospel reading for the Fourth Sunday of Lent), Mary and Martha are unafraid to be known as Jesus's followers. Lazarus comes out of the tomb wrapped in a "cloth" or shroud, a common method of Jewish burial in the first century meant to aid decomposition. After eleven months, the tomb would have been unsealed and the bones placed in a bone box and stored on a shelf in the tomb. Raising Lazarus seals Jesus's fate; it leads directly to the decision to put Jesus to death (vv. 45-53).

Ponder

In our readings, death and rising from the dead take many forms. In Ezekiel, death is akin to hopelessness, and resurrection is its reversal—the infusion of hope into an exiled, suffering community. For Paul, resurrection is linked with righteousness and new life with Christ through the death of sin. And in the Gospel, the raising of Lazarus is a literal, physical return to life from death, and with it a shift from mourning to celebration. Consider the areas of death in your own life and in the world around you—those spaces of hopelessness, brokenness, and mourning. What spaces need new life, and what would resurrection look like in those spaces?

Resurrection is an intimate experience of union with God. It is a call and response, a physical and spiritual drawing out from death into new life. In Ezekiel, God calls the exiled community out of the grave through the loving refrain "O my people" and clothes them with flesh, sinew, and breath. In our responsorial psalm, it is the psalmist who cries out from the depths, trusting in God's redemption. And finally, Jesus calls Lazarus to "come out" from the tomb, and Lazarus responds. Jesus both calls us and hears our cries for help. He embraces us in our suffering, lifts our burdens, and beckons us to come out from the areas of death and sin in our own lives. Spend time in prayer with Jesus this week. Call to him, be honest about what burdens you, and listen for his call to "come out" and be set free.

Palm Sunday of the Passion of the Lord

Servant Song

FIRST READING

ISAIAH 50:4-7

The Lord GOD has given me
  a well-trained tongue,
that I might know how to speak to the weary
  a word that will rouse them.
Morning after morning
  he opens my ear that I may hear;
and I have not rebelled,
  have not turned back.
I gave my back to those who beat me,
  my cheeks to those who plucked my beard;
my face I did not shield
  from buffets and spitting.

The Lord GOD is my help,
  therefore I am not disgraced;
I have set my face like flint,
  knowing that I shall not be put to shame.

For context on the book of Isaiah and its major divisions, consult the First Sunday of Advent. Our reading draws from the third of four "Servant Songs" in Second Isaiah (42:1-4; 49:1-6; 50:4-11; 52:13–53:12). We will read from the fourth Servant Song on Good Friday. This third song combines two voices: the servant's (vv. 4-9) and God's (vv. 10-11). The servant equates himself twice with a disciple or one who is "well-trained" (literally "one who is taught"). We see this in the first sentence of the above reading in reference to "a well-trained tongue." Yet this same expression is lost in the above translation of the second sentence (compare with this literal translation: "Morning by morning he wakens—wakens my ear to listen *as those who are taught.* The Lord God has opened my ear, and I have not rebelled, have not turned back"; emphasis added). The servant listens before he speaks; he then speaks directly to the weary and afflicted. His words make him a physical target, yet he suffers nonviolently and acclaims God through his words. This servant is an anonymous male who has been identified with numerous figures, including the prophet Isaiah or another unknown prophet, Zion/Jerusalem, the exiled Judeans, and a future savior figure. Christian tradition views the servant as Jesus.

RESPONSORIAL PSALM   PSALM 22:8-9, 17-18, 19-20, 23-24

My God, my God, why have you abandoned me?

SECOND READING   PHILIPPIANS 2:6-11

Christ Jesus, though he was in the form of God,
    did not regard equality with God
    something to be grasped.
Rather, he emptied himself,
    taking the form of a slave,
    coming in human likeness;
    and found human in appearance,
    he humbled himself,
    becoming obedient to the point of death,
    even death on a cross.
Because of this, God greatly exalted him
    and bestowed on him the name
    which is above every name,
    that at the name of Jesus
    every knee should bend,
    of those in heaven and on earth and under the earth,
    and every tongue confess that
    Jesus Christ is Lord,
    to the glory of God the Father.

The hymn in today's reading from Philippians is one of the oldest texts in the New Testament. It describes the entire mystery of Christ, who was in the physical "form" (Greek *morphē*) of God and was hence equal to God, yet he did not regard this equality as "something to be grasped" (the Greek term *harpagmos* is rare and may mean to be held on to by force or to be exploited in some way). According to traditional biblical scholarship, the hymn describes how Christ "emptied" himself, not of his divinity but of his status of glory, and "humbled" (or literally "humiliated") himself through incarnation and crucifixion.

The humble one is then exalted (literally "super-exalted") and adored by the entire universe in his new title as "Lord" (Greek *Kyrios*).

GOSPEL   MATTHEW 26:14–27:66 OR 27:11-54 (HERE 27:33-54)

And when they came to a place called Golgotha
  —which means Place of the Skull—,
  they gave Jesus wine to drink mixed with gall.
But when he had tasted it, he refused to drink.
After they had crucified him,
  they divided his garments by casting lots;
  then they sat down and kept watch over him there.
And they placed over his head the written charge against him:
  This is Jesus, the King of the Jews.
Two revolutionaries were crucified with him,
  one on his right and the other on his left.
Those passing by reviled him, shaking their heads and saying,
  "You who would destroy the temple and rebuild it in
      three days,
  save yourself, if you are the Son of God,
  and come down from the cross!"
Likewise the chief priests with the scribes and elders mocked him
    and said,
  "He saved others; he cannot save himself.
So he is the king of Israel!
Let him come down from the cross now,
  and we will believe in him.
He trusted in God;
  let him deliver him now if he wants him.
For he said, 'I am the Son of God.'"
The revolutionaries who were crucified with him
  also kept abusing him in the same way.

From noon onward, darkness came over the whole land
  until three in the afternoon.
And about three o'clock Jesus cried out in a loud voice,
  "Eli, Eli, lema sabachthani?"
  which means, "My God, my God, why have you forsaken me?"
Some of the bystanders who heard it said,
  "This one is calling for Elijah."

depth of human suffering

Immediately one of them ran to get a sponge;
    he soaked it in wine, and putting it on a reed,
    gave it to him to drink.
But the rest said,
    "Wait, let us see if Elijah comes to save him."
But Jesus cried out again in a loud voice,
    and gave up his spirit.

(Here all kneel and pause for a short time.)

And behold, the veil of the sanctuary
    was torn in two from top to bottom.
The earth quaked, rocks were split, tombs were opened,
    and the bodies of many saints who had fallen asleep
        were raised.
And coming forth from their tombs after his resurrection,
    they entered the holy city and appeared to many.
The centurion and the men with him who were keeping watch
      over Jesus
    feared greatly when they saw the earthquake
    and all that was happening, and they said,
    "Truly, this was the Son of God!"

In each Gospel account, Jesus makes a final statement from the cross before he dies. In Luke's Gospel, Jesus quotes from Psalm 31:6: "Into your hands I commend my spirit" (see Luke 23:46; see also Acts 7:59, where Stephen, the first martyr in Acts, echoes these words before he dies). In John's Gospel, Jesus says simply, "It is finished" (in reference to his completed mission; 19:30). In contrast, Mark's and Matthew's Gospels emphasize Jesus's humanity in his cry of agonizing faith in Aramaic, quoting Psalm 22:2: "My God, my God, why have you abandoned me?" (Mark 15:34; Matt 27:46; alternative translations for "abandoned me" are "forsaken me" or "left me"). Here and throughout Matthew's passion narrative, Jesus experiences the depths of human suffering that come not only from physical pain and humiliation but also from the sense of utter abandonment by God and all those around him. The word "passion" comes from the Latin word *passio*, meaning passivity in the sense of internal submission to great difficulty. Whereas much of Matthew's Gospel focuses on Jesus's activity, here we turn to Jesus's passivity, meaning not a lack of involvement but deep involvement in his submission to the divine plan. Through his submission (his passivity or passion) Jesus accomplishes something far greater than any of his prior activities, and when he dies, Jesus is instantly recognized as the Son of God. The entire reading is too long to include here, but it is worth meditating on throughout Holy Week, particularly its rich themes of friendship and betrayal, love and forgiveness, and commitment and the great cost of discipleship.

Ponder

The beauty of Isaiah's Servant Song lies in the mystery of the servant's identity. In his anonymity, the servant stands for all those who have suffered injustice yet remain peaceful and firm in their commitment to God and in their vision of a just world. His qualities of humility, gentleness, steadfastness, and selfless love are mirrored in the description of Jesus throughout the passion narrative. According to Philippians, these are the qualities of God and the markers of real power, in contrast to human displays of violence, brute force, and humiliation. This week, ponder your understanding of power. Do you connect power to gentleness, humility, and steadfast love? How and where do you see these qualities manifest in the world and in the anonymous servants around you? *Power over self or power over others?*

The long Gospel readings today, from the entry into Jerusalem (read at the procession) and the passion, reveal human fickleness as well as loyalty. Throngs of people who initially proclaim Jesus soon deny him, turn their backs on him, even abuse him. But not everyone. For example, we hear of the many women standing by Jesus as he dies and who remain by his side even as he is entombed. They are the quiet and steadfast followers, the ones who suffer with Jesus throughout his passion. These true disciples are easy to miss in all the noise. The beginning of Holy Week is a time to examine honestly our own tendencies toward fickleness and our loyalty as followers of Christ. What are our failures and successes in Christian discipleship? When we examine our hearts and actions, to what—or to whom—are we most deeply committed?

Easter Sunday of the Resurrection of the Lord

FIRST READING   ACTS 10:34a, 37-43

Peter proceeded to speak and said:
"You know what has happened all over Judea,
    beginning in Galilee after the baptism
    that John preached,
    how God anointed Jesus of Nazareth
    with the Holy Spirit and power.
He went about doing good
    and healing all those oppressed by the devil,
    for God was with him.
We are witnesses of all that he did
    both in the country of the Jews and in Jerusalem.
They put him to death by hanging him on a tree.
This man God raised on the third day and granted that he
        be visible,
    not to all the people, but to us,
    the witnesses chosen by God in advance,
    who ate and drank with him after he rose from the dead.
He commissioned us to preach to the people
    and testify that he is the one appointed by God
    as judge of the living and the dead.
To him all the prophets bear witness,
    that everyone who believes in him
    will receive forgiveness of sins through his name."

Throughout the Easter season, the Acts of the Apostles will take the place of the Hebrew Bible in our first reading. Acts is the sequel to Luke's Gospel, and we call the author of both books "Luke," though the author is not identified in either book. Acts recounts the time from Jesus's ascension until Paul's house arrest in Rome, focusing on the early Jerusalem church, the apostles Peter and Paul, the spread of the gospel through their missionary endeavors, and the continuity between Judaism and early Christianity. The author describes the ideal Gentile convert as one who practices Jewish acts of piety like almsgiving and prayer (10:2) and other practices that maintain association with Jews (in other words, avoiding practices that were offensive to Jewish customs, such as eating meat sacrificed to idols; 15:20). Our reading comes from a key story in which God directs Peter to include the Gentiles in his mission. The story deals with the conversion of Cornelius, an officer in the Roman army who sends for Peter after receiving a vision from God. Peter simultaneously receives a vision in which God dissolves Jewish dietary regulations. Peter travels to Cornelius's house, where a group of Gentiles are assembled, and he tells those gathered the story of Jesus's life, death, and resurrection. Immediately after this excerpt, Peter witnesses the Holy Spirit being poured out among those assembled, and he calls for their baptism (10:44-48).

RESPONSORIAL PSALM   PSALM 118:1-2, 16-17, 22-23

This is the day the Lord has made; let us rejoice and be glad.

SECOND READING   COLOSSIANS 3:1-4 (ALT. 1 COR 5:6b-8)[1]

Brothers and sisters:
If then you were raised with Christ, seek what is above,
    where Christ is seated at the right hand of God.
Think of what is above, not of what is on earth.
For you have died, and your life is hidden with Christ in God.
When Christ your life appears,
    then you too will appear with him in glory.

For background on the letter to the Colossians, see The Holy Family of Jesus, Mary, and Joseph. One of the letter's key arguments is that baptism makes one full or complete in Christ. Through baptism, believers undergo a death and resurrection that fully transforms their reality and way of being. As a result of baptism, believers are to

---

1. For commentary on the alternative reading from 1 Corinthians, see *Ponder: Year B*.

set aside old ways of life and act in accordance with the new reality of "Christ in you" (1:27). No longer is their reality that of a fleeting, earthly life; instead, it is eternal and "above," rooted in Christ and in the kingdom of God. The author echoes Psalm 110:1 in referring to Christ as "seated at the right hand of God" in this eternal realm. In the final line, the author affirms that when Christ "appears" or returns in the fullness of time, this final and full revelation will glorify all those who have been baptized and reborn into life with Christ (see also 1 John 3:2).

GOSPEL   MATTHEW 28:1-10 (ALT. JOHN 20:1-9)[2]

After the sabbath, as the first day of the week was dawning,
    Mary Magdalene and the other Mary came to see the tomb.
And behold, there was a great earthquake;
    for an angel of the Lord descended from heaven,
    approached, rolled back the stone, and sat upon it.
His appearance was like lightning
    and his clothing was white as snow.
The guards were shaken with fear of him
    and became like dead men.
Then the angel said to the women in reply,
    "Do not be afraid!
I know that you are seeking Jesus the crucified.
He is not here, for he has been raised just as he said.
Come and see the place where he lay.
Then go quickly and tell his disciples,
    'He has been raised from the dead,
    and he is going before you to Galilee;
    there you will see him.'
    Behold, I have told you."
Then they went away quickly from the tomb,
    fearful yet overjoyed,
    and ran to announce this to his disciples.
And behold, Jesus met them on their way and greeted them.

---

2. This is the Gospel reading for the Easter Vigil in Year A. For commentary on John 20:1-9, the Gospel for the Mass of Easter Day, see *Ponder: Year B*.

They approached, embraced his feet, and did him homage.
Then Jesus said to them, "Do not be afraid.
Go tell my brothers to go to Galilee,
   and there they will see me."

Every year on Easter Sunday, we read the post-crucifixion account according to John 20:1-9. Another option for Sunday's reading is a Synoptic version of the same story, which we read at Saturday night's Easter Vigil. This year, the Synoptic account comes from Matthew, which in many ways follows Mark 16:1-8 (Mark was likely the earliest Gospel written and was used as a guide by Luke and Matthew). According to Mark, three women go to the tomb to prepare the body of Jesus for burial (Mary Magdalene; James's mother, Mary; and Salome). They encounter a young man in white within the tomb, who tells them that Jesus has risen and orders them to inform the disciples. They flee from the tomb and, according to the short account, tell no one about their experience out of fear (Mark 16:8). According to Matthew, only two women are at the tomb: Mary Magdalene and "the other Mary" (who is identified as the mother of James and Joseph in 27:56). Matthew transforms Mark's description of the young man in white to an angel who descends from heaven amid the sounds of a "great earthquake," echoing the description of the earthquake after Jesus's death (27:51). Though the guards are "shaken with fear" at the sight of the angel descending, as are the centurion and guards at Jesus's death (27:54), the women's joy overcomes their fear. Unlike the shorter version in Mark, the women run to tell the disciples. These women are then the first to whom Jesus appears. Twice they are told not to fear, first by the angel and then by Jesus. When they encounter Jesus on the road, they physically touch him and experience that he is indeed alive.

Ponder

Mary Magdalene and the other Mary were Easter people. When the angel descended, he told them not to fear but to come and see that the body was missing and then to "go quickly and tell." Yet the women did not even look into the tomb. Instead, they rushed off instantly to proclaim that life had emerged from the grave. On the way, they encountered the living Jesus. They were Easter people. So are we. We, too, are invited away from the tomb to embrace the living Jesus, the life and hope that breaks us out of darkness. Imagine the angel telling you to "go quickly," to be a messenger of hope wherever it is needed. On the journey, you will find Jesus. Where and to whom will you go?

"Alleluia!"—"Praise Yah [YHWH, the Divine Name]!" We will sing this joyful acclamation throughout the Easter season. It encapsulates the mystery of Christ and the human journey of forgiveness and transformation. Today, we renew our baptismal promises alongside the newly baptized and affirm with Colossians that we have been and will be raised up with Christ. We have only to remember and live into this reality, day by day, in our lives and communities. Throughout Holy Week and the Triduum, we concentrate on Jesus. But Easter Sunday points back to us. What will *we* do with the new life we have been given?

Second Sunday of Easter
(or Sunday of Divine Mercy)

FIRST READING   ACTS 2:42-47

They devoted themselves
    to the teaching of the apostles and to the communal life,
    to the breaking of bread and to the prayers.
Awe came upon everyone,
    and many wonders and signs were done through the apostles.
All who believed were together and had all things in common;
    they would sell their property and possessions
    and divide them among all according to each one's need.
Every day they devoted themselves
    to meeting together in the temple area
    and to breaking bread in their homes.
They ate their meals with exultation and sincerity of heart,
    praising God and enjoying favor with all the people.
And every day the Lord added to their number those who were
        being saved.

We begin our journey through Acts this Easter season with the author's vision of community among the early believers, which includes ongoing instruction or teaching, communal life and care, and right worship (see also 4:32-37; 5:12-16). Early Christian worship centered around the meal (the "breaking of bread") and small house churches, which eventually developed into the eucharistic celebrations in our churches today. The twice-used word "devoted" (vv. 42 and 46) denotes a dedication that is not easy but instead takes work and perseverance (from the Greek *proskartereō*). The author of Acts continually emphasizes the divine guidance behind the church's growth (e.g., 6:5-7; 9:31). The communal life characterized here may seem unattainable or unrealistically optimistic, and it was likely more of an ideal than a reality, yet how could any healthy community *not* be built upon the foundation of care, justice, and equitable distribution for each and all of its members?

RESPONSORIAL PSALM   PSALM 118:2-4, 13-15, 22-24

Give thanks to the Lord for he is good, his love is everlasting.
or: Alleluia.

SECOND READING   1 PETER 1:3-9

Blessed be the God and Father of our Lord Jesus Christ,
    who in his great mercy gave us a new birth to a living hope
    through the resurrection of Jesus Christ from the dead,
    to an inheritance that is imperishable, undefiled, and unfading,
    kept in heaven for you
    who by the power of God are safeguarded through faith,
    to a salvation that is ready to be revealed in the final time.
In this you rejoice, although now for a little while
    you may have to suffer through various trials,
    so that the genuineness of your faith,
    more precious than gold that is perishable even though tested
        by fire,
    may prove to be for praise, glory, and honor
    at the revelation of Jesus Christ.
Although you have not seen him you love him;
    even though you do not see him now yet believe in him,
    you rejoice with an indescribable and glorious joy,
    as you attain the goal of your faith, the salvation of your souls.

This week, we begin a semi-continuous reading of 1 Peter, a pastoral letter that was likely written at the end of the first century CE by a later disciple of Simon Peter. The author writes to Gentile converts to Christianity in Asia Minor (modern Turkey) who have become marginalized by their wider communities because of their belief in Jesus Christ. The author encourages readers to follow in Jesus's footsteps (2:21) and suffer without complaint for their faith, living in hope of their own perfect and mysterious "inheritance" in Jesus's resurrection (1:4). Our reading is an expression of praise to God, who has given Christians a "new birth" (baptism) into this "living hope," a hope that is ongoing and eternal. "Faith" has a wide range of meanings in 1 Peter; here, it refers to the trust in God that is essential for salvation. The "salvation that is ready to be revealed" is one that will occur in the end times, which early Christians believed would happen in their own generation. They look forward (not "up") to heaven as they reach toward this revelation within the context of their suffering. The author speaks of rejoicing as an "indescribable and glorious joy" rooted in salvation, a joy that far surpasses any trials in this life.

GOSPEL   JOHN 20:19-31

On the evening of that first day of the week,
   when the doors were locked, where the disciples were,
   for fear of the Jews,
   Jesus came and stood in their midst
   and said to them, "Peace be with you."
When he had said this, he showed them his hands and his side.
The disciples rejoiced when they saw the Lord.
Jesus said to them again, "Peace be with you.
As the Father has sent me, so I send you."
And when he had said this, he breathed on them and said
     to them,
   "Receive the Holy Spirit.
Whose sins you forgive are forgiven them,
   and whose sins you retain are retained."

Thomas, called Didymus, one of the Twelve,
   was not with them when Jesus came.
So the other disciples said to him, "We have seen the Lord."
But he said to them,
   "Unless I see the mark of the nails in his hands
   and put my finger into the nailmarks
   and put my hand into his side, I will not believe."

Now a week later his disciples were again inside
   and Thomas was with them.
Jesus came, although the doors were locked,
   and stood in their midst and said, "Peace be with you."
Then he said to Thomas, "Put your finger here and see my hands,
   and bring your hand and put it into my side,
   and do not be unbelieving, but believe."

Thomas answered and said to him, "My Lord and my God!"
Jesus said to him, "Have you come to believe because you have
    seen me?
Blessed are those who have not seen and have believed."

Now, Jesus did many other signs in the presence of his disciples
    that are not written in this book.
But these are written that you may come to believe
    that Jesus is the Christ, the Son of God,
    and that through this belief you may have life in his name.

We read this Gospel account from John every year on the Second
Sunday of Easter. In this single story, the Gospel writer summarizes
the mysteries of resurrection, ascension, and Pentecost. According
to John, after the resurrection Jesus first appears to Mary Magdalene
(20:11-18) and then to this unnumbered group of disciples. These
disciples are currently paralyzed by the shock and fear of crucifixion, hiding from those who had sought Jesus's death (keep in mind
that "Jews" is a code word in John's Gospel for those who oppose
Jesus; Jesus and all the disciples are also Jews). "Peace be with you"
is a traditional Jewish greeting (see 14:27). Jesus shows the disciples
his wounded body to prove he is not a ghost, and they rejoice. Jesus
then commissions the disciples and breathes the Spirit on them. The
Greek word for "breathe" (*emphysaō*) is a unique term that is attested
only here and in the Greek translation of Ezekiel 37:9, where God
breathes upon the bones of the dead to bring them back to life. In both
Greek and Hebrew, "breath" is synonymous with "wind" and "spirit."
In Catholic tradition, Jesus's statement about forgiving and retain-
ing sins (v. 23) provides the origins of the sacrament of reconciliation. Note Jesus's gentleness with Thomas, whereas elsewhere Jesus is
sharply critical of those who demand signs (4:48). Jesus complies with
Thomas's request, and Thomas calls Jesus "Lord" and "God" (Greek
Kyrios Theos), a translation of the Hebrew name for the "Lord our
God" (*Yahweh Elohim*). We do not know whether Thomas touches
Jesus, but we do know that he makes the most complete affirmation
of Christ's true nature out of anyone in the Gospel. Jesus's words in
response transcend the scene and speak to Christians across time.

Ponder

"Although you have not seen him you love him," writes the author of 1 Peter. Like his early Christian audience, we were not present at the crucifixion. We have not seen Jesus's wounds or touched his resurrected body. But we have experienced him in some capacity because there is no such thing as "secondhand faith."[1] For many of us, faith comes through the witness of others, by seeing Jesus enfleshed among those brave enough to be expressions of love, reconciliation, and justice in the midst of a broken world. Faith also comes through the records of communal memories shared in our sacred Scriptures. As Jesus says, we are the truly blessed ones for believing without seeing. And yet we do see. Where and through whom do you see the crucified and resurrected Jesus?

In the Gospel, Jesus offers his disciples both his peace and his very real wounds to see and touch. This double offering reminds us that peace is not an easy or trite choice, but it comes through the experience of crucifixion and dares to believe in an alternative path to violence and sin. Peace is a manifestation of divine mercy, connecting us with the Body of Christ and with suffering as a shared universal experience. Jesus entrusts his followers to be this path of peace, as does the author of 1 Peter. Imagine Jesus offering you his wounds, calling you to touch the places of suffering and brokenness in and around you. Imagine him simultaneously breathing his peace upon you, calling you forward on the path of healing and reconciliation. How do you respond to his double call?

---

1. Barbara E. Reid, *Abiding Word: Sunday Reflections for Year A* (Collegeville, MN: Liturgical Press, 2013), 36.

Third Sunday of Easter

Then Peter stood up with the Eleven,
   raised his voice, and proclaimed:
   "You who are Jews, indeed all of you staying in Jerusalem.
Let this be known to you, and listen to my words.
You who are Israelites, hear these words.
Jesus the Nazorean was a man commended to you by God
   with mighty deeds, wonders, and signs,
     which God worked through him in your midst, as you
      yourselves know.
This man, delivered up by the set plan and foreknowledge
   of God,
   you killed, using lawless men to crucify him.
But God raised him up, releasing him from the throes of death,
   because it was impossible for him to be held by it.
For David says of him:
   I saw the Lord ever before me,
     with him at my right hand I shall not be disturbed.
   Therefore my heart has been glad and my tongue has exulted;
     my flesh, too, will dwell in hope,
   because you will not abandon my soul to the netherworld,
     nor will you suffer your holy one to see corruption.
   You have made known to me the paths of life;
     you will fill me with joy in your presence.

"My brothers, one can confidently say to you
   about the patriarch David that he died and was buried,
   and his tomb is in our midst to this day.
But since he was a prophet and knew that God had sworn an
     oath to him
   that he would set one of his descendants upon his throne,
   he foresaw and spoke of the resurrection of the Christ,
   that neither was he abandoned to the netherworld
   nor did his flesh see corruption.
God raised this Jesus;
   of this we are all witnesses.

Exalted at the right hand of God,
   he received the promise of the Holy Spirit from the Father
   and poured him forth, as you see and hear."

The setting is Shavuot (also called the feast of Weeks or Pentecost, meaning "fiftieth" in Greek), the spring harvest that takes place fifty days after Passover (see Lev 23:15-21; Acts 2:1; notes on Pentecost Sunday). Shavuot was one of three pilgrimage festivals that brought Jews to Jerusalem from all over the known world. In the beginning of Acts 2, the Holy Spirit descends upon the crowds, and the disciples begin to speak in foreign languages (2:1-13). Then Peter stands up to make the long speech from which our reading comes (vv. 14-36). In it, he reinterprets the Hebrew Scriptures in light of Jesus's life, crucifixion, and resurrection, emphasizing both human responsibility and divine fulfillment in Jesus's death (v. 23). Quoting from Psalm 16:8-11, Peter creatively adapts the psalm to Jesus, ascribing to King David a dual role as Jesus's ancestor and as a prophet who foretells his coming. Peter declares Jesus's superiority to David by juxtaposing David's mortality with Jesus being "raised" from the tomb (v. 24). Peter states that the Holy Spirit was "poured" out by the ascending Jesus (v. 33), while in contrast, Jesus states that the Holy Spirit will be "the promise of the Father" (see 1:4). On the Fourth Sunday of Easter, we will read the conclusion of this speech and about the mass conversion that follows.

RESPONSORIAL PSALM   PSALM 16:1-2, 5, 7-8, 9-10, 11

Lord, you will show us the path of life.
   or: Alleluia.

SECOND READING   1 PETER 1:17-21

Beloved:
If you invoke as Father him who judges impartially
   according to each one's works,

conduct yourselves with reverence[1] during the time of your
   sojourning,
realizing that you were ransomed from your futile conduct,
handed on by your ancestors,
not with perishable things like silver or gold
but with the precious blood of Christ
as of a spotless unblemished lamb.

He was known before the foundation of the world
   but revealed in the final time for you,
   who through him believe in God
   who raised him from the dead and gave him glory,
   so that your faith and hope are in God.

The section from 1 Peter that our reading draws from (1:13–2:10) is an extended appeal to the community to "be holy" as God is holy (1:15-16; see also Lev 19:2). As Gentile converts who now call God "Father," they must live and act as God's children. Like the Israelites who lived in a foreign culture during the exile, these believers are to live with "reverence" or "reverent fear" (see footnote) during their own time of "sojourning" or exile in hostile surroundings. They have been "ransomed" (Greek *lutroō*) or purchased by Christ (see also Luke 24:21) from their previously "futile conduct," a phrase that refers to their actions prior to conversion. The "spotless unblemished lamb" alludes to a number of themes: animals involved in temple sacrifice (Lev 3:1), Isaiah's Suffering Servant who was the "lamb led to slaughter" (Isa 53:7), the Passover lamb, and Jesus as the "Lamb of God" (John 1:29, 36). The final verses assume that events in "the final time" have already taken place and root Christian faith and hope in God, who acts through Christ.

GOSPEL   LUKE 24:13-35

That very day, the first day of the week,
   two of Jesus' disciples were going

1. Greek *phobos*, translated here as "reverence," can also mean "fear" or "terror" (the NRSV translates this as "reverent fear").

to a village seven miles from Jerusalem called Emmaus,
   and they were conversing about all the things that had
      occurred.
And it happened that while they were conversing and debating,
   Jesus himself drew near and walked with them,
   but their eyes were prevented from recognizing him.
He asked them,
   "What are you discussing as you walk along?"
They stopped, looking downcast.
One of them, named Cleopas, said to him in reply,
   "Are you the only visitor to Jerusalem
   who does not know of the things
   that have taken place there in these days?"
And he replied to them, "What sort of things?"
They said to him,
   "The things that happened to Jesus the Nazarene,
   who was a prophet mighty in deed and word
   before God and all the people,
   how our chief priests and rulers both handed him over
   to a sentence of death and crucified him.
But we were hoping that he would be the one to redeem Israel;
   and besides all this,
   it is now the third day since this took place.
Some women from our group, however, have astounded us:
   they were at the tomb early in the morning
   and did not find his body;
   they came back and reported
   that they had indeed seen a vision of angels
   who announced that he was alive.
Then some of those with us went to the tomb
   and found things just as the women had described,
   but him they did not see."
And he said to them, "Oh, how foolish you are!
How slow of heart to believe all that the prophets spoke!
Was it not necessary that the Christ should suffer these things
   and enter into his glory?"
Then beginning with Moses and all the prophets,
   he interpreted to them what referred to him
   in all the Scriptures.

emass

As they approached the village to which they were going,
    he gave the impression that he was going on farther.
But they urged him, "Stay with us,
    for it is nearly evening and the day is almost over."
So he went in to stay with them.
And it happened that, while he was with them at table,
    he took bread, said the blessing,   *eucharist*
    broke it, and gave it to them.
With that their eyes were opened and they recognized him,
    but he vanished from their sight.
Then they said to each other,
    "Were not our hearts burning within us
    while he spoke to us on the way and opened the Scriptures
        to us?"
So they set out at once and returned to Jerusalem
    where they found gathered together
    the eleven and those with them who were saying,
    "The Lord has truly been raised and has appeared to Simon!"
Then the two recounted
    what had taken place on the way
    and how he was made known to them in the breaking
        of bread.

"That very day," the same day of Jesus's resurrection, we come upon two otherwise unknown disciples, Cleopas and his companion (perhaps his wife?). They are leaving Jerusalem and heading toward Emmaus, the site of a great Judean victory over the Seleucid army in 166 BCE, recounted in 1 Maccabees and celebrated in the holiday of Hanukkah. When Jesus appears, "their eyes were prevented from recognizing him" as if by divine intervention. Cleopas describes Jesus as a prophet, a man, and (hopefully) the Jewish messiah, but not as a divine being. To "redeem" or "ransom" in verse 21 (Greek *lytroō*) is to be set free, and it is the same verb that we find in 1 Peter 1:18 with the sense of being "purchased" by Christ. It is also a word used in 1 Maccabees 4:11 to describe God as the one who "redeems and delivers" Israel from the Seleucid army. These disciples, it seems, were still hoping for a powerful messiah who would deliver a crushing victory over the Romans. They did not yet understand the nature of

Jesus's power. When Jesus remarks on their foolishness, he begins to reinterpret the Hebrew Scriptures in light of his life, death, and resurrection. This practice of artful reinterpretation is a Jewish mode of textual interpretation or study called *midrash*, which Peter also employs in our reading from Acts. When the three gather for a meal, the description echoes the words of both the Last Supper (22:19; Acts 2:42) and the feeding of the five thousand (Luke 9:16-17). It is a meal that emphasizes both hospitality and revelation. The passage as a whole follows the contours of the Mass: the disciples come to the celebration with concerns and doubts, they recite Scripture and hear a sermon, and finally they gather together in fellowship over the meal as a sign of revelation, hope, and renewal. Rather than continue away from Jerusalem, the disciples are then set free from their "downcast" state and return "at once" to bear witness.

Ponder

"Were not our hearts burning within us while he spoke to us on the way and opened the Scriptures to us?" The power and mystery of the Scriptures burn through our readings today. Just as the disciples' hearts "burn" within them when Jesus breaks open the Scriptures for them, so too can we imagine the people in Acts experiencing an inward flame as they hear Peter preach. Peter also has this flame deep within, ignited by faith and fueled by the Scriptures and the Spirit that set him on fire to proclaim Christ. All of us have this fire of faith in us. Sometimes it burns intensely, while at other times it feels like fragile embers. But it is there. As you pray with our readings, can you feel this inward fire, whether it is a flickering flame or a roaring blaze? What helps to fuel the fire?

We are all, at times, on the road to Emmaus. Emmaus symbolizes a place of escape when life is painful, confusing, or overwhelming. While Emmaus is not a place to remain for long, the road itself is a necessary space. In the Gospel, it is a space of nourishment and healing, of prayer and honest searching, and of conversion when the risen Jesus reveals himself to the downcast. He draws the disciples away from Emmaus, back to himself and to their task of proclaiming the resurrection from Jerusalem. Ultimately, it is resurrection that makes this transformation possible and gives the disciples "faith and hope" in God, as we read in 1 Peter. Wherever you are on your faith journey this week, spend time meditating on the resurrection, the great linchpin of our faith. Allow our readings to draw you ever deeper into its mystery and beauty.

Fourth Sunday of Easter

Good Shepherd Sunday

FIRST READING   ACTS 2:14a, 36-41

Then Peter stood up with the Eleven,
    raised his voice, and proclaimed:
"Let the whole house of Israel know for certain
    that God has made both Lord and Christ,[1]
    this Jesus whom you crucified."

Now when they heard this, they were cut to the heart,
    and they asked Peter and the other apostles,
    "What are we to do, my brothers?"
Peter said to them,
    "Repent and be baptized, every one of you,
    in the name of Jesus Christ for the forgiveness of your sins;
    and you will receive the gift of the Holy Spirit.
For the promise is made to you and to your children
    and to all those far off,
    whomever the Lord our God will call."
He testified with many other arguments, and was exhorting them,
    "Save yourselves from this corrupt generation."
Those who accepted his message were baptized,
    and about three thousand persons were added that day.

Our reading contains the beginning and end of Peter's long speech in Acts 2. First, we repeat verse 14 from the Third Sunday of Easter. Then, we jump to the end of the speech and its resulting baptisms. In these verses, Peter declares that Jesus is the Jewish messiah by calling him "Lord and Christ" while contrasting God's actions ("God has made both Lord and Christ") with those of humans ("whom you crucified"). His words are clearly effective (his hearers were "cut to the heart"), and he catalogs the proper response to his message: repentance, baptism, forgiveness of sins, and reception of the Holy Spirit. Elsewhere in Acts, we see the same list in a different order (see 8:15-17; 10:44-48; 19:1-6). In early Judaism, baptism was sometimes associated with repentance

---

1. "Christ" (Greek *Christos*) can also translate as "Messiah" or "Anointed One."

(e.g., Isa 1:16), yet baptism "in the name of Jesus Christ" claims this community as unique. The ultimate promise is the salvation offered to Israel through Jesus (see Acts 13:23), yet it expands across space and time, to their children as well as to all people who will hear the gospel ("those far off"; v. 39). The phrase "corrupt generation" draws from the Hebrew Bible (e.g., the "fickle generation" in Deut 32:20 and the "defiant generation" in Ps 78:8). The final summary statement about people "added" to the community repeats throughout Acts with some variation (e.g., 5:14; 6:7).

RESPONSORIAL PSALM   PSALM 23:1-3a, 3b-4, 5, 6

The Lord is my shepherd; there is nothing I shall want.
  or: Alleluia.

SECOND READING   1 PETER 2:20b-25

Beloved:
If you are patient when you suffer for doing what is good,
  this is a grace before God.
For to this you have been called,
  because Christ also suffered for you,
  leaving you an example that you should follow in his footsteps.
He committed no sin, and no deceit was found in his mouth.

When he was insulted, he returned no insult;
  when he suffered, he did not threaten;
  instead, he handed himself over to the one who judges justly.
He himself bore our sins in his body upon the cross,
  so that, free from sin, we might live for righteousness.
By his wounds you have been healed.
For you had gone astray like sheep,
  but you have now returned to the shepherd and guardian of
    your souls.

Our reading draws from a code of conduct in 1 Peter 2:11–3:12 that organizes the family into a system of subordination and focuses specifically on those at the bottom of the ladder: wives and enslaved people. Ultimately, the point is to compare these lowest members of the household with Christians in Greco-Roman society; they serve as a metaphor for how all Christians are to act within unjust and degrading social systems. Directly preceding our reading, the author exhorts slaves to accept the authority of their masters with reverence regardless of whether those masters are kind or "perverse" (v. 18). The reason given is that it is a grace to bear "the pain of unjust suffering" (v. 19) and to do "what is good" (v. 20), thereby imitating Christ. The ultimate hope is that the ones enslaved will convert their masters through their own righteousness. The description of Christ's suffering throughout our reading may come from an old hymn based on Isaiah's Suffering Servant (see especially Isa 53:3-9). Once vindicated, Christ (like the Suffering Servant) becomes the "shepherd and guardian" of their souls, meaning the audience of Gentile converts (v. 25). In our contemporary context, we unequivocally condemn slavery and seek to dismantle social structures that degrade the dignity of the human person. Within its own context, however, the return of Christ was thought to be imminent, a return that would naturally turn the existing social system on its head. While waiting for this return, therefore, our reading undercuts and judges the existing system and returns to the powerless a sense of power and self-worth. The direct address to enslaved people is a Jewish and Christian innovation. The author of 1 Peter is presenting not a God who ordains or requires suffering but a God who redeems those who suffer unjustly due to human sin and evil.

GOSPEL   JOHN 10:1-10

Jesus said:
"Amen, amen, I say to you,
    whoever does not enter a sheepfold through the gate
    but climbs over elsewhere is a thief and a robber.
But whoever enters through the gate is the shepherd of
        the sheep.
The gatekeeper opens it for him, and the sheep hear his voice,
    as the shepherd calls his own sheep by name and leads
        them out.
When he has driven out all his own,
    he walks ahead of them, and the sheep follow him,
    because they recognize his voice.

But they will not follow a stranger;
   they will run away from him,
   because they do not recognize the voice of strangers."
Although Jesus used this figure of speech,
   the Pharisees did not realize what he was trying to tell them.

So Jesus said again, "Amen, amen, I say to you,
   I am the gate for the sheep.
All who came before me are thieves and robbers,
   but the sheep did not listen to them.
I am the gate.
Whoever enters through me will be saved,
   and will come in and go out and find pasture.
A thief comes only to steal and slaughter and destroy;
   I came so that they might have life and have it more
      abundantly."

Every year on the Fourth Sunday of Easter (often called "Good Shepherd Sunday"), we read a portion of John 10. In ancient Israel, the sheep of a village were kept within a common "fold" or rock enclosure that provided protection against thieves, and shepherds would call and lead their sheep from within this common fold. Because of how common shepherding was in ancient Israel, the Hebrew Bible contains a rich tradition of depicting prophets and kings as literal and figurative shepherds of Israel whose duty it is to protect their flock (Israel). Such shepherds include Moses, a shepherd who guides his people out of Egypt (Exod 3:1), and King David, who begins as a shepherd boy and becomes the great shepherd of Israel (2 Sam 5:2). Many other leadership figures of Israel, however, were ultimately failed or false shepherds (e.g., Ezek 34). The ultimate shepherd is God (Ps 23; Ezek 34:31). Our reading builds upon this metaphor to describe Jesus as both the gate to the sheepfold (vv. 1-2, 7-10) and the "good shepherd" (v. 11). He contrasts himself with false shepherds or robbers (i.e., religious leaders), whose intentions are not to protect the sheep and who do not enter by way of the gate (v. 1). The true shepherd has open entry into the sheepfold with the help of the gatekeeper (God). Both the gatekeeper and the sheep distinguish easily between the call of their shepherd and the "stranger," and the sheep will only follow their own shepherd. Jesus then describes himself as the gate itself that swings in and out into abundant or eternal life (v. 10). Jesus's words are directed specifically to religious leaders who work against God as they "steal" the trust of their people, failing to guide, protect, or act as living witnesses of love and justice.

Ponder

Underlying our readings is the call to ongoing *metanoia,* the transformation of heart, mind, and actions. In Acts, God's promise of redemption is for all people who are "cut to the heart" and willing to be changed. Although the author of 1 Peter primarily speaks to those who are suffering unjustly, behind his message is a second audience and a call to reform for those who abuse others within corrupt systems of power and greed. Finally, John's Gospel is an open invitation into the sheepfold through the gate (Jesus) so one does not have to try to break in through selfishness, laziness, manipulations of authority, or distorted visions of truth. Ongoing *metanoia* is the natural result of listening and following the true shepherd. It happens through God's grace, and it leads to the still waters of Psalm 23. How are you listening and following today?

Sometimes the Gospels describe the path to abundant life as "narrow" and "constricted" (Matt 7:14), yet in today's Gospel, the gate swings easily and widely for all sheep to flow in and out. The gate is an apt metaphor for the spiritual life, in which we first come "in" to Christ for rest, nourishment, and protection, and then follow Christ out with strength, confidence, and purpose to be prophetic witnesses. All of our readings depict this movement in and out, from Peter moving out as a public witness in Acts to the call for inward rest in 1 Peter. Explore your own sheepfold this week, the quiet space of prayer and renewal. How does Jesus, who calls himself the Gate, beckon you in and out? By following this beckoning, the ultimate promise is that we will not only enter the gate but *become* the gate through which others enter into abundant life.

Fifth Sunday of Easter

As the number of disciples continued to grow,
   the Hellenists complained against the Hebrews
   because their widows
   were being neglected in the daily distribution.
So the Twelve called together the community of the disciples
     and said,
   "It is not right for us to neglect the word of God to serve
     at table.
Brothers, select from among you seven reputable men,
   filled with the Spirit and wisdom,
   whom we shall appoint to this task,
   whereas we shall devote ourselves to prayer
   and to the ministry of the word."
The proposal was acceptable to the whole community,
   so they chose Stephen, a man filled with faith and the
     Holy Spirit,
   also Philip, Prochorus, Nicanor, Timon, Parmenas,
   and Nicholas of Antioch, a convert to Judaism.
They presented these men to the apostles
   who prayed and laid hands on them.
The word of God continued to spread,
   and the number of the disciples in Jerusalem increased greatly;
   even a large group of priests were becoming obedient to
     the faith.

Our reading depicts the realistic internal difficulties that often characterize communities of faith, especially as they become larger and more diverse. At this point, the communities of believers are all Jewish, so the tension is internal: between Hellenists (Greek-speaking Jews from the Diaspora) and Hebrews (Aramaic-speaking Jews). Though we do not know whether this depiction of inner-Jewish tension is historically accurate, it seems probable that social and cultural differences would have led to conflicts that included problems with food distribution. Widows were among the most vulnerable members of ancient society, and the Hebrew Bible is filled with admonitions to care for widows, orphans, and immigrants (e.g., Deut 14:28-29; 24:17-21; Isa 10:1-2; Zech 7:10). The "Twelve" is an expression for the twelve disciples/apostles whom Jesus originally called (see Luke 6:13); the term now includes Matthias as Judas Iscariot's replacement (Acts 1:26). To "serve at table" could refer to the literal feeding of the hungry or to more general service, such as the keeping of records for food distribution among the needy. The seven men are carefully chosen by reputation, though we never hear of them carrying out their designated function later in Acts; instead, Stephen and Philip are depicted specifically as preachers (see next Sunday's reading). Later tradition identifies these "seven" as the first deacons, and all of them likely come from Hellenistic Jewish families with the exception of Nicholas, a Gentile convert. Prayers and the laying on of hands was a common Jewish ritual of appointment that invoked God's blessing and power upon the one designated (e.g., Num 8:10; 27:23; 1 Tim 4:14; 2 Tim 1:6). Our reading concludes with the common summary statement in Acts of an increase in believers (e.g., 2:41; 9:31; 12:24). Elsewhere, the author states that few Jews accepted Jesus as the messiah and that priests were especially resistant to the message (e.g., 5:17), yet in this account even priests become "obedient to the faith" (6:7).

RESPONSORIAL PSALM   PSALM 33:1-2, 4-5, 18-19

Lord, let your mercy be on us, as we place our trust in you.
or: Alleluia.

SECOND READING   1 PETER 2:4-9

Beloved:
Come to him, a living stone, rejected by human beings
    but chosen and precious in the sight of God,
    and, like living stones,
    let yourselves be built into a spiritual house
    to be a holy priesthood to offer spiritual sacrifices
    acceptable to God through Jesus Christ.

For it says in Scripture:
Behold, I am laying a stone in Zion,
a cornerstone, chosen and precious,
and whoever believes in it shall not be put to shame.
Therefore, its value is for you who have faith, but for those
    without faith:
The stone that the builders rejected
has become the cornerstone,
and
A stone that will make people stumble,
and a rock that will make them fall.
They stumble by disobeying the word, as is their destiny.

You are "a chosen race, a royal priesthood,
    a holy nation, a people of his own,
    so that you may announce the praises" of him
    who called you out of darkness into his wonderful light.

This week, we move backward instead of forward in 1 Peter with an excerpt from the beginning of chapter 2. Here, the author reassures his Gentile converts of their true worth by comparing society's rejection of them to the rejection of Christ. The author first quotes from Isaiah 28:16, then draws from Psalm 118:22 and Isaiah 8:14 to reinterpret these texts in light of Jesus Christ. As a "living stone," Christ was rejected by humans but was "precious in the sight of God" and "chosen" to build up a new house. Believers who join themselves to Christ also become "living stones" of this new temple or "spiritual house," bound by the Spirit in Christ through baptism to become "a people of his own." This house is not physical but is a spiritual body through which the people will be a "holy priesthood," offering up a continual sacrifice through the witness of their lives. In the Hebrew Bible, Israel is often described as "chosen" or elected (Isa 43:20), a royal priesthood and "a holy nation" (Exod 19:6). Here we find these same terms applied to the community of those who have faith in Christ (v. 9). As this "holy nation" and "royal priesthood," the people have been called into the "wonderful light" of Christ to live each day as a sacred act, manifesting Christ's sacrifice through lives that continually "announce [his] praises."

GOSPEL   JOHN 14:1-12

Jesus said to his disciples:
  "Do not let your hearts be troubled.
You have faith in God; have faith also in me.
In my Father's house there are many dwelling places.
If there were not,
  would I have told you that I am going to prepare a place
    for you?
And if I go and prepare a place for you,
  I will come back again and take you to myself,
  so that where I am you also may be.
Where I am going you know the way."
Thomas said to him,
  "Master, we do not know where you are going;
  how can we know the way?"
Jesus said to him, "I am the way and the truth and the life.
No one comes to the Father except through me.
If you know me, then you will also know my Father.
From now on you do know him and have seen him."
Philip said to him,
  "Master, show us the Father, and that will be enough for us."
Jesus said to him, "Have I been with you for so long a time
  and you still do not know me, Philip?
Whoever has seen me has seen the Father.
How can you say, 'Show us the Father'?
Do you not believe that I am in the Father and the Father is
  in me?
The words that I speak to you I do not speak on my own.
The Father who dwells in me is doing his works.
Believe me that I am in the Father and the Father is in me,
  or else, believe because of the works themselves.
Amen, amen, I say to you,
  whoever believes in me will do the works that I do,
  and will do greater ones than these,
  because I am going to the Father."

This speech begins Jesus's famous last discourse to his disciples at
the Last Supper, which we focus on toward the end of the Easter

season. Although there is plenty for the disciples to be troubled about (Jesus has just told them that he is going away, that they cannot follow him, and that two of them will deny him), he comforts them by reframing his death as departure and his departure as preparation for his return and abiding presence with them. The disciples are continually concerned with where Jesus will be, and he describes not a geographical place but an interior state, a house or intimate dwelling based on relationship and faith that he will "prepare" for them (v. 2). When Jesus says that they "know the way," Thomas misinterprets his words and, still concerned with physical place, says that they do not know where this place is (vv. 4-5). Jesus then clarifies that it is not about *where* but about *who* (vv. 6-7). He describes himself as the incarnation of divinity, linking himself with the mysterious divine name "I AM" ("I am the way and the truth and the life") that God declared to Moses in Exodus 3:14. Here, "truth" signifies a personal relationship (not an intellectual experience) that leads to "life," while the language of "knowing" and "seeing" further denotes intimacy. In other words, to know Jesus is to know God, to see Jesus is to see God, and to be "in" Jesus is to be in relationship with God or to "dwell" in God's house. The final reference to one's "works" includes not only miracles and ministry but also the willingness to offer up one's life as Jesus is about to do.

Ponder

A foundation holds a building in place, acting as an anchor between the frame and the earth below. Yet all buildings are impermanent, no matter the strength of their foundation. First Peter calls us into a different sort of building, one made not of physical material but of flesh and spirit, built upon a permanent, divine foundation. This is not a building but a body, and we are the "living stones," anchored not in rigid, lifeless concrete but in a person, a Spirit who moves and breathes and manifests in and through the changing shape of humanity. Like the early church as its communities expanded and diversified, this spiritual house is rooted solidly while at the same time adaptable and open to creative change. As you ponder these combined traits of rootedness and adaptability, where and how do they manifest in your own life and community? Are there places where the building is in danger of crumbling?

Today's Gospel is often read at funeral liturgies to remind us that dying means coming home to Christ. And yet it also speaks to a deep sense of being home or belonging with Christ *now*. The passage juxtaposes homelessness with homecoming, separation with belonging. Homelessness takes many forms, including the human tragedies of physical homelessness and the suffering many experience in their own "homes." Yet our passage also speaks to a broader human yearning to belong. We all seek the place where we feel safe, loved, and at rest. Where, or with whom, is this place for you? Do you believe you have this place of deep belonging with Jesus? We all bear the responsibility to reach out compassionately and invite others in. There are many rooms, and everyone needs a home.

Sixth Sunday of Easter

FIRST READING   ACTS 8:5-8, 14-17

Philip went down to the city of Samaria
    and proclaimed the Christ to them.
With one accord, the crowds paid attention to what was said by
        Philip
    when they heard it and saw the signs he was doing.
For unclean spirits, crying out in a loud voice,
    came out of many possessed people,
    and many paralyzed or crippled people were cured.
There was great joy in that city.

Now when the apostles in Jerusalem
    heard that Samaria had accepted the word of God,
    they sent them Peter and John,
    who went down and prayed for them,
    that they might receive the Holy Spirit,
    for it had not yet fallen upon any of them;
    they had only been baptized in the name of the Lord Jesus.
Then they laid hands on them
    and they received the Holy Spirit.

After Stephen was stoned at the end of Acts 7, persecution broke
out against the early church in Jerusalem, and many of its members
scattered into the rural areas of Judea and Samaria (8:1). Samaria was
the region north of Judea, part of the northern kingdom of Israel
in the preexilic period before it collapsed at the hands of the Neo-
Assyrian Empire around 722 BCE. In the preexilic period, Samaria
was a central city in Israel, and its name was used interchangeably
with Israel for the kingdom itself (much like Jerusalem was used for
Judah). The long and complicated history between Judah (Jerusalem)
and Israel (Samaria) continued into the first century CE between
Samaritans (descendants of Samaria, whose central worship site was
on Mount Gerizim) and Jews (descendants of Judah, whose central
worship site was in Jerusalem). Much of the Hebrew Bible and all
of the New Testament come from Judah's perspective, a perspective

that contemporary Jews and Christians inherit. In a sense, then, we are all Judah's descendants. According to Acts 6:5, Philip was one of the seven tasked with feeding the poor, yet many references to him in the second century CE consider him to be one of the twelve apostles (Luke 6:14; Acts 1:13). The response to Philip's preaching and miracles in Samaria is similar to the initial response to Peter in Jerusalem (Acts 5:12-16). Philip therefore fulfills Jesus's exhortation in Acts 1:8 to be one of his "witnesses" throughout Judea and Samaria and "to the ends of the earth." The presence of Peter and John in this passage signals apostolic cooperation with Philip's work. Our text mirrors the church's sacramental process, which separates baptism from confirmation (the reception of the Holy Spirit).

RESPONSORIAL PSALM   PSALM 66:1-3, 4-5, 6-7, 16, 20

Let all the earth cry out to God with joy.
   or: Alleluia.

SECOND READING   1 PETER 3:15-18

Beloved:
Sanctify Christ as Lord in your hearts.
Always be ready to give an explanation
   to anyone who asks you for a reason for your hope,
   but do it with gentleness and reverence,
   keeping your conscience clear,
   so that, when you are maligned,
   those who defame your good conduct in Christ
   may themselves be put to shame.
For it is better to suffer for doing good,
   if that be the will of God, than for doing evil.

For Christ also suffered for sins once,
   the righteous for the sake of the unrighteous,
   that he might lead you to God.
Put to death in the flesh,
   he was brought to life in the Spirit.

According to the author of 1 Peter, the believer's responsibility is to imitate Christ, specifically Christ's suffering for what is right or "good" (v. 17; see also 2:20). Here, the author expands upon previous exhortations to those who are enslaved (see 2:18-25 and notes for the Fourth Sunday of Easter) and directs similar words of encouragement to the general population. In word as well as in action, Christians must be ready to give an "explanation" or defense (Greek *apologia*) for their faith or their deep-seated "hope" in Christ (v. 15). Living as exiles within Greco-Roman society, hope in Christ is the very essence of their motivation. "Put to death in the flesh" underscores Jesus's human death, while "brought to life in the Spirit" emphasizes his divine life and inheritance (v. 18). The entire reading is rooted in the call to continually "[s]anctify" (Greek *hagiazō*) Christ (literally "make Christ holy") within one's heart in the midst of an unbelieving, ignorant, or hostile world (v. 15).

GOSPEL   JOHN 14:15-21

Jesus said to his disciples:
   "If you love me, you will keep my commandments.
And I will ask the Father,
   and he will give you another Advocate to be with you always,
   the Spirit of truth, whom the world cannot accept,
   because it neither sees nor knows him.
But you know him, because he remains with you,
   and will be in you.
I will not leave you orphans; I will come to you.
In a little while the world will no longer see me,
   but you will see me, because I live and you will live.
On that day you will realize that I am in my Father
   and you are in me and I in you.
Whoever has my commandments and observes them
   is the one who loves me.
And whoever loves me will be loved by my Father,
   and I will love him and reveal myself to him."

This week, our Gospel reading begins close to where we left off in Jesus's final discourse to his disciples on the Fifth Sunday of Easter.

Through the repetition of the word "in," our reading speaks of the deepest intimacy between Jesus and his disciples, the indwelling of the Spirit. This Spirit will be "in" the disciples just as Jesus will be "in" the Father, and the disciples will be "in" Jesus, and Jesus will be "in" the disciples. In describing the coming of this Spirit, Jesus links love for him with external actions or observance of the commandments. According to Jesus, all commandments are rooted in love and reveal love. If the disciples love Jesus, then they will "keep" or, literally, "guard" (Greek *tēreō*) his commandments. To help them, God will send the "Advocate" or "Spirit of truth" (vv. 16-17). Both of these expressions for the Spirit are unique to John's writings, though "Spirit of truth" is also found in texts from Qumran, where it refers to an inward moral force that comes from God. The term for "Advocate," Greek *paraklētos* or "Paraclete," is richly nuanced. It means literally "one who stands beside" another, and it can have a legal sense (think defense attorneys) or a broader sense of one who supports, comforts, sustains, teaches, or mediates. This passage influenced later Christian theology regarding the nature and role of the Holy Spirit. The Spirit guides the church in and into truth, abiding in the church and in every believer. This Spirit is visible only to the eye of faith, and it lives within each of us, sustaining and guiding our actions, drawing us into ever-deepening communion with God.

Ponder

"Sanctify Christ as Lord in your hearts," writes the author of 1 Peter. This is a beautiful and mysterious statement. It is both a promise and a challenge. Directed specifically to people who are marginalized and suffering, this call to sanctify Christ inwardly in all contexts challenges them—and us—to respond to the world not by mirroring its brokenness and sinfulness but by living from the reality and possibility of faith. We walk this path through a continual process of inward sanctification and renewal. The promise is that we are born into God, belong to God, and contain God's Spirit in us. This week, meditate on the call to sanctify Christ in your heart. How does this call invite you to live day by day, moment by moment?

St. Augustine wrote, "See that your praise of God comes from your whole being; . . . praise God not with your lips and voices alone, but with your minds, your lives and all your actions."[1] To grow into this full-bodied praise of God is part of the journey of faith. Acts describes the starting point of this journey through conversion stories and through the disciples' journey to become witnesses to the whole world. First Peter reveals the journey of suffering people who learn to praise God in the midst of adverse circumstances. Such full-bodied praise is not about fleeting happiness. It is not dependent on external circumstances. It comes from a deep, inward communion with Christ through the Spirit. Christ is in all of us, and we are in Christ. Once we know this, joy and praise become a limitless well from which we drink and live.

---

1. St. Augustine, *A Discourse on the Psalms.*

The Ascension of the Lord[1]

FIRST READING   ACTS 1:1-11

In the first book, Theophilus,
  I dealt with all that Jesus did and taught
  until the day he was taken up,
  after giving instructions through the Holy Spirit
  to the apostles whom he had chosen.
He presented himself alive to them
  by many proofs after he had suffered,
  appearing to them during forty days
  and speaking about the kingdom of God.
While meeting with them,
  he enjoined them not to depart from Jerusalem,
  but to wait for "the promise of the Father
  about which you have heard me speak;
  for John baptized with water,
  but in a few days you will be baptized with the Holy Spirit."

When they had gathered together they asked him,
  "Lord, are you at this time going to restore the kingdom to
      Israel?"
He answered them, "It is not for you to know the times or
      seasons
  that the Father has established by his own authority.
But you will receive power when the Holy Spirit comes upon you,
  and you will be my witnesses in Jerusalem,
  throughout Judea and Samaria,
  and to the ends of the earth."
When he had said this, as they were looking on,
  he was lifted up, and a cloud took him from their sight.
While they were looking intently at the sky as he was going,
  suddenly two men dressed in white garments stood
      beside them.
They said, "Men of Galilee,

---

1. In some dioceses in the United States, the solemnity of the Ascension of the Lord is celebrated on a Thursday, while in others it is celebrated on the following Sunday.

why are you standing there looking at the sky?
This Jesus who has been taken up from you into heaven
    will return in the same way as you have seen him going into
        heaven."

The ascension narrative is about waiting. It is also about the promise that the locus of Jesus's work will soon transfer from Jesus to the disciples through the Spirit. Jesus ascends, yet the Spirit will descend, and the disciples will become Christ's hands and feet on earth. The first verse links Acts with Luke's Gospel (the "first book") as two parts of the story, which were written by the same author for an individual named Theophilus (see Luke 1:3). In these opening verses, the author retells and expands upon essential information from the end of his Gospel (Luke 24:13-53). In the Gospel, Jesus's resurrection and ascension occur on the same day, but in Acts, Jesus lingers among the disciples for a forty-day period (a number signifying completeness), teaching and preparing them for ministry. After this time, the disciples remain unsure of the future and ask Jesus if the coming of the Spirit will be the moment when he will "restore the kingdom to Israel." He tells them to focus not on this question but instead on their task to be his "witnesses" (Greek *martys*, meaning "witness" or "martyr") to the entire world. Four times in vv. 10-11, the author emphasizes the "heaven[s]" or "sky" (Greek *ouranos*) into which Jesus ascends. The stories of Moses and Elijah are key to understanding this account. Both prophetic figures are associated with forty-day periods and with ascending into the clouds or heavens (Exod 24:18; 1 Kgs 19:8; 2 Kgs 2:11). Also note that at the transfiguration, clouds overshadow Moses and Elijah along with Jesus (Luke 9:34-36). In 2 Kings 2:1-25, Elijah ascends and so transfers his power to Elisha, while Moses shifts his prophetic spirit to Joshua when he dies (Deut 34:9). Similar to these prophetic shifts of power, Jesus's ascension marks the shift of his own power to his disciples through the Spirit. Perhaps we are to imagine that the two men "dressed in white" are Elijah and Moses. As the disciples await the coming of the Spirit, so too we all wait for the ultimate return of Christ.

RESPONSORIAL PSALM   PSALM 47:2-3, 6-7, 8-9

God mounts his throne to shouts of joy: a blare of trumpets for
    the Lord.
    or: Alleluia.

SECOND READING   EPHESIANS 1:17-23

Brothers and sisters:
May the God of our Lord Jesus Christ, the Father of glory,
    give you a Spirit of wisdom and revelation
    resulting in knowledge of him.
May the eyes of your hearts be enlightened,
    that you may know what is the hope that belongs to his call,
    what are the riches of glory
    in his inheritance among the holy ones,
    and what is the surpassing greatness of his power
    for us who believe,
    in accord with the exercise of his great might,
    which he worked in Christ,
    raising him from the dead
    and seating him at his right hand in the heavens,
    far above every principality, authority, power, and dominion,
    and every name that is named
    not only in this age but also in the one to come.
And he put all things beneath his feet
    and gave him as head over all things to the church,
    which is his body,
    the fullness of the one who fills all things in every way.

This prayer for wisdom and knowledge is one of the richest in Paul's
letters. Though deeply monotheistic, it is addressed not to Christ but
to "the God of our Lord Jesus Christ," and the focus is God's work
through Christ. The first half of the prayer emphasizes wisdom and
hope, while the second half carries hope further in describing Jesus's
dominance over all present and future powers. The passage depends
upon the psalms, particularly in references to Christ sitting "at [the]
right hand" of God (Ps 110:1) and "put[ting] all things beneath his feet"
(Ps 8:7). Drawing upon these psalms, Paul depicts Jesus as authoritative

and highly exalted, the climax of God's creation and the rightful earthly descendant of King David. The phrase "every principality, authority, power, and dominion" represents all spiritual powers that Christ subjects to himself (see also 1 Cor 15:20-28). In the final verse, Christ is the fullness of all reality and of the cosmos as the head of the church. The church is the clearest expression of this presence and reality as the embodiment of Christ and of God's purpose on earth.

GOSPEL   MATTHEW 28:16-20

The eleven disciples went to Galilee,
    to the mountain to which Jesus had ordered them.
When they saw him, they worshiped, but they doubted.
Then Jesus approached and said to them,
    "All power in heaven and on earth has been given to me.
Go, therefore, and make disciples of all nations,
    baptizing them in the name of the Father,
    and of the Son, and of the Holy Spirit,
    teaching them to observe all that I have commanded you.
And behold, I am with you always, until the end of the age."

According to the Synoptic Gospels, Jesus's resurrection and ascension occur in a single day. While Luke's Gospel and Mark's longer ending refer to his ascension directly (Luke 24:51; Mark 16:19), Matthew's Gospel only hints at it in these verses, when Jesus commissions the remaining eleven disciples (Judas will be replaced in Acts 1:12-26). Earlier, an angel had instructed the disciples to go to Galilee, promising that they would encounter the risen Jesus (28:7). They encounter him on top of a mountain, a space of revelation and prayer throughout Matthew's Gospel (e.g., 5:1; 14:23; 15:29). Mountains also link Jesus with Moses, who similarly gave his final instructions from a mountaintop (Deut 32:48–33:29). The disciples doubt even as they believe, a common theme in the Gospels, which suggests that faith and doubt are not mutually exclusive (see Matt 14:31-33; John 20:24-29). Now that Jesus has been resurrected, his domain extends across "heaven" and "earth" (v. 18). Like our first reading from Acts, Jesus commissions the disciples to make disciples of "all nations" and alludes to the coming of the Spirit through the statement that he will be with them "always, until the end of the age" (vv. 19-20). We find similar statements in the Hebrew Bible when God commissions prophets (e.g., Exod 4:12; Jer 1:19). Though Jesus tells the disciples to baptize in the name of the Father, Son, and Holy Spirit, the understanding of God as Trinity does not become an integral part of Christian theology until the second century CE. The Gospel ends here, yet we assume that Jesus is subsequently lifted into the skies.

Ponder

Faith is a path of winding growth into knowledge of Christ. This is not intellectual knowledge but a deeply intimate relationship. Paul describes it as enlightenment, meaning that the Spirit will literally give light to the "eyes" of our "hearts" (Greek *dianoia* also translates as "mind," "thought," or "intention"; Eph 1:18). It is this enlightenment, the Spirit's suffusion of light into our entire being, that guides us into the fullness of knowledge and hope in Christ. We hope in the One who was raised up and who has and will raise us up with him, the One who is intimately present with us "always" (Matt 28:20). Take time to ponder hope this week— what it means to you, where it is present or seemingly absent. How does hope guide your life?

Galilee is an important backdrop to Jesus's ascension in the Gospel. Situated far to the north of Judea, it was a region peripheral to Jerusalem and an area populated with Gentiles (Matt 4:15). It is the place where Jesus finds refuge as a child (Matt 2:22) and where he later calls his disciples (Matt 4:18). It is therefore fitting that the end of the Gospel draws us back to the beginning, back to Galilee and the marginal places. It is into these places where Jesus calls each of us and sends us out to do his work. His ascension raises us up and into him and simultaneously transforms us into his prophetic witnesses, his hands and his feet in the Galilees of our world. We are to be voices of hope, sources of justice and compassion to those who are marginalized, suffering, and in despair. Where are your Galilees? Where and to whom are you called?

Seventh Sunday of Easter

FIRST READING   ACTS 1:12-14

After Jesus had been taken up to heaven the apostles
    returned to Jerusalem
    from the mount called Olivet, which is near Jerusalem,
    a sabbath day's journey away.

When they entered the city
    they went to the upper room where they were staying,
    Peter and John and James and Andrew,
    Philip and Thomas, Bartholomew and Matthew,
    James son of Alphaeus, Simon the Zealot,
    and Judas son of James.
All these devoted themselves with one accord to prayer,
    together with some women,
    and Mary the mother of Jesus, and his brothers.

Our first reading picks up immediately after Jesus's ascension. The Holy Spirit's descension will come in our Pentecost Sunday reading from Acts 2:1-11. Fittingly, this last Sunday of Easter places us in between these two experiences, into a scene of waiting, expectation, and prayer. According to Luke-Acts, Jesus's ascension concludes his post-resurrection appearances with the unique exception of his later appearance to Saul/Paul in Acts 9. The ascension also marks the very beginning of the early church, as the responsibility for Jesus's mission shifts from Jesus to the disciples. The "mount called Olivet," or Mount of Olives (whose eastern slope borders Bethany; see Luke 24:50), lies about a half mile east of Jerusalem, over a steep descent and ascent through the Kidron Valley. A "sabbath day's journey" denotes the short distance one may travel on the Sabbath, about a half mile. When the apostles return to Jerusalem, the setting of all important paschal events, we are reintroduced to the remaining eleven apostles (see lists given in Luke 6:14-16; Mark 3:16-19). It is as if the disciples are beginning their mission anew and with deeper significance. The three key apostles in Acts appear first in this list: Peter, John, and James. Together, all those who devote themselves to prayer become the nucleus of the emerging church. The final line also reminds us that women were central to Jesus's mission and the shaping of the early church. This is the last reference to Mary in Luke-Acts.

RESPONSORIAL PSALM   PSALM 27:1, 4, 7-8

I believe that I shall see the good things of the Lord in the land of
   the living.
or: Alleluia.

SECOND READING   1 PETER 4:13-16

Beloved:
Rejoice to the extent that you share in the sufferings of Christ,
   so that when his glory is revealed
   you may also rejoice exultantly.
If you are insulted for the name of Christ, blessed are you,
   for the Spirit of glory and of God rests upon you.
But let no one among you be made to suffer
   as a murderer, a thief, an evildoer, or as an intriguer.
But whoever is made to suffer as a Christian should not be
   ashamed
   but glorify God because of the name.

Today we reach the end of our time with 1 Peter. The letter concludes with advice to the persecuted, a section from which our reading draws (4:12-19), followed by advice to the entire community (5:1-11) and farewell statements (5:12-14). Though the author discusses the role of persecution frequently in the letter, here it is expressed in more ardent terms. According to the author, to be a person of faith necessarily involves suffering, a reality that Christians should not only endure but in which we should "rejoice" (v. 13) and "glorify God" (v. 16). The word "glory" and its verbal form "glorify" (Greek *doxa* and *doxazō*) are central to the idea that through suffering, believers reach a deeper participation in the mystery of Christ and manifest his presence or glory (see the Gospel notes for a fuller discussion of the term "glory"). In the Greek, the word "Christian" appears only here and in Acts 11:26 and 26:28. In the context of 1 Peter, to be Christian means communion with Christ in suffering.

GOSPEL   JOHN 17:1-11a

Jesus raised his eyes to heaven and said,
    "Father, the hour has come.
Give glory to your son, so that your son may glorify you,
    just as you gave him authority over all people,
    so that your son may give eternal life to all you gave him.
Now this is eternal life,
    that they should know you, the only true God,
    and the one whom you sent, Jesus Christ.
I glorified you on earth
    by accomplishing the work that you gave me to do.
Now glorify me, Father, with you,
    with the glory that I had with you before the world began.

"I revealed your name to those whom you gave me out of
        the world.
They belonged to you, and you gave them to me,
    and they have kept your word.
Now they know that everything you gave me is from you,
    because the words you gave to me I have given to them,
    and they accepted them and truly understood that I came
        from you,
    and they have believed that you sent me.
I pray for them.
I do not pray for the world but for the ones you have given me,
    because they are yours, and everything of mine is yours
    and everything of yours is mine,
    and I have been glorified in them.
And now I will no longer be in the world,
    but they are in the world, while I am coming to you."

Each year on the Seventh Sunday of Easter, we read a portion of John 17, which is also known as Jesus's "high priestly prayer" (a phrase that goes back to the sixteenth century). The setting is the Last Supper in John's Gospel, when Jesus delivers his farewell discourse to his disciples (chaps. 14–17), preparing them for his impending departure and promising the coming of the Paraclete, or Holy Spirit. The prayer has three sections: Jesus prays first for himself (vv. 1-5), then for all those who believe in him (vv. 6-19), and lastly for all future believers (vv. 20-26). This Sunday, we read from the first half of the prayer. Although the Synoptic Gospels (Matthew, Mark, Luke) frequently mention Jesus in prayer, only rarely do they give the content of his prayers (e.g., the "Our Father" in Matt 6 and Luke 11; Jesus's prayer at Gethsemane the night before his death). This prayer not only provides detailed content, but it also sums up the significance of Jesus's life. John's Gospel also presents a unique picture of Jesus in these final hours before his crucifixion. For example, compare his calm and authority here to the Synoptic accounts of Jesus praying before his arrest, when he is deeply troubled and prays to be released from the suffering to come (Mark 14:32-36; Matt 26:36-46; Luke 22:39-46). Key to this passage, as in our second reading, is the word "glory" and its verbal form "glorify," which carry a similar resonance to the Hebrew *kābôd* ("glory," "honor," or "weightiness"). The Hebrew word stems from literal heaviness or wealth, and in its less literal form it refers to both human honor and divine glory. In the Hebrew Bible, this "glory" is characterized as an awesome, radiant manifestation of God's presence. For example, in the exodus story, Moses climbs Mount Sinai to speak with God, whose glory is like a "consuming fire" (24:17). When Moses descends from the mountain, his own face is a radiant mirror of God's glory, so much so that he must wear a veil (34:29-35). Here, Jesus is the physical "weight" or manifestation of God's glory, yet this glory has and will also continue to express itself in diverse ways, including through the disciples (v. 10).

Ponder

Prayer is a powerful tool that unites Jesus's followers as they await Pentecost. We do not know how they, still in mourning over the loss of Jesus, felt in that Upper Room. Were they overcome with hope and expectation? Were they lonely or perhaps afraid of the weight of their responsibility? Whatever their emotions, prayer was the primary support that sustained and unified them in this in-between time. In the Gospel, it is Jesus who prays, both for himself and for his disciples, in an impending period of suffering and uncertainty. In our own difficult and in-between times, prayer heals, encourages, and binds us with each other and with God. What is the role of prayer in your life? What does it feel like to imagine Jesus praying for you?

In the face of his death, Jesus has a calm certainty and sense of completion in John's Gospel, culminating in his last words from the cross: "It is finished" (19:30). His behavior can be hard to square with our own experiences of death, which do not always leave us with a sense of completion, yet Jesus's words can help us to envision a different kind of completion, one that is not physical but spiritual. It is a completion that comes from belonging to God. As Jesus describes in the Gospel, our deepest identity is in God, and we are fulfilled when we welcome God within us and manifest God's love and justice in this world. As John Shea writes, when we carry out this task that Jesus leaves for us, "God is glorified, the work is accomplished, and life is complete."[1] Do we believe this?

1. John Shea, *The Spiritual Wisdom of the Gospels for Christian Preachers and Teachers, Year A: On Earth as It Is in Heaven* (Collegeville, MN: Liturgical Press, 2004), 196.

Pentecost Sunday

FIRST READING   ACTS 2:1-11

When the time for Pentecost was fulfilled,
 they were all in one place together.
And suddenly there came from the sky
 a noise like a strong driving wind,
 and it filled the entire house in which they were.
Then there appeared to them tongues as of fire,
 which parted and came to rest on each one of them.
And they were all filled with the Holy Spirit
 and began to speak in different tongues,
 as the Spirit enabled them to proclaim.

Now there were devout Jews from every nation under heaven
  staying in Jerusalem.
At this sound, they gathered in a large crowd,
 but they were confused
 because each one heard them speaking in his own language.
They were astounded, and in amazement they asked,
 "Are not all these people who are speaking Galileans?
Then how does each of us hear them in his native language?
We are Parthians, Medes, and Elamites,
 inhabitants of Mesopotamia, Judea and Cappadocia,
 Pontus and Asia, Phrygia and Pamphylia,
 Egypt and the districts of Libya near Cyrene,
 as well as travelers from Rome,
 both Jews and converts to Judaism, Cretans and Arabs,
 yet we hear them speaking in our own tongues
 of the mighty acts of God."

Pentecost (Greek for "fiftieth") occurs fifty days after Passover, during the yearly barley festival of Shavuot, also called the "feast of Weeks" (see Lev 23:15-21). Shavuot celebrates the giving of the Torah on Mount Sinai, and historically, it was one of three pilgrimage festivals that attracted devout Jews to Jerusalem. Yet the Jews in our reading are "residents" (Greek *katoikountes*) of Jerusalem, not visitors from afar. The Spirit descending echoes the divine presence descending in fire in Exodus 19:16-18 to impart the commandments to Israel, and it also draws from the prophetic image of God's "spirit" pouring itself out "upon all flesh" (Joel 3:1-5). The scene also parallels Jesus receiving the Spirit in Luke 3:21-22. The image of "tongues as of fire" is common in the Hebrew Bible (e.g., Isa 5:24), and both fire and wind symbolize divine presence and cleansing (e.g., Gen 1:2; Exod 3:2; 14:24; 19:18). Every known nation is listed here, foreshadowing the spread of Christianity. Unlike Paul's discussion of "speaking in tongues" in 1 Corinthians 14:6-19, the languages spoken here are understood by native speakers from Iran (Parthians, Medes, Elamites), Turkey (Cappadocia, Pontus, Asia, Phrygia, Pamphylia), northern Africa, and Rome. In the story of the tower of Babel (Gen 11:1-9), God divided humans by creating different languages after they built a tower to attempt to break the divine-human barrier (the story attempts to explain the origin of variety in languages and cultures). Here, the diversity of speech is a cause for unification.

RESPONSORIAL PSALM   PSALM 104:1, 24, 29-30, 31, 34

Lord, send out your Spirit, and renew the face of the earth.
or: Alleluia.

SECOND READING   1 CORINTHIANS 12:3b-7, 12-13

Brothers and sisters:
No one can say, "Jesus is Lord," except by the Holy Spirit.

There are different kinds of spiritual gifts but the same Spirit;
    there are different forms of service but the same Lord;
    there are different workings but the same God
    who produces all of them in everyone.
To each individual the manifestation of the Spirit
    is given for some benefit.

As a body is one though it has many parts,
    and all the parts of the body, though many, are one body,
    so also Christ.
For in one Spirit we were all baptized into one body,
    whether Jews or Greeks, slaves or free persons,
    and we were all given to drink of one Spirit.

First Corinthians is Paul's appeal for unity against divisive conflicts in the Corinthian community. A key conflict was the perceived hierarchy of spiritual gifts. Some church members claimed higher status because of their gifts (it also seems that speaking in tongues was at the top of the hierarchy; see 1 Cor 13:1). Paul interrupts both the hierarchy and the idea that spiritual gifts are an individual's achievement. In our reading, he emphasizes that nothing comes through the power of the individual and affirms the equality of all who confess that "Jesus is Lord." Those who confess this receive "gifts" (Greek *charismata*) from the Holy Spirit, the diversity of which benefits the common good and builds up the Body of Christ. We skip over verses 8-11, which describe the various manifestations of the Spirit: wisdom, knowledge, faith, healing, miracles, prophecy, discernment of spirits, and the gift of tongues and their interpretation (he lists the gift of tongues last purposefully, to counter those who would claim it was a higher gift). Our reading leads into the rest of 1 Corinthians 12 and 13, where Paul continues his discussion of gifts of the Spirit by outlining a "still more excellent way," the greatest manifestation of the Holy Spirit: love (12:31).

GOSPEL   JOHN 20:19-23

On the evening of that first day of the week,
    when the doors were locked, where the disciples were,
    for fear of the Jews,
    Jesus came and stood in their midst
    and said to them, "Peace be with you."
When he had said this, he showed them his hands and his side.
The disciples rejoiced when they saw the Lord.
Jesus said to them again, "Peace be with you.
As the Father has sent me, so I send you."
And when he had said this, he breathed on them and said
        to them,
    "Receive the Holy Spirit.
Whose sins you forgive are forgiven them,
    and whose sins you retain are retained."

Unlike the longer timeline presented in our reading from Acts, in John's Gospel the resurrection, the ascension, and the outpouring of the Holy Spirit (known as the "Johannine Pentecost") all occur on a single day. After appearing first to Mary Magdalene and ascending to God (20:1-18),[1] the risen Christ breathes the Holy Spirit upon the disciples and commissions them. Compare this to the Acts story, in which the Spirit appears as the powerful, divine force of God. Here in John, the Holy Spirit is a flesh-and-blood experience, the literal breath (Greek *pneuma*) of the crucified and risen Christ. This scene echoes the second creation story, in which God breathes into Adam the "breath of life" (Gen 2:7), and it recalls the spirit that breathes life back into the dead bones of Israel (Ezek 37:6-10). In our reading, the disciples receive this breath and, with it, the ability to forgive and heal. In the last verse of the reading, the word "sins" in the phrase "whose sins you retain" is absent in the Greek. Instead, the phrase may speak to the apostles "retain[ing]" or literally "taking possession of" (Greek *krateō*) not sins but people, as Jesus seeks to hold on to anyone who might be lost. The disciples are therefore commissioned into a holy responsibility to forgive, heal, and hold on to others as Christ would. According to Catholic tradition, the origins of the sacrament of reconciliation are found in this reading. We read a longer version of this passage on the Second Sunday of Easter, which leads into the story of Thomas (John 20:24-31).

---

1. Raymond Brown noted that in John's account of the ascension, there is no "levitation" or "visible departure" of Jesus into heaven as in Luke 24:50-53. Rather, Jesus's ascension in John's Gospel is a theological and invisible one, a rapid completion of his resurrection and glorification. See Brown, *The Gospel and Epistles of John: A Concise Commentary* (Collegeville, MN: Liturgical Press, 1988), 98.

Ponder

Pentecost celebrates diversity in the unity of Christ. In Acts, the Spirit descends upon "all" and reveals itself through the diversity of language. First Corinthians describes a range of spiritual gifts that build up Christ's Body, the church. In the Gospel, the disciples receive the gift to unify through forgiveness. Our readings challenge us to view diversity as essential for unity. Diversity is the path to a harmonious whole when we foster each other's unique gifts, embrace our differences, listen to each other, and work to build bridges instead of trenches. It is the Spirit who helps us to walk the path of honest and authentic wholeness as the Body of Christ and the glory of God. How do you walk this path in your daily life?

Tongues of fire, driving wind, Jesus's breath: the Spirit is irreducible to a single metaphor. From these metaphors, it can be tempting to view the Spirit as something that is solely "out there," descending upon us. Yet according to Paul, its source is not outside but within. God "produces" or "activates" (Greek *energeō*) this Spirit in us, which emanates into the world as different "workings" or "activities" (Greek *energēma*; 1 Cor 12:6). The words "energy" and "energize" derive from these Greek terms. In other words, the Spirit is both our own creative energy and the energizing force that sustains us. The Spirit unleashes this power and energy into the world, and it is our responsibility to manifest it in our lives. Are we ready?

The Most Holy Trinity

FIRST READING   EXODUS 34:4b-6, 8-9

Early in the morning Moses went up Mount Sinai
   as the LORD had commanded him,
   taking along the two stone tablets.

Having come down in a cloud, the LORD stood with Moses there
   and proclaimed his name, "LORD."
Thus the LORD passed before him and cried out,
   "The LORD, the LORD, a merciful[1] and gracious God,
   slow to anger and rich in kindness[2] and fidelity."
Moses at once bowed down to the ground in worship.
Then he said, "If I find favor with you, O LORD,
   do come along in our company.[3]
This is indeed a stiff-necked people; yet pardon our wickedness
   and sins,
   and receive us as your own."[4]

Earlier in Exodus, Moses climbs Mount Sinai for the first time to receive the covenant between Israel and God. When he comes down from the mountain, he brings with him a token of the covenant in the form of two stone tablets. These tablets were made by God and "inscribed by God's own finger" (Exod 31:18). Moses then smashes the tablets after learning that the Israelites had violated the covenant while waiting for him to return; they had created a figurine of a calf through which to worship God, thus breaking the commandment not to create idols (Exod 20:4) or, more specifically, "gods of silver" and "gods of gold" (Exod 20:23). (Note that in earlier Israelite and Canaanite traditions, calves and bulls were common images of the divine.) The above reading draws from the renewal of the covenant

---

1. "Merciful" also translates as "compassionate" (Hebrew *raḥûm*). The term derives from *reḥem*, "womb."

2. "Rich in kindness" translates literally as "abounding in loving-kindness."

3. "Come along in our company" translates literally as "come into our midst" or "come among us."

4. "Receive" translates literally as "inherit" or "possess" (Hebrew *nāḥal*).

after God forgives the people of this incident. God tells Moses to return to Mount Sinai, where God will again meet Moses and reinscribe the covenant on two new stone tablets. This time, however, it is Moses who makes the tablets, not God. Throughout the Hebrew Bible, God commonly manifests within a cloud (e.g., Exod 19:9, 16; 24:15). According to Acts, Jesus's ascension raises him up back into this cloud (Acts 1:1-11; see the first reading for the feast of the Ascension of the Lord). In today's reading from Exodus, God first appears to Moses, then lists key divine attributes in verse 6 ("merciful," "gracious," "slow to anger," "abounding in love and fidelity"). We skip verse 7, which lists justice (including punishment when people err) as another divine attribute and a necessary corollary to mercy and forgiveness. This list of divine attributes is known as God's "Thirteen Attributes" in Jewish tradition, and it is recited as a prayer for forgiveness on various occasions and holy days. Moses then entreats God to pardon the people's sins, to come into their midst ("come along in our company"), and to inherit or "receive" them again as God's treasured possession (see footnote on the Eleventh Sunday in Ordinary Time for Exod 19:5).

RESPONSORIAL PSALM   DANIEL 3:52, 53, 54, 55

Glory and praise forever!

SECOND READING   2 CORINTHIANS 13:11-13

Brothers and sisters, rejoice.
Mend your ways,[5] encourage one another,
   agree with one another, live in peace,
   and the God of love and peace will be with you.
Greet one another with a holy kiss.
All the holy ones greet you.

The grace of the Lord Jesus Christ
   and the love of God
   and the fellowship[6] of the Holy Spirit be with all of you.

5. "Mend your ways" can also translate as "Put things in order" (NRSV) or "Aim for restoration" (ESV). The Greek term is *katartizō* ("to mend, restore, or strengthen").
6. "Fellowship" (Greek *koinōnia*) also translates as "participation" and "partnership."

Paul ends his second letter to the Corinthians in typical Pauline style. A few verses earlier, he exhorts the community of believers as follows: "Examine yourselves to see whether you are living in faith. Test yourselves. Do you not realize that Jesus Christ is in you?" (13:5). In today's reading, he describes what "living in faith" and having Christ "in" them looks like as a community: like joy or rejoicing; like the restoration or strengthening of relationships; like encouragement, unity, and peacefulness. When the people act this way, through the grace of Jesus Christ, God will be present with them. Paul concludes with the trinitarian formula as a bookend to the beginning of the letter, where he explains the work of the Trinity among us: God gives believers "security" in Christ, anoints them, and gives them the Spirit as a "first installment" or down payment (borrowing from economic terminology; 1:21-22). In other words, the Spirit is the assurance of the fulfillment of God's promises through Christ.

GOSPEL   JOHN 3:16-18

God so loved the world that he gave his only Son,
    so that everyone who believes in him might not perish
    but might have eternal life.
For God did not send his Son into the world to condemn
        the world,
    but that the world might be saved through him.
Whoever believes in him will not be condemned,
    but whoever does not believe has already been condemned,
    because he has not believed in the name of the only Son
        of God.

This short Gospel reading originates within the story of Nicodemus, a religious leader who comes to Jesus secretly by night to question him and learn from him. In John's Gospel, darkness and night, in contrast to light and day, signify spiritual blindness. The first line of our reading is the summation of Christian theology: "God so loved the world that he gave his only Son." It is this first phrase—"God so loved"—that expresses the source of the Christian mystery. God poured out this remarkable love into the world through the gift of

Jesus. The gift is expressed through the verb "gave," which encapsulates both birth (incarnation) and death (crucifixion). Jesus testifies to God's love through his life and death, both of which are necessary for human salvation. The contrast between those who "perish" and those who "have eternal life" implies that eternal life is not inherent to a person; rather, it is given or withheld based on belief. The verb "condemn" (Greek *krinō*), which translates literally as "judge" and is juxtaposed with the concepts of belief and salvation, repeats three times in this short reading. There is a delicate dance between judgment and salvation in these verses. On the one hand, Jesus came to this earth because of God's immense love, *not* to judge or condemn, but as a gift of salvation. On the other hand, judgment happens as a present reality (not a future event) through the active human choice to "believe" or not. The verse following our reading further clarifies that humans are responsible for their own judgment: "And this is the verdict [or judgment], that the light came into the world, but people preferred darkness to light, because their works were evil." Ultimately, then, our own actions condemn us ("people preferred darkness"; "their works were evil"), and there is always a present choice either to remain in this state or to "prefer" the light (Jesus) and his willingness to transform and save us (v. 19).

Ponder

We begin our transition into Ordinary Time by meditating on the Trinity, the mystery awaiting us on the other side of Lent and Easter. This great mystery—the divine reality of three-in-one—lies beyond the shore of reason. According to Augustine, if we think we understand it, then what we understand is not God.[7] Yet our readings are carefully chosen to reveal aspects of this mystery to us. The Trinity is the powerful God coming in a cloud to form a covenant with Israel. It is the gift of divinity embodied in Jesus Christ, who comes to embrace the world. And it is the Spirit permeating all things. Give yourself time this week to contemplate the Trinity, to rest in its mystery, and to open your heart to awe and wonder.

What we can know about the Trinity, we know through relationships. After the Israelites' grave misstep in Exodus, Moses pleads with God to forgive them and inherit them again as God's treasured people. This story is our own, reminding us that our God is a compassionate and ever-forgiving God who is always present among us and between us, drawing us into relationship. As Christians, we experience this relationship through the Trinity, which theologians have likened to a "dance" or "choreography" (Greek *perichōrēsis*). The Trinity dances in and around us, pulling us into the divine embrace through the greatness of God, the humanity of the Son, and the Spirit that breathes us into union. The Trinity calls us tirelessly to join this dance through our own relationships and commitments. How are you being called into relationship this week?

7. St. Augustine, "Si enim comprehendis, non est Deus [If you understand, it is not God]," *Sermon* 117.5.

The Most Holy Body and Blood
of Christ (Corpus Christi)

FIRST READING   DEUTERONOMY 8:2-3, 14b-16a

Moses said to the people:
"Remember how for forty years now the LORD, your God,
has directed all your journeying in the desert,
so as to test you by affliction
and find out whether or not it was your intention
to keep his commandments.
He therefore let you be afflicted with hunger,
and then fed you with manna,
a food unknown to you and your fathers,
in order to show you that not by bread alone does one live,
but by every word that comes forth from the mouth of
the LORD.

"Do not forget the LORD, your God,
who brought you out of the land of Egypt,
that place of slavery;
who guided you through the vast and terrible desert
with its saraph serpents and scorpions,
its parched and waterless ground;
who brought forth water for you from the flinty rock
and fed you in the desert with manna,
a food unknown to your fathers."

The book of Deuteronomy is the fifth and last book of the Torah
or Pentateuch (Genesis through Deuteronomy). It is set across
the Jordan River east of Israel, where Moses and the Israelites are
poised to enter the Promised Land after forty years of desert wandering from Egypt. The book is comprised of a series of discourses
in which Moses rehearses the trajectory of the wilderness period
from the books of Exodus, Leviticus, and Numbers in order to reit-
erate God's commandments and covenant with Israel. The primary
focus is the importance of remembrance or memory of the past for

future generations. The above reading draws from the second and longest of these discourses (Deut 4:44–28:68) and from a particular subsection (5:1–11:30) in which Moses reviews the covenant made at Mount Sinai (also called Mount Horeb), originally narrated in the book of Exodus. In chapter 8, he warns the Israelites never to forget God, especially in times of prosperity. Wealth and success are divine gifts and never personal rights. He describes how the Israelites were humbled and afflicted in the wilderness period in order to test their willingness to follow God. Throughout this time, they survived on manna alone, a wafer-like substance and "wretched food" (Num 21:5), to learn the valuable lesson that only God has the power to sustain life. For more on the consumption of manna, see Exodus 16. On "saraph serpents and scorpions," see the episode in Numbers 21:6-9. On water coming from a "flinty rock," see Exodus 17:1-7 (also Num 20:2-13), in which Moses strikes the rock at Massah and Meribah after the people complain of lack of water, and water bursts forth. The point is that in the desert, Israel has had to learn to depend solely on God, not on "bread alone" or their own preferences. This lesson is one that must never be forgotten.

RESPONSORIAL PSALM   PSALM 147:12-13, 14-15, 19-20

Praise the Lord, Jerusalem.
or: Alleluia.

SECOND READING   1 CORINTHIANS 10:16-17

Brothers and sisters:
The cup of blessing that we bless,
    is it not a participation in the blood of Christ?[1]
The bread that we break,
    is it not a participation in the body of Christ?
Because the loaf of bread is one,
    we, though many, are one body,
    for we all partake of the one loaf.

---

1. "Participation" (Greek *koinōnia*) translates literally as "fellowship" or "communion."

For background information on 1 Corinthians, consult the Second Sunday in Ordinary Time. This short reading takes place within an extended discussion on the dangers of idolatry in 1 Corinthians 10, especially Paul's concern with eating meat that comes from pagan sacrifice. In the midst of this discussion, Paul offers this beautiful description of the unity and interconnectedness of the early Christian community. By joining together to partake in the Lord's Supper, the community participates or shares with each other in Christ's self-sacrifice, becoming the body and blood of Christ (see also 1 Cor 11:17-34).

GOSPEL   JOHN 6:51-58[2]

Jesus said to the Jewish crowds:
   "I am the living bread that came down from heaven;
   whoever eats this bread will live forever;
   and the bread that I will give
   is my flesh for the life of the world."

The Jews quarreled among themselves, saying,
   "How can this man give us his flesh to eat?"
Jesus said to them,
   "Amen, amen, I say to you,
   unless you eat the flesh of the Son of Man and drink his blood,
   you do not have life within you.
Whoever eats my flesh and drinks my blood
   has eternal life,
   and I will raise him on the last day.
For my flesh is true food,
   and my blood is true drink.
Whoever eats my flesh and drinks my blood
   remains in me and I in him.

2. See also the Gospel notes for the Twentieth Sunday in Ordinary Time on John 6:51-58 in *Ponder: Year B*. Readers may wish to consult the Seventeenth through Twenty-First Sundays in Ordinary Time in that volume for further information on John 6.

> Just as the living Father sent me
>   and I have life because of the Father,
>   so also the one who feeds on me
>   will have life because of me.
> This is the bread that came down from heaven.
> Unlike your ancestors who ate and still died,
>   whoever eats this bread will live forever."

John 6 is a lengthy chapter that invites readers to reflect on the sustenance that comes from Christ. Our reading follows a discussion in which Jesus calls himself the true "bread of life" (v. 35), in contrast to the manna sent from heaven to sustain Israel in the wilderness. This discussion then develops into a teaching on the Eucharist. Jesus refers to himself as the "living bread" sent by the "living Father" for salvation. He gives his "flesh" in a double sense: through his crucifixion and in the ongoing eucharistic meal from which the people will eat (v. 51). To his Jewish audience, Jesus's words about eating his "flesh" and drinking his "blood" would have been repellant and offensive for two reasons: first, because they sound cannibalistic (see, e.g., prophetic statements in Jer 19:7-10 and Lam 2:16-21 regarding eating flesh in times of war and famine); and second, because the Hebrew Bible admonishes against eating an animal's blood along with its flesh (see Gen 9:4; Lev 7:26-27; Deut 12:23). Often, Jesus's teachings are metaphors. Here, however, the point seems to be literal, as demonstrated by Jesus's insistence and his repetitive, direct statements and graphic language, including the words "flesh" and "eat." Elsewhere, accounts of the Last Supper refer not to the "flesh" but to the "body" (e.g., Mark 14:22). Together, "flesh" and "blood" refer to the totality of the human person. In verse 54 ("Whoever eats my flesh and drinks my blood has eternal life"), the verb "eat" shifts from the Greek *phagein* to *trōgein*, which refers not to human eating but to an animal munching or gnawing. It seems that Jesus is purposely trying to shock his disciples with this imagery, for directly following our reading, many of them say, "This saying is hard; who can accept it?" Jesus then responds, "Does this shock you?" (vv. 60-61). The answer must be yes, for many of the disciples then abandon him (v. 66).

Ponder

Deuteronomy is about memory. Repeatedly, Moses tells the people to remember. Remember God, he says, who led you out of slavery and made you a treasured possession (see Exod 19:5-6). Remember that "not by bread alone does one live." It is God who sustains all life. For Jews, the exodus is the central religious event to remember; it is a birth narrative out of Egypt and into relationship with God. For Christians, Easter is the central religious event, another birth narrative out of slavery and into a new relationship with God through Christ. At the heart of this event is Christ's body and blood poured out for the world. This is the Eucharist, the great Christian Mystery that collapses past into present and calls us to remember, to recreate, and to participate. Imagine Christ calling you to remember through the Eucharist. What does active remembrance look like in your daily life and actions?

Jesus's words in the Gospel are meant to shock. Why? Perhaps to call us to task. He reminds us that the Eucharist is not something we consume mindlessly, nor is it a ritual commemorating a past event. Instead, it is a present gift and an obligation. To participate in the Eucharist is to become what we consume: Christ's flesh and blood given for others. As Christ gifts his entire being to us, so we commit to becoming that gift for others. To be a eucharistic people is to acknowledge Christ flowing through our blood, binding us as one body. It is to walk the path that Jesus walked, caring for the least among us, committing ourselves to the task of unity, justice, and truth. This road may not be easy, but it is simple in light of the gift. As you meditate on the Eucharist this week, how do you experience it as both gift and obligation?

Second Sunday in Ordinary Time

FIRST READING   ISAIAH 49:3, 5-6

The LORD said to me: You are my servant,
   Israel, through whom I show my glory.
Now the LORD has spoken
   who formed me as his servant from the womb,
that Jacob may be brought back to him
   and Israel gathered to him;
and I am made glorious in the sight of the LORD,
   and my God is now my strength!
It is too little, the LORD says, for you to be my servant,
   to raise up the tribes of Jacob,
   and restore the survivors of Israel;
I will make you a light to the nations,
   that my salvation may reach to the ends of the earth.

We enter Ordinary Time through the second of four "Suffering Servant" poems in Isaiah (see the notes on Isaiah from The Baptism of the Lord). This second poem identifies the servant explicitly with Israel (as a collective singular), who is a prophetic witness to God's salvation for the world. God calls the servant from the womb like a prophet (see Jer 1:5; Gal 1:15) to reflect God's glory and to help bring about Jacob's/Israel's restoration. Written within the context of the Babylonian exile (586–536 BCE), God reassures Israel that its suffering will serve a broader purpose—not only for its own redemption but for the redemption of all people. The boundaries between prophet and Israel collapse in this poem, for the servant is both a prophet *to* Israel and a prophet *as* Israel. Through the servant (prophet), God will bring back Israel, while the servant (Israel) will simultaneously bring other nations to God. It is unfortunate that our reading skips verse 4, which describes God as the one in whom the servant trusts unwaveringly despite his suffering.

RESPONSORIAL PSALM   PSALM 40:2, 4, 7-8, 8-9, 10

Here am I, Lord; I come to do your will.

SECOND READING   1 CORINTHIANS 1:1-3

Paul, called to be an apostle of Christ Jesus by the will of God,
    and Sosthenes our brother,
    to the church of God that is in Corinth,
    to you who have been sanctified in Christ Jesus,
        called to be holy,
    with all those everywhere who call upon the name of our Lord
        Jesus Christ, their Lord and ours.
Grace to you and peace from God our Father
    and the Lord Jesus Christ.

As we begin Ordinary Time, we also begin a semi-continuous reading of 1 Corinthians 1–4 that will continue through the Eighth Sunday in Ordinary Time (or until Lent begins). Paul wrote the letter
around 54 CE from Ephesus to the community of believers he had
founded a few years prior in Corinth. At the time, Corinth was a
prosperous and diverse city with great economic possibilities as
well as disparities. The community to whom Paul writes was mainly
composed of Gentile converts, many of whom were of lesser social
standing and means, though Paul also baptized a few elites. After
Paul left, arguments and factions arose in the community about a
variety of disputes that Paul addresses in this letter, including community factions, the marginalization of certain members, flagrant
violations of ethical behavior, and the spreading of religious views
contrary to the gospel. Underlying the letter is a call for unity as part
of a deeper belonging in Christ, and Paul continually counsels the
community to seek love above all else (see 8:1-3, 13). As always, the
letter begins with a prescription and greeting in the first few verses.
Paul refers to himself as an apostle or, literally, "one who has been
sent." He names the community both in terms of its geographical
setting and its broader identity as "the church of God." Paul refers
to Sosthenes, who was likely an official of the Corinthian synagogue

(see also Acts 18:17). He also stresses the importance of holiness, stating that the community has already been "sanctified" (made holy) by God in Christ Jesus, yet is simultaneously called to respond to this sanctification by continuing to "be holy" through their actions.

John the Baptist saw Jesus coming toward him and said,
    "Behold, the Lamb of God, who takes away the sin of
        the world.
He is the one of whom I said,
    'A man is coming after me who ranks ahead of me
    because he existed before me.'
I did not know him,
    but the reason why I came baptizing with water
    was that he might be made known to Israel."
John testified further, saying,
    "I saw the Spirit come down like a dove from heaven
    and remain upon him.
I did not know him,
    but the one who sent me to baptize with water told me,
    'On whomever you see the Spirit come down and remain,
    he is the one who will baptize with the Holy Spirit.'
Now I have seen and testified that he is the Son of God."

Each year, we mark the shift from the Christmas season into Ordinary Time by reading from the beginning of Jesus's ministry according to the Gospel of John. We will not read from this Gospel again until Lent. Directly preceding our reading, Jewish authorities question John the Baptist while he prophesies Jesus's coming (1:19-28). The next day, he sees Jesus for the first time. John then exclaims to his receptive audience to stop and "[b]ehold," or look upon, Jesus, who is the "Lamb of God." The term "Lamb" is noteworthy and links Jesus in part to the sacrificial Passover lamb from Exodus 12. Later, in John's account of the crucifixion, Jesus's bones remain unbroken on the cross (19:36), a clear reference to the admonition that the Passover lamb's bones were to remain unbroken (Exod 12:46). However, John's use of the term "lamb" is multilayered, playing on the Aramaic *ṭalyâ*, a word that can translate as "lamb," "servant," or "child" (Aramaic was Jesus's language and the spoken language among commoners in first century Palestine/Israel). In this case, there may be a deeper connection to Isaiah's Suffering Servant passages, particularly Isaiah 53:7, where the servant is compared to a lamb who quietly and willingly goes to slaughter. In our reading, John the Baptist reiterates twice that he did not know Jesus but that God had revealed Jesus to him through the descending dove (see the accounts of Jesus's baptism in the Synoptic Gospels, e.g., Luke 3:21-22). John's Gospel seeks to divinize Jesus as much as possible and so refrains from stating explicitly that John baptized Jesus. The Spirit "remain[s]" on Jesus after his baptism, a word that signals belonging and attachment and is used consistently in John's Gospel and in 1–2 John. The reference to "Spirit" draws upon the meaning of "spirit" in the Hebrew Bible, God's vital power that remains permanently with Jesus. The early Christian sense of "Holy Spirit" develops after Jesus's death, when the Spirit is breathed into the disciples (John 20:22) and pours itself out on the community following the resurrection (Acts 2:4).

Ponder

As we transition from Christmas to Ordinary Time, the call to discipleship is strong and urgent. Our readings bridge the two seasons by remaining with the Suffering Servant poems in Isaiah and with John the Baptist at the beginning of Jesus's ministry. The servant and John have a deep connection with God, as does Paul. God formed each of these figures to be unique prophetic witnesses and lights to the world. God has also formed each of us as unique witnesses. Now that we have celebrated Jesus's birth, Ordinary Time invites us to meditate upon this great gift and ponder our response. What does it mean to be called forth by God as a witness? Are we open to hearing the call, and are we ready to respond with the power of the psalmist: "Here am I, Lord; I come to do your will"?

Witness begins with recognition. In the Gospel, John the Baptist is waiting for Jesus and is receptive to God's revelation. Twice he states that he "did not know" Jesus. Yet he still recognizes Jesus instantly, stating, "He is the one." He calls his audience to stop and behold the Son of God, who will heal the collective brokenness of the world and bridge us back to a relationship with God. John recognizes that Jesus is the one he has been waiting and longing for, the one who will not disappoint. As you pray with the Gospel, imagine yourself in John's shoes saying the same words about Jesus: "He is the one." What is this experience like? Today, in the context of your own life, can you describe what (or whom) you are waiting and longing for most?

Third Sunday in Ordinary Time (Sunday of the Word of God)

First the LORD degraded the land of Zebulun
    and the land of Naphtali;
    but in the end he has glorified the seaward road,
    the land west of the Jordan,
    the District of the Gentiles.

Anguish has taken wing, dispelled is darkness:
    for there is no gloom where but now there was distress.

The people who walked in darkness
    have seen a great light;
upon those who dwelt in the land of gloom
    a light has shone.
You have brought them abundant joy
    and great rejoicing,
as they rejoice before you as at the harvest,
    as people make merry when dividing spoils.
For the yoke that burdened them,
    the pole on their shoulder,
and the rod of their taskmaster
    you have smashed, as on the day of Midian.

In these verses, the prophet proclaims Assyria's fall and the return of a righteous king from David's line (see also the broader context in Isa 8:16–9:7). This prophecy follows the Syro-Ephraimite war (735–732 BCE), when Syria and the northern kingdom of Israel (Ephraim) joined together to fight unsuccessfully against the Assyrians. The result was Assyria's subjugation of the northernmost areas of Israel, including Zebulun and Naphtali, along with the province of Dor (the "seaward road"), Gilead ("the land west of the Jordan"), and Megiddo ("District of the Gentiles"). Isaiah promises that God will eventually remove the burden of this oppressive empire, transforming darkness and distress into light, joy, and rejoicing. The yoke, pole, and rod are symbols of Assyrian oppression. The "day of Midian" is a reference to Judges 7:15-25, when God helps Gideon defeat Midian and deliver Israel from its oppressors.

RESPONSORIAL PSALM   PSALM 27:1, 4, 13-14

The Lord is my light and my salvation.

SECOND READING   1 CORINTHIANS 1:10-13, 17

I urge you, brothers and sisters, in the name of our Lord
    Jesus Christ,
    that all of you agree in what you say,[1]
    and that there be no divisions among you,
    but that you be united[2] in the same mind and in the same
      purpose.
For it has been reported to me about you, my brothers and sisters,
    by Chloe's people, that there are rivalries among you.
I mean that each of you is saying,
    "I belong to Paul," or "I belong to Apollos,"
    or "I belong to Cephas," or "I belong to Christ."
Is Christ divided?
Was Paul crucified for you?
Or were you baptized in the name of Paul?
For Christ did not send me to baptize but to preach the gospel,
    and not with the wisdom of human eloquence,
    so that the cross of Christ might not be emptied of its meaning.

After Paul left Corinth, other missionaries arrived. Factions formed, which were reported to Paul through "Chloe's people" (Chloe was likely well known in Corinth, though she is otherwise unmentioned in the New Testament). Some followed Apollos, a Jewish-Christian

---

1. A simpler translation is "that all of you be in agreement" (in other words, this is not simply about agreement in what is spoken).

2. "United" (Greek *katartizō*) means "to restore, put in order" and suggests adaptation and mutual adjustment, a readiness to give in to one another in the interests of harmony.

teacher from Alexandria, Egypt, and an "eloquent speaker" (see Acts 18:24-28). It seems that others followed Peter (or Cephas, meaning "rock" in Aramaic), though we have no historical evidence that Peter was ever in Corinth. Meanwhile, most of the lower-class believers remained attached to Paul. Paul uses a slogan that was shouted by fans rooting for performers in the amphitheater (i.e., "I belong to Paul") to caricature these factions. His final statement ("I belong to Christ") reminds the community of their true belonging. He concludes with rhetorical questions to make two key points: (1) there is only one Savior, Christ, in whom all people are united through baptism, no matter who administers it; and (2) Paul's mission was to preach the gospel, not to baptize (though Paul held baptism in high regard). For Paul, the power of the gospel manifests through authentic preaching that is focused on the cross. In contrast, false preachers focus on building themselves up by sounding clever or attractive.

GOSPEL   MATTHEW 4:12-23 [OR 4:12-17]

When Jesus heard that John had been arrested,
    he withdrew to Galilee.
He left Nazareth and went to live in Capernaum by the sea,
    in the region of Zebulun and Naphtali,
    that what had been said through Isaiah the prophet
    might be fulfilled:
        Land of Zebulun and land of Naphtali,
            the way to the sea, beyond the Jordan,
            Galilee of the Gentiles,
        the people who sit in darkness have seen a great light,
        on those dwelling in a land overshadowed by death
            light has arisen.
From that time on, Jesus began to preach and say,
    "Repent, for the kingdom of heaven is at hand."

As he was walking by the Sea of Galilee, he saw two brothers,
    Simon who is called Peter, and his brother Andrew,
    casting a net into the sea; they were fishermen.
He said to them,
    "Come after me, and I will make you fishers of men."
At once they left their nets and followed him.

He walked along from there and saw two other brothers,
    James, the son of Zebedee, and his brother John.
They were in a boat, with their father Zebedee, mending
        their nets.
He called them, and immediately they left their boat and
        their father
    and followed him.
He went around all of Galilee,
    teaching in their synagogues, proclaiming the gospel of the
        kingdom,
    and curing every disease and illness among the people.

When Jesus calls his first disciples, he has just emerged from a forty-day sojourn in the desert following his baptism. According to the Synoptic Gospels, Jesus calls his first disciples while his identity remains a mystery, after John the Baptist is arrested (see also Mark 1:14-20; Luke 5:1-11). In contrast, in John's Gospel, the first disciples follow Jesus in John the Baptist's presence and at his urging (1:35-42; see also the Gospel notes for the Second Sunday in Ordinary Time). In our reading, after Jesus learns that John has been arrested by Herod Antipas, ruler of Galilee, he leaves the sleepy village of Nazareth and follows John's path to danger. His move is purposeful: to pick up John's torch and fulfill John's prophecies. Galilee was a remote area of northern Israel formerly allotted to the tribes of Zebulun and Naphtali (see the first reading from Isaiah). Capernaum was a bustling village in this region, on the northwest shore of the Sea of Galilee and at the crossroads of the international trade route called the *Via Maris*, the "Way of the Sea." Fishing was a key economic activity in the region. Jesus begins by proclaiming that the kingdom of God has come, meaning that the long-standing desires and yearnings of the people are being fulfilled. They are to repent, or return, to God in response to the good news. As Jesus passes Simon and Andrew, James and John, these first disciples leave their work instantly to follow him. We do not know why. Jesus's identity has not yet been revealed to them. All Jesus tells them (or at least tells Simon and Andrew) is that he will make them "fishers" of people.

Ponder

Jesus calls people who have something to leave behind. In rapid succession, he calls his first disciples, and they abandon their families and occupations to follow him. Jesus is also calling us, asking us to examine our own lives for that which prevents us from following him freely, that which can be left behind. This could be a job, a half-hearted commitment to faith, or perhaps a passive acceptance of social structures that degrade the dignity of the human person. Maybe it is attachment to our own opinions that feed divisions in our families, communities, and church. Each day is an invitation to search our hearts and let go of that which contradicts our baptismal callings in order to hear him and follow freely.

The psalmist longs for God, seeking to "gaze" upon God and "dwell in the house of the LORD / all the days" of his life. Can you feel this longing? Like the psalmist, we often experience God most intimately in our churches, where the Real Presence resides in the tabernacle. Yet we also experience God intimately through our sacred Scriptures. Today is Sunday of the Word of God, a reminder that we dwell with God not only in sacred buildings but in the sacredness of God's word. By meditating upon the written word, we encounter *the* Word, who greets us "with great love" and "speaks" intimately with us.[3] As you pray with the readings this week, ponder the role of the Scriptures in your life. How are they—or how might they become—a refuge, a place to experience and communicate with God?

3. *Dei Verbum* 21.

Fourth Sunday in Ordinary Time

Seek the LORD, all you humble of the earth,
   who have observed[1] his law;
seek justice,[2] seek humility;
   perhaps you may be sheltered
   on the day of the LORD's anger.

But I will leave as a remnant in your midst
   a people humble and lowly,
who shall take refuge in the name of the LORD:
   the remnant of Israel.
They shall do no wrong
   and speak no lies;
nor shall there be found in their mouths
   a deceitful tongue;
they shall pasture and couch their flocks
   with none to disturb them.

Zephaniah is a short prophetic book of three chapters. It is set in the eighth century BCE, when King Josiah instituted religious reforms and tried to establish political independence from Assyria (see 2 Kgs 16–23 for his story). Likely, the book was added to after the Babylonian exile and into the fifth century BCE. Zephaniah (whose name means "the Lord has stored up" or "the Lord has hidden") begins by announcing the coming "Day of the Lord" with powerful imagery of divine judgment that has been reimagined over the centuries. For example, a thirteenth-century-CE Christian hymn called the *Dies Irae* (or "Day of Wrath") draws from the imagery of Zephaniah's "Day of the Lord" and is included in the Mass for the Dead. The term *shoah* (*šō 'āh*, the Hebrew word for "disaster" or "ruin") in Zephaniah 1:15 has also become a synonym for the devastation of European Jews during the Holocaust. We hear from Zephaniah only twice during

---

1. A closer translation of "observed" (Hebrew *pā 'al*) is "to do" or "to fulfill."
2. "Justice" translates more literally as "righteousness" (Hebrew *ṣedeq*).

our three-year lectionary cycle. This Sunday's reading begins with one verse from the book's core prophecies of God's judgment against the nations. Zephaniah calls Judah to seek justice and humility in order to escape judgment. We then skip to the end of the book to visions of Jerusalem's renewal. God speaks to the Holy City, describing the righteous remnant, the humble and lowly, who will remain "in your midst." Our reading repeats the term "humble" (Hebrew *ānow*) or "humility" (*ănāwâ*) three times for emphasis. This term also translates as "poor," "meek," or "oppressed" and refers to literal and internal states of being. As the first verse of our reading explains, the deepest meaning of humility is fidelity to God's law.

RESPONSORIAL PSALM   PSALM 146:6-7, 8-9, 9-10

Blessed are the poor in spirit; the kingdom of heaven is theirs!

SECOND READING   1 CORINTHIANS 1:26-31

Consider your own calling, brothers and sisters.
Not many of you were wise by human standards,[3]
    not many were powerful,
    not many were of noble birth.
Rather, God chose the foolish of the world to shame the wise,
    and God chose the weak of the world to shame the strong,
    and God chose the lowly and despised of the world,
    those who count for nothing,
    to reduce to nothing those who are something,
    so that no human being[4] might boast before God.
It is due to him that you are in Christ Jesus,
    who became for us wisdom from God,
    as well as righteousness, sanctification, and redemption,
    so that, as it is written,
    "Whoever boasts, should boast in[5] the Lord."

---

3. "Human standards": the Greek translates literally as "according to the flesh."
4. "No human being": the Greek translates literally as "no flesh."
5. "In" could also translate as "of."

Within his call for unity in Christ (see last Sunday's reading), Paul turns to the single unifying event for all believers: the cross. Paul calls the community of believers to "proclaim Christ crucified" (1:23), a message that seems like "foolishness" (1:18) to those of the world. Here, Paul adopts terms that Greek writers used to describe major class divisions and flips them on their head; "wise," "powerful," and "noble" represented the wealthy, while "foolish," "weak," and "lowly and despised" represented the poor. According to Paul, God did not choose the wealthy but the lowly, despised, and weak (in other words, those deemed "foolish" by human standards). He stresses the importance of being chosen by repeating the verb three times ("chose," Greek *eklegomai*, means to "pick out," "choose," or "select"). For Paul, to be "in" Christ is to be drawn into a new understanding of reality through Christ, who embodies divine wisdom, righteousness, sanctification (holiness), and redemption (freedom from sin or death) through his death and resurrection. This list of divine attributes echoes language in the Hebrew Bible (see especially Jer 9:23-24, which also describes true "boasting" as knowledge of God).

GOSPEL   MATTHEW 5:1-12a

When Jesus saw the crowds, he went up the mountain,
  and after he had sat down, his disciples came to him.
He began to teach them, saying:
  "Blessed are the poor in spirit,
    for theirs is the kingdom of heaven.
  Blessed are they who mourn,
    for they will be comforted.
  Blessed are the meek,
    for they will inherit the land.
  Blessed are they who hunger and thirst for righteousness,
    for they will be satisfied.
  Blessed are the merciful,
    for they will be shown mercy.
  Blessed are the clean of heart,
    for they will see God.
  Blessed are the peacemakers,
    for they will be called children of God.

Blessed are they who are persecuted for the sake of
    righteousness,
  for theirs is the kingdom of heaven.
Blessed are you when they insult you and persecute you
    and utter every kind of evil against you falsely because of me.
Rejoice and be glad,
  for your reward will be great in heaven."

This week brings us to Jesus's beatitudes (from the Latin *beatus*, meaning "blessed" or "favored by God"). The beatitudes mark the beginning of Jesus's famous Sermon on the Mount in Matthew's Gospel (5–7). Compare to Luke's much briefer Sermon on the Plain (6:17–7:1), which contains four beatitudes to Matthew's nine as well as four "woes" and a more concrete emphasis on this world (e.g., "Blessed are you who are poor" rather than "Blessed are the poor in spirit"). The focus on beatitudes, or blessings, given to those who are faithful to God's laws comes from the prophets and the Wisdom tradition of ancient Israel (e.g., Isa 30:18; 32:20; Prov 3:13; 28:14). Each blessing begins in the third-person plural ("Blessed are they"; Greek *makarioi hoi*) and therefore assumes communal living and relationship. In other words, these are not blessings for the individual. Matthew stresses that believers will receive these blessings fully in God's kingdom (see also Isa 61:1-2), though he does not advise passive waiting until then. While some of the beatitudes speak concretely to states that threaten people's well-being (e.g., grief, poverty, persecution), others speak to active states of communal care that help bring about God's kingdom (e.g., righteousness, mercy, peacemaking). A few of these expressions necessitate a bit more explanation; for example, "poor in spirit" is not an acceptance of poverty but an inward freedom and receptiveness to God that leads to the pursuit of righteousness above all else. The word "meek" means those who are poor, afflicted, or humble (see Ps 37:11), while "mercy" is one of God's primary attributes (along with justice; see Ps 145:7-9). To be "clean of heart" refers to pure motives and a clean conscience (see Ps 24:4; 73:1). The beatitudes are not unattainable or future promises alone. Instead, they assure us that happiness and favor are possible in this life when we pursue God's kingdom with all that we have.

Ponder

The kingdom of God belongs to those who are "humble and lowly." What do these words mean? To Zephaniah, humility means faithfulness to God. It means recognizing one's dependence on God (i.e., to "take refuge in" God), seeking righteousness and humility. For Paul, the "lowly" are those whom the world counts as "nothing." Our responsorial psalm and the Gospel perhaps encompass these terms best with the phrase "poor in spirit." All of these terms embrace the totality of oneself: internal disposition as well as physical poverty and suffering. God's kingdom upends social hierarchies and esteem, and it condemns all structures and people who live at the expense of others' well-being. The poor and lowly will bring about the kingdom, and the kingdom belongs to them. In our world today, do we truly believe this message? How does it call us to live *now*?

To understand the beatitudes is to understand the audience. Jesus is speaking to people at the bottom of the social ladder. These people seek in Jesus another world of possibility beyond their suffering. He offers them this world (God's kingdom) from a mountaintop, a biblical place of revelation and vision. Moses once revealed the commandments from a mountain; now Jesus reveals a vision of God's reign from this same space. He gives people hope and encourages them to trust beyond what they can see. He promises that *they* are the truly blessed ones, not those who are rich, comfortable, or complacent now. He gives them strength to trust in God's promises, to remain faithful and work for the kingdom. These beatitudes are not superficial sayings. They are radical, demanding one's life and fidelity. They both convict and comfort. As you pray with the beatitudes, how do they speak to you today?

Fifth Sunday in Ordinary Time

FIRST READING   ISAIAH 58:7-10

Thus says the LORD:
  Share your bread with the hungry,
    shelter the oppressed and the homeless;
  clothe the naked when you see them,
    and do not turn your back on your own.
  Then your light shall break forth like the dawn,
    and your wound shall quickly be healed;
  your vindication shall go before you,
    and the glory of the LORD shall be your rear guard.
  Then you shall call, and the LORD will answer,
    you shall cry for help, and he will say: Here I am!
  If you remove from your midst
    oppression, false accusation and malicious speech;
  if you bestow your bread on the hungry
    and satisfy the afflicted;
  then light shall rise for you in the darkness,
    and the gloom[1] shall become for you like midday.

Our reading comes from the final chapters of Isaiah, amid calls for communal repentance and the continued promise of Judah's restoration. Set in postexilic Judah in the late sixth or fifth centuries BCE, the broader context suggests that the people were still in a period of distress after the Babylonian exile. In the verses preceding our reading, God orders the prophet to proclaim aloud the people's transgressions (v. 1). "They seek me day after day," says God, desiring to "know my ways" and "draw near to [me]" (v. 2). The people fast, a traditional act of repentance and humility, yet God finds their fasting empty and selfish (vv. 4-5). God then describes what genuine "fasting" means in verses 6-14: to practice communal care, especially for the

---

1. The words "light" and "gloom" that are set parallel to each other in these last two lines translate more literally as "your light" and "your darkness." In other words, it is "*your* light" that "shall rise for you in the darkness" and "*your* gloom" that "shall become for you like midday."

poor and suffering, and to work for justice. The people must feed, clothe, and have compassion upon those who are hungry, oppressed, and homeless. They must cease to perpetuate oppression, lies, and maliciousness. Only then, God says, will the community's true restoration take place. Their "darkness" and "gloom" will transform into "light" (see footnote), they will be healed, and their "vindication" (or "vindicator," depending on the translation) will protect them. The concern for the poor in these verses is a hallmark of biblical tradition, as seen in last Sunday's readings (see also Exod 22:21-26; Lev 19:9-10; Deut 14:28-29).

RESPONSORIAL PSALM   PSALM 112:4-5, 6-7, 8-9

> The just man is a light in darkness to the upright.
> *or:* Alleluia.

SECOND READING   1 CORINTHIANS 2:1-5

> When I came to you, brothers and sisters,
>   proclaiming the mystery[2] of God,
>   I did not come with sublimity[3] of words or of wisdom.
> For I resolved to know nothing while I was with you
>   except Jesus Christ, and him crucified.
> I came to you in weakness and fear and much trembling,
>   and my message and my proclamation
>   were not with persuasive words of wisdom,
>   but with a demonstration of Spirit and power,
>   so that your faith might rest not on human wisdom
>   but on the power of God.

Paul continues to build upon his message from last week, where he spoke of God reversing human notions of power and weakness and choosing the lowly to turn the world upside down. Here, he maintains this focus while turning his attention to his own experience.

---

2. Other ancient manuscripts replace "mystery" with "testimony."
3. "Sublimity" (Greek *hyperochē*) also translates as "loftiness" or "authority."

The "mystery" of God is God's plan for salvation through Jesus and the cross. Paul argues that his ambition was never the wisdom or "sublimity" of his own speech but only to know Jesus Christ and "him crucified." He juxtaposes his own weakness with the power of the Spirit that works through him when he strips himself of any pretense and orients himself fully to God. Paul wants the community to understand that "human wisdom" counts as nothing in relation to "the power of God." Paul chooses words associated with Hellenistic rhetoric (e.g., "sublimity of words," "persuasive words," "demonstration," "power") to undermine those who rely on rhetoric and impressive speeches (something the people of Corinth would have been accustomed to among the philosophers of the day). He therefore reorients the focus from any charismatic human performance to a single-minded focus on God working through Christ. Ironically, Paul makes this argument with great rhetorical skill; his self-deprecation only strengthens his message about the power of the cross. For Paul, God's mystery working through Christ and the cross is *everything*, the sum of the gospel message.

GOSPEL   MATTHEW 5:13-16

> Jesus said to his disciples:
>   "You are the salt of the earth.
> But if salt loses its taste, with what can it be seasoned?
> It is no longer good for anything
>   but to be thrown out and trampled underfoot.
> You are the light of the world.
> A city set on a mountain cannot be hidden.
> Nor do they light a lamp and then put it under a bushel basket;
>   it is set on a lampstand,
>   where it gives light to all in the house.
> Just so, your light must shine before others,
>   that they may see your good deeds
>   and glorify your heavenly Father."

This Sunday, we continue reading from the Sermon on the Mount. While the prophetic voice in our Isaiah reading details specific actions linked to a life of fidelity to God—actions of communal care and compassion—Jesus describes how these actions will transform a community, using metaphors that are ordinary and necessary for daily life: salt and light. Salt was everyday seasoning, and the lamp was the single light used in one-room peasant houses in ancient Israel. Light is also a common metaphor for God and God's people throughout the Hebrew Bible and the New Testament, as we see here and in our reading from Isaiah (see also Isa 42:6; Dan 12:3; Prov 6:23; John 1:4-5; Phil 2:15). Jesus says that his disciples are "no longer good for anything" if they lose their distinctiveness or "salty flavor" or if they are no longer visible witnesses to God's kingdom. Yet there is something more to these metaphors. Is it really possible for salt to lose its flavor? Or is it possible to hide a city on a mountain? Would anyone dare waste a lamp's fuel or run the risk of setting a house on fire by putting a lamp "under" a basket? Jesus's rhetorical questions remind his audience that as true disciples, it is simply impossible *not* to be witnesses in the world, just as light cannot help but be light and salt cannot help but season.

Ponder

For Paul, belief in Christ means belief in a God who chose to become human and vulnerable. Through our own vulnerability, we are drawn closer together, bound more intimately to God, and we become truly strong. This is a strength that comes from a deep understanding of our inherent "weakness" and a dependence on God's strength. This is the same strength the psalmist describes in the one who "shall never be moved" and whose heart is "firm" and "steadfast." Society can pressure us to be strong and independent, but this self-oriented "strength" is fake, an illusion. This week, explore the relationship between weakness and humility, power and strength. Can you relate to Paul's experience of strength that comes through weakness?

Jesus uses common, essential objects (salt, light, and lamps) to illustrate the path of discipleship. Salt and light are most effective when they do not draw attention to themselves. Salt should flavor but not overpower a meal, and light should illuminate for the sake of its surroundings. Similarly, to be a disciple is to focus not on ourselves but on Christ crucified. Our actions are not about self-glory but about the glory of God. Light and salt are so common that they may be easy to take for granted, but they are also impossible to miss, like a city on a hill. This metaphor of salt and light symbolizes the work of communal care described in Isaiah and today's psalm. This essential, often understated work is the path of true discipleship, and it promises true transformation—in ourselves and our communities.

Sixth Sunday in Ordinary Time

FIRST READING   SIRACH 15:15-20

If you choose you can keep the commandments, they will
    save you;
  if you trust in God, you too shall live;
he has set before you fire and water;
  to whichever you choose, stretch forth your hand.
Before man are life and death, good and evil,
  whichever he chooses shall be given him.
Immense is the wisdom of the Lord;
  he is mighty in power, and all-seeing.
The eyes of God are on those who fear him;
  he understands man's every deed.
No one does he command to act unjustly,
  to none does he give license to sin.

For background on Sirach, see notes for The Holy Family of Jesus, Mary, and Joseph. The social world of Ben Sira (the book's writer) was organized in terms of dualities: good and evil, fire and water, life and death. Our reading concludes a longer section (15:11-20) that stresses human responsibility to choose one of two paths: life and its generation (water, good, and wisdom), or death and destruction (fire and evil). Prior to and at the end of our reading, the author states that God bears no responsibility for human sin (vv. 11-13, 20). The Bible is ambivalent on this point, however. Sometimes, the Hebrew Bible emphasizes human responsibility to choose between life or death (Deut 30:15-20). At other times, it seems that God can cause people to sin for a larger purpose (e.g., Exod 11:10; 2 Sam 24:1). In our reading, though, Ben Sira focuses on free will: God "created human beings / and made them subject to their own free choice" (v. 14). The expression "free choice" (Greek *diaboulion*, or "deliberation") draws from the Hebrew *yēṣer* for "intent" or "inclination." This intent can be positive (Isa 26:3) or negative (Gen 6:5; 8:21). Later rabbinic tradition speaks of two *yetsers*, meaning a good and bad "inclination." According to the Hebrew Bible, humans can master our negative inclination to sin, but it is hard to do. A key example is the story of Cain and Abel, where God tells Cain that "sin lies in wait at the door: its urge is for you, yet you can rule over it" (Gen 4:7). Cain then fails to "rule" it and kills his brother. However, in Sirach and other Wisdom texts, the human choice between good and bad is easier. Throughout the book, Ben Sira stresses that God is "all-seeing" and will reward the righteous and punish sinners (e.g., 16:17-23).

RESPONSORIAL PSALM   PSALM 119:1-2, 4-5, 17-18, 33-34

Blessed are they who follow the law of the Lord!

SECOND READING   1 CORINTHIANS 2:6-10

Brothers and sisters:
We speak a wisdom to those who are mature,[1]
   not a wisdom of this age,
   nor of the rulers of this age who are passing away.
Rather, we speak God's wisdom, mysterious, hidden,
   which God predetermined before the ages for our glory,
   and which none of the rulers of this age knew;
   for, if they had known it,
   they would not have crucified the Lord of glory.
But as it is written:
   What eye has not seen, and ear has not heard,
      and what has not entered the human heart,
   what God has prepared for those who love him,
   this God has revealed to us through the Spirit.

For the Spirit scrutinizes everything, even the depths of God.

In last Sunday's reading, Paul claimed that his preaching was not wise or eloquent by human standards, but that its very weakness communicated God's power (which itself is paradoxical, made manifest in Christ crucified). Here he continues, saying that his words express a divine wisdom that is "mysterious" and "hidden" and makes sense

---

1. "Mature" (Greek *teleios*) designates one who is fully developed or initiated.

only to those who are mature or fully initiated in faith. This wisdom is powerful enough to transform those who are open to hearing it, despite the simplicity of his preaching. The deepest meaning of this "wisdom" is knowledge of Christ crucified (1 Cor 2:2), "which God predetermined before the ages," or before creation. The phrase "our glory" looks ahead to the fullness of salvation that will come about in the end times (see also Rom 5:2; 2 Cor 3:18). The "rulers of this age" are the world's political rulers and, possibly, cosmic powers hostile to God. The quote that Paul cites does not come from the Hebrew Bible, though it resembles Isaiah 52:15 and 64:3. As in previous readings, Paul undermines common perceptions of what makes for good preaching or apostleship, in this case wisdom as determined by human standards (especially the elite or learned).

GOSPEL   MATTHEW 5:17-37 [OR 5:20-22a, 27-28, 33-34a, 37]

Jesus said to his disciples:
"Do not think that I have come to abolish the law or the
    prophets.
I have come not to abolish but to fulfill.
Amen, I say to you, until heaven and earth pass away,
    not the smallest letter or the smallest part of a letter
    will pass from the law,
    until all things have taken place.
Therefore, whoever breaks one of the least of these
    commandments
    and teaches others to do so
    will be called least in the kingdom of heaven.
But whoever obeys and teaches these commandments
    will be called greatest in the kingdom of heaven.
I tell you, unless your righteousness surpasses
    that of the scribes and Pharisees,
    you will not enter the kingdom of heaven.

"You have heard that it was said to your ancestors,
    You shall not kill; and whoever kills will be liable to judgment.
But I say to you,
    whoever is angry with his brother
    will be liable to judgment;

and whoever says to his brother, 'Raqa,'[2]
  will be answerable to the Sanhedrin;
  and whoever says, 'You fool,'
  will be liable to fiery Gehenna.
Therefore, if you bring your gift to the altar,
  and there recall that your brother
  has anything against you,
  leave your gift there at the altar,
  go first and be reconciled with your brother,
  and then come and offer your gift.
Settle with your opponent quickly while on the way to court.
Otherwise your opponent will hand you over to the judge,
  and the judge will hand you over to the guard,
  and you will be thrown into prison.
Amen, I say to you,
  you will not be released until you have paid the last penny.

"You have heard that it was said,
  You shall not commit adultery.
But I say to you,
  everyone who looks at a woman with lust
  has already committed adultery with her in his heart.
If your right eye causes you to sin,
  tear it out and throw it away.
It is better for you to lose one of your members
  than to have your whole body thrown into Gehenna.
And if your right hand causes you to sin,
  cut it off and throw it away.
It is better for you to lose one of your members
  than to have your whole body go into Gehenna.

"It was also said,
  Whoever divorces his wife must give her a bill of divorce.
But I say to you,
  whoever divorces his wife—unless the marriage is unlawful—
  causes her to commit adultery,
  and whoever marries a divorced woman commits adultery.

---

2. "Raqa" is an obscure Aramaic word and insult. An alternative translation of the phrase "whoever says to his brother, 'Raqa'" is "whoever insults his brother."

"Again you have heard that it was said to your ancestors,
Do not take a false oath,
but make good to the Lord all that you vow.
But I say to you, do not swear at all;
   not by heaven, for it is God's throne;
   nor by the earth, for it is his footstool;
   nor by Jerusalem, for it is the city of the great King.
Do not swear by your head,
   for you cannot make a single hair white or black.
Let your 'Yes' mean 'Yes,' and your 'No' mean 'No.'
Anything more is from the evil one."

This week, in the Sermon on the Mount, we shift to teachings on the Torah (meaning the law or commandments), which Jesus seeks to uphold and perfect. The phrases that mark the beginning of his teachings ("Amen, I say to you" and "until . . .") refer to the end times, and they also imply that Matthew's community of Jewish believers continued to follow the Torah precepts. Throughout this section of the sermon, Jesus repeats the phrase "You have heard that it was said" to introduce a particular law, and his authority is then emphasized through the statement "But I say to you" and the explanation that follows. When Jesus speaks of righteousness that "surpasses that of the scribes and Pharisees," he is setting a high bar; historically, scribes and Pharisees were considered to be particularly righteous. Perhaps, too, his statement contains the undercurrents of possible religious hypocrisy (replace "Pharisee" with "priest" or "bishop" today, and you'll get a sense of how complicated these terms of religious authority can be). On murder (v. 21), see, for example, Deuteronomy 5:17. The Sanhedrin was the highest Jewish court or council, and "Gehenna" is hell, named after a valley in southern Israel that was associated with child sacrifice (Matt 5:22). In referencing gifts at the altar (vv. 23-24), Jesus assumes ongoing temple sacrifice. On adultery (v. 27), see, for example, Exodus 20:14. On divorce (vv. 31-32), see, for example, Deuteronomy 24:1-4. Note that in the Hebrew Bible, divorce is allowed but frowned upon. Jesus enters an ongoing debate in early Judaism on how to interpret the Bible's teachings on divorce, and he sets a high standard based, in part, on his concern for the economic well-being of the woman. Finally, on oath-making

(vv. 33-37), see, for example, Exodus 20:7. Jesus extends the Torah's prohibitions against swearing in the name of God to a prohibition against all oaths.

Ponder

"Open my eyes," the psalmist prays, "that I may consider / the wonders of your law." The *wonders* of your law. This phrase is worth pondering. "Law" is *tôrâ* in Hebrew, meaning "teaching" or "Torah." For the psalmist, God's Torah is wondrous. What does this mean to us? Christians often have an uneasy relationship with the Old Testament laws. The old stereotype is that they are harsh regulations that oppose Jesus's law of love, but the reality is that the laws come from the eternal Law, the heart of our merciful God, and they are guideposts to draw us back to God. In Sirach, the Torah is the path to life and true wisdom. As you pray with these readings, what does it mean to you to "open your eyes" to the "wonders" of God's law?

Jesus insists on the Torah's enduring value, and he enters a dynamic conversation in early Judaism over the deepest meaning and ongoing interpretation of the laws or teachings. For Jesus, the deepest meaning connects with our deepest selves. In other words, in order to reject those actions that weaken our relationship with God and each other, we have to understand the root of these actions deep within us. For Jesus, daily prayer and reflection (what we might call an "examination of conscience") are the necessary path to this inward understanding, along with recognition of our dependence on God. What role does daily prayer and self-reflection play in your life?

Seventh Sunday in Ordinary Time

FIRST READING   LEVITICUS 19:1-2, 17-18

The LORD said to Moses,
  "Speak to the whole Israelite community and tell them:
  Be holy, for I, the LORD, your God, am holy.

"You shall not bear hatred for your brother or sister in your heart.
Though you may have to reprove your fellow citizen,
  do not incur sin because of him.
Take no revenge and cherish no grudge against any of
     your people.
You shall love your neighbor as yourself.
I am the LORD."

At the heart of the book of Leviticus is the Holiness Code (chaps. 17–26). In chapters 1–16, holiness is generally relegated to the religious sanctuary and the priesthood, yet within the Holiness Code, this vision spans out to include the whole community of Israel and even the land itself. At the heart of this call to holiness is God's desire that humans mirror, imitate, or image God. In one sense, this is an unattainable goal, for humans can never perfectly imitate God or God's holiness. In another sense, it is an aspiration to live for because it is God's desire for us. Holiness is therefore about striving to live a life of godliness because this is what we were made for. At the heart of the Holiness Code is Leviticus 19, a series of ethical and ritual commands formed around the call to love one's "neighbor" (v. 18), meaning a fellow Israelite. The call then extends out to the "alien" or foreigner at the end of the chapter ("you shall love the alien as yourself; for you too were once aliens in the land of Egypt"; v. 34). In these verses, love is not a feeling but an active commitment that includes all people. In Matthew 22:37-40, Jesus quotes verse 18 alongside Deuteronomy 6:5 ("Therefore, you shall love the LORD, your God, with your whole heart, and with your whole being, and with your whole strength") as the two great commandments.

RESPONSORIAL PSALM   PSALM 103:1-2, 3-4, 8, 10, 12-13

The Lord is kind and merciful.

SECOND READING   1 CORINTHIANS 3:16-23

Brothers and sisters:
Do you not know that you are the temple of God,
    and that the Spirit of God dwells in you?
If anyone destroys God's temple, God will destroy that person;
    for the temple of God, which you are, is holy.

Let no one deceive himself.
If any one among you considers himself wise in this age,
    let him become a fool, so as to become wise.
For the wisdom of this world is foolishness in the eyes of God,
    for it is written:
        God catches the wise in their own ruses,
    and again:
        The Lord knows the thoughts of the wise,
            that they are vain.

So let no one boast about human beings, for everything belongs
        to you,
    Paul or Apollos or Cephas,
    or the world or life or death,
    or the present or the future:
    all belong to you, and you to Christ, and Christ to God.

This Sunday's reading from 1 Corinthians shifts back to the central theme of unity in Christ (see the Third Sunday in Ordinary Time). Speaking to the entire Corinthian community ("you" is a plural form), Paul calls them a "temple of God," for God's Spirit dwells in them as a believing body (see also 6:17; Eph 1:19-22; Ezek 37:26-28). What "destroys" this temple is disunity and rivalry. Paul's imagery of destruction is intentionally provocative, for both Jews and Gentiles considered the desecration of a temple to be a horrible crime. Maintaining this focus on unity versus disunity, Paul draws upon his previous discussion of wisdom versus foolishness to emphasize the ultimate source of wisdom and the reality of unity in God. He quotes from Job 5:12-13 ("God catches the wise . . .") and Psalm 94:11 ("The Lord knows . . .") to underscore his point. Ultimately, the entire community, including its various teachers or apostles, belongs to God. In the end times, Paul envisions not only the unity of all believers in God through Christ but also the ultimate destruction of death itself and the final collapse of time (see also Rom 8:38-39).

GOSPEL   MATTHEW 5:38-48

Jesus said to his disciples:
   "You have heard that it was said,
   An eye for an eye and a tooth for a tooth.
But I say to you, offer no resistance to one who is evil.
When someone strikes you on your right cheek,
   turn the other one as well.
If anyone wants to go to law with you[1] over your tunic,
   hand over your cloak as well.
Should anyone press you into service for one mile,
   go for two miles.
Give to the one who asks of you,
   and do not turn your back on one who wants to borrow.

"You have heard that it was said,
   You shall love your neighbor and hate your enemy.
But I say to you, love your enemies
   and pray for those who persecute you,
   that you may be children of your heavenly Father,
   for he makes his sun rise on the bad and the good,
   and causes rain to fall on the just and the unjust.
For if you love those who love you, what recompense will
     you have?
Do not the tax collectors do the same?
And if you greet your brothers only,
   what is unusual about that?
Do not the pagans do the same?
So be perfect, just as your heavenly Father is perfect."

---

1. "Go to law with you": literally "sue you."

end, goal, purpose

hate! Drinking poison and waiting for the other person to die.

This week, we continue with Jesus's teachings on the Torah (see last week). In the Hebrew Bible, measure-for-measure punishments helped to limit disproportionate retribution and to break cycles of violence and revenge (e.g., Exod 21:23-34). Jesus further explores these cycles and calls people to the higher standard of nonviolent resistance through four examples in different areas of civil life: physical abuse, legal action, forced labor, and requests for gifts or loans. In the first example, offering one's other cheek to an abuser would point a mirror back on the abuser to shame them. In the second example of a lawsuit, most people owned only two garments: the tunic (the long shirt worn close to the body) and the outer cloak (the heavier garment). If the creditor were to take one's tunic as a pledge of payment, then giving over one's cloak would render oneself naked in the court of law and, again, turn a mirror on the creditor. Note, too, that in the Hebrew Bible, interest is forbidden on loans, and it was unjust to keep a person's garments overnight as a pledge of payment (see Exod 22:25-26: "If you take your neighbor's cloak as a pledge, you shall return it to him before sunset; for this is his only covering; it is the cloak for his body. What will he sleep in?") In the third example, Roman soldiers could enlist people to carry their gear for one mile; Jesus tells them to go a second mile, once again to prove a point and turn a mirror on an unjust system. Finally, in terms of giving and borrowing, tithing and generosity are mandated in the Torah and are first and foremost expressions of gratitude to God (e.g., Deut 12:5-6). The expression "love your neighbor" quotes from Leviticus 19:18, but "hate your enemy" is not found in the Hebrew Bible. Perhaps "enemy" here refers to persecutors of the early church community, for Jesus links love of enemies to prayer for persecutors. Tax collectors were Jewish, yet they collaborated with the Romans, while the negative connotation of the word "pagans" (or Gentiles; Greek *ethnikos*) is unusual in Matthew's Gospel. The word "perfect" (Greek *teleios*) occurs only in Matthew (see also Matt 19:21) and James (1:4; 3:2); it refers not to moral perfection but to wholeness, completeness, or maturity and is linked with the commandment to love (see Matt 19:19). The Lukan parallel calls upon hearers to be "merciful" (Luke 6:36), while the equivalent in the Hebrew Bible is the call to be "holy" (Lev 19:2; see the first reading).

anger - expressive desire for revenge

Ponder

A key component of the Civil Rights Movement was nonviolent resistance. This was no easy path. Before boarding buses to the segregated South, activists were asked if they were prepared that day—spiritually, mentally—to respond to abuse nonviolently. If they said "no," they did not board the bus. In the Gospel, Jesus calls for similar nonviolent measures to break cycles of violence and injustice. In his examples, discipleship takes a creative extra step, stripping societal mechanisms of their power and, in so doing, striving to transform them. We all know the flutter of hope that comes through the witnesses of those who respond to greed with generosity, violence with nonviolence, hostility with love. Who inspires us to transformation in our own communities? What if this is up to us?

In calling us to be "holy," "perfect," "temples of God," our readings speak not of moral perfection but of a profound wholeness rooted in God. In Leviticus, the path to wholeness or holiness is a recognition of God's desire for us, for God made us in the divine image. For Paul, we are holy as the Body of Christ through the Spirit's indwelling. Paul's vision of wholeness is one that neither overestimates oneself nor indulges in hero worship but understands that, together, we are a precious, holy temple. Perhaps this sense of wholeness is why there is no need to insist on one's rights in the Gospel. To be "perfect" or whole, as Jesus says, is to be rooted in the knowledge of God's love and generosity. When we know this, it leads to a deep sense of personal and communal dignity that needs no external validation. How does the call to wholeness resonate within you?

Eighth Sunday in Ordinary Time

FIRST READING   ISAIAH 49:14-15

Zion said, "The LORD has forsaken me;
  my Lord has forgotten me."
Can a mother forget her infant,
  be without tenderness for the child of her womb?
Even should she forget,
  I will never forget you.

For context on the book of Isaiah and its major divisions, consult the First Sunday of Advent. Buried within Second Isaiah is our reading, one of a few instances in the Hebrew Bible where God is compared to a mother. These two verses come within a series of prophecies that promise Jerusalem's (or Zion's) impending restoration. The prophet speaks to the exiled Judean community living in Babylon in the late sixth century BCE, a community that questions God's care for them and God's power to protect them in a foreign nation. Directly before these verses, the prophet calls the natural world to rejoice and sing because redemption is near; God comforts and will have compassion on the people (v. 13). In the first line of our reading, Zion responds as a woman to voice the concerns of the destroyed city and the people in exile, certain that God has "forsaken" and "forgotten" her. God then responds poetically, repeating the word "forget" three times for emphasis. Is it possible, asks God, for a mother to "forget her infant" (literally, "nursing child"; Hebrew *ʿûl*) or to "be without tenderness" (or "compassion"; Hebrew *rāḥam*) for her own child? The answer, of course, is no. And yet even if she were to forget the child of her own "womb," or body, God insists, "I will never forget you." In the subsequent verse, God continues with a tender and memorable image: "See, upon the palms of my hands I have engraved you" (v. 16). In other words, the future plan of the city and its people is inscribed into God's own being.

RESPONSORIAL PSALM   PSALM 62:2-3, 6-7, 8-9

Rest in God alone, my soul.

SECOND READING   1 CORINTHIANS 4:1-5

Brothers and sisters:
Thus should one regard us: as servants of Christ
    and stewards of the mysteries of God.
Now it is of course required of stewards
    that they be found trustworthy.
It does not concern me in the least
    that I be judged by you or any human tribunal;
    I do not even pass judgment on myself;
    I am not conscious of anything against me,
    but I do not thereby stand acquitted;
    the one who judges me is the Lord.
Therefore do not make any judgment before the appointed time,
    until the Lord comes,
    for he will bring to light what is hidden in darkness
    and will manifest the motives of our hearts,
    and then everyone will receive praise from God.

This is the last week we will read from 1 Corinthians this season. We will return to it on the Second Sunday in Ordinary Time in Year B. The broader context for our reading is a series of metaphors in which Paul describes himself and Apollos as God's farmworkers (3:6-9), construction laborers (3:9-15), and finally, household "servants" or "stewards" (4:1-5). The point is to continue to emphasize unity and collegiality over disunity and rivalry, as Paul does throughout the letter. In these verses, the word "servant" (Greek *hypēretēs*) designates a rower or under-rower on a ship's crew, one who works on the lowest bank of the galleys. The term "steward" (Greek *oikonomos*) refers to the servant who is entrusted with the administration of the house. The apostles, then, are Christ's "servants," or grunt force labor, as well as the household "stewards" of God's mysteries, entrusted with preaching divine revelation rather than their own doctrines. Such stewards must be "trustworthy" or dependable in maintaining absolute devotion to the interests of the master of the house (God). When Paul states that he is unconcerned about being judged by a "human tribunal" (v. 3), the Greek means literally "by man's day," signifying human judgment or criticism in contrast to God's judgment or the day when "the Lord comes" (v. 5). Not even Paul himself can judge the faithfulness of his ministry. Only God can do this at the "appointed time," when Christ returns. This return is not a warning but a promise, a day to receive God's "praise."

GOSPEL   MATTHEW 6:24-34

Jesus said to his disciples:
　"No one can serve two masters.
He will either hate one and love the other,
　or be devoted to one and despise the other.
You cannot serve God and mammon.

"Therefore I tell you, do not worry about your life,
　what you will eat or drink,
　or about your body, what you will wear.
Is not life more than food and the body more than clothing?
Look at the birds in the sky;
　they do not sow or reap, they gather nothing into barns,
　yet your heavenly Father feeds them.
Are not you more important than they?
Can any of you by worrying add a single moment to your
　　life-span?
Why are you anxious about clothes?
Learn from the way the wild flowers grow.
They do not work or spin.
But I tell you that not even Solomon in all his splendor
　was clothed like one of them.
If God so clothes the grass of the field,
　which grows today and is thrown into the oven tomorrow,
　will he not much more provide for you, O you of little faith?
So do not worry and say, 'What are we to eat?'
　or 'What are we to drink?' or 'What are we to wear?'
All these things the pagans seek.
Your heavenly Father knows that you need them all.

But seek first the kingdom of God and his righteousness,
   and all these things will be given you besides.
Do not worry about tomorrow; tomorrow will take care of itself.
Sufficient for a day is its own evil."

At the heart of this reading is the question of what is central to the disciples' lives: God or mammon? The Aramaic term "mammon" is linked to the word *'āman* ("trust" or "support"), meaning that thing (other than God) in which one places one's trust (see Luke 16:9-13). Here, mammon means both money and possessions and is personified as an evil master. The teaching is simple: Jesus's disciples cannot have divided loyalties. Taken with the preceding warnings not to store up treasures on earth but in heaven (6:19-21) and the reminder that one unhealthy part of the body can infect the whole (6:22-23), Jesus is calling for wholehearted loyalty to God. Three times Jesus repeats the term "worry," referring to a type of anxiety that, like mammon, divides heart and mind and steals one's loyalty from God. Those listening to Jesus were not the wealthiest members of society but instead peasants and laborers, those living hand-to-mouth, many of whom were concerned about daily survival. He is not ignoring these concerns, nor is he telling them to stop working for a living. Instead, Jesus is saying that when the search for God and God's righteousness are at the center of one's life, these qualities support and sustain all else. This is a teaching for the poorest and the wealthiest, and it is simultaneously a call to become support and sustenance for others. Jesus then employs a rabbinic argument that begins with a lesser and more obvious point in order to reach a greater and more complex conclusion, moving from the natural environment to humans. Birds work busily, yet they take only what they need, leaving the rest for others. Flowers and grass grow without effort through a process of inner, natural unfolding. On Solomon's splendor, see 1 Kings 10. The final line of our reading translates best as "Today's trouble is enough for today."

Ponder

In what do we place our trust? Our readings call us to trust in God, not as a superficial feeling but as an abiding certainty in God's care for us. In Hebrew, "tenderness" or compassion derives from the word for "womb." In comparing God to a nursing mother, Isaiah captures the truest meaning of compassion as something that emanates from our deepest core or "womb." The psalmist then calls the soul (which means the physical "life force"; Hebrew *nepeš*) to trust or "[r]est in God alone." Paul trusts in God in the pivotal moment when God sees the truth in our hearts, while Jesus tells us that God cares for us better than we can care for ourselves. In living from a deep trust in God, our lives are more easeful, and we are better able to care for ourselves and others. In what, or in whom, do you place your trust?

Jesus is not encouraging indifference or irresponsibility about life's practicalities. His concern is how we integrate material goods into our lives. When these things become central to our hearts and minds, they turn into an insatiable, ceaseless striving for more. They enslave us and become our sole focus. As Pope Francis warned, the great danger in today's world is the "desolation and anguish" that comes from a "covetous heart" and the "feverish pursuit of frivolous pleasures."[1] But when God is central, we are free to live more creatively and fully. We accumulate less so others can have more. We are less anxious about what we do not have. In pursuing first God and God's righteousness, we become what we were made to be: Jesus's disciples, working with God to nurture and care for all life.

---

1. Pope Francis, The Joy of the Gospel (*Evangelii Gaudium*), 2.

Ninth Sunday in Ordinary Time

FIRST READING   DEUTERONOMY 11:18, 26-28, 32

Moses told the people,
"Take these words of mine into your heart and soul.
Bind them at your wrist as a sign,
and let them be a pendant on your forehead.

"I set before you here, this day, a blessing and a curse:
a blessing for obeying the commandments of the LORD,
your God,
which I enjoin on you today;
a curse if you do not obey the commandments of the LORD,
your God,
but turn aside from the way I ordain for you today,
to follow other gods, whom you have not known.
Be careful to observe all the statutes and decrees
that I set before you today."

For background context on the book of Deuteronomy, consult The Most Holy Body and Blood of Christ (Corpus Christi). Our reading draws from a broader section in Deuteronomy (5:1–11:30) in which Moses reviews the covenant made between Israel and God on Mount Sinai from the book of Exodus. The section begins with Moses telling the people to remember and continually make the past present (chap. 5), and it concludes with his call to fidelity to the covenant (here in chap. 11). This call to fidelity is addressed to the whole community in the plural "you," which emphasizes that loyalty to God is a collective responsibility. If the people love God with their whole "heart and soul" (or, literally, their whole "being"; Hebrew *nepeš*; 11:13, 18), holding fast to God's commandments, then the "blessing" (v. 26) is that they will live harmoniously in the land of Israel. But if they are disloyal to God, as described above, then as a natural consequence or "curse," they will be driven from the land. This is not because God is unkind but because God's law is carved deeply into the rhythms and patterns of creation. In the ancient Middle East, the word "curse" was a political term for sanctions related to the violation of treaties. In terms of biblical history, the narrative of Deuteronomy takes place before the people enter and occupy the land of Israel, according to the book of Joshua. In reality, however, Deuteronomy was written and edited much later by scribes looking back and attempting to make sense of Israel's past. These warnings of blessings and curses therefore already anticipate the Babylonian exile in the sixth century BCE. The binding of Moses's words to the wrist and forehead is a metaphor for taking the commandments to heart. This exhortation developed into the wearing of phylacteries (from the Greek *phylaktērion*, meaning "amulet") or tefillin (small, cube-shaped leather cases that contain Torah texts, worn by observant Jewish men during morning prayer).

RESPONSORIAL PSALM   PSALM 31:2-3, 3-4, 17, 25

Lord, be my rock of safety.

SECOND READING   ROMANS 3:21-25, 28

Brothers and sisters,
Now the righteousness of God has been manifested apart from
    the law,
    though testified to by the law and the prophets,
    the righteousness of God through faith in Jesus Christ
    for all who believe.
For there is no distinction;
    all have sinned and are deprived of the glory of God.
They are justified freely by his grace
    through the redemption in Christ Jesus,
    whom God set forth as an expiation,
    through faith, by his blood.
For we consider that a person is justified by faith
    apart from works of the law.

Paul's monumental letter to the Romans will carry us through the Twenty-Fourth Sunday in Ordinary Time. For further context on the letter, consult both the First and Fourth Sundays of Advent. Prior to our reading, Paul begins to build his argument concerning justification through faith. In chapter 2, he urges the community of believers, both Jews and Gentiles, not to pass judgment on each other, for God shows no partiality and will repay in fair measure all who do good and all who do evil (vv. 9-11). This sense of God's impartiality provides the foundation for Paul's grappling with the role of the Jewish law in this new, inclusive community of faith. For Paul, the law is good and written on a person's heart, whether Jew or Gentile, and those who are justified are those who act in accordance with God's law (2:12-16). However, the reality of universal sin means that no one is able to measure up to the righteousness that the law requires (3:9-20). But now, "apart from the law," believers can be made righteous through faith in Christ. The term "righteousness" (Greek *dikaiosynē*) is synonymous with being "justified" or pronounced righteous (Greek *dikaioō*). Originally, the term "justified" was a legal term relating to acquittal in a court of law, and in early Judaism it came to mean "righteousness" in the sense of fulfilling God's law. In our reading, to be justified through faith is not a passive state; rather, it means active participation in God's righteousness through Christ. "[T]he law and the prophets" refers to the entirety of the Hebrew Scriptures (v. 21). According to Jewish tradition, God's "glory" was taken from Adam in Genesis 3; Paul implies that it will return through salvation in Christ (v. 23). The language of Christ as "expiation" draws from rituals surrounding Yom Kippur, or the "Day of Atonement," the holiest day of the Jewish year (see Lev 16:13-15). "Expiation" refers to the place of forgiveness or atonement (Greek *hilastērion*) or the "mercy seat" (Hebrew *kappōret*), meaning the place that covers over sins. Here, the blood that sets people free of their sins is not that of a bull or a goat (see Lev 16:14-15) but that of Jesus Christ. Paul concludes this section by arguing that justification by faith does not annul the law but instead supports it because God's desire is justification, and God is the ultimate source of the law (v. 31).

GOSPEL   MATTHEW 7:21-27

Jesus said to his disciples:
  "Not everyone who says to me, 'Lord, Lord,'
  will enter the kingdom of heaven,
  but only the one who does the will of my Father in heaven.

Many will say to me on that day,
  'Lord, Lord, did we not prophesy in your name?
Did we not drive out demons in your name?
Did we not do mighty deeds in your name?'
Then I will declare to them solemnly,
  'I never knew you. Depart from me, you evildoers.'

"Everyone who listens to these words of mine and acts on them
  will be like a wise man who built his house on rock.
The rain fell, the floods came,
  and the winds blew and buffeted the house.
But it did not collapse; it had been set solidly on rock.
And everyone who listens to these words of mine
  but does not act on them
  will be like a fool who built his house on sand.
The rain fell, the floods came,
  and the winds blew and buffeted the house.
And it collapsed and was completely ruined."

This Sunday, we read the conclusion of the Sermon on the Mount. Referring back to all of his teachings throughout the sermon, Jesus tells his listeners to listen to and act upon "these words of mine" in order to achieve righteousness and "enter the kingdom of heaven" (vv. 21, 24). The phrase "on that day" refers to the day of judgment (v. 22). Jesus quotes from Psalm 6:9 in referring to "evildoers" (literally "workers of lawlessness"). Upon first glance, these evildoers seem to be doing nothing wrong; they refer to Jesus respectfully with the title "Lord" (a title that hints at his divine nature), and the acts they perform are considered worthy of praise elsewhere (e.g., Matt 10:8). To perform "mighty deeds" in the name of Jesus is to invoke his name as a source of power. Yet they are not acting in accordance with God's will, perhaps because the appropriate intention does not undergird their displays of power and their confessions of faith (e.g., Matt 6:1-18).

Ponder

Moses and Jesus call their audiences to remember and act on "these words of mine." These are not human words but divine words originating in the Word of God. In Judaism, adherence to "these words," the commandments, draws one back to God and into all righteousness. For Christians, righteousness comes through faith in Jesus Christ, Word made flesh. For both Jews and Christians, observance of "these words" begins internally, by binding the commandments to our hearts. Elsewhere in the Hebrew Bible, God inscribes the law on the heart (Jer 31:33), and Paul also views the law as written on the human heart (Rom 2:15). In both religious traditions, to follow "these words" begins by listening to the Word deep within us, as intimate to us as our own breath. What is it like to imagine "these words," God's Word, bound within your heart and soul?

Although we may find some tension between Romans and the Gospel, they reflect two sides of the same coin. Paul states that people are "justified" or made righteous through faith apart from works. Jesus says that not everyone who professes faith in him will enter the kingdom of heaven, only those who do God's will. Both are right. Action must be rooted in faith or right intention, otherwise it is brittle and performative. But profession of faith, too, can be a performance. True faith manifests in actions that are in alignment with God's will, and actions point back to the truth in one's heart (see Rom 2:9-15; Jas 2:14-17). This week, take time to examine your actions and intentions. In what, or in whom, are your actions rooted?

Tenth Sunday in Ordinary Time

FIRST READING   HOSEA 6:3-6

In their affliction, people will say:
"Let us know, let us strive to know the LORD;
    as certain as the dawn is his coming,
    and his judgment shines forth like the light of day!
He will come to us like the rain,
    like spring rain that waters the earth."
What can I do with you, Ephraim?
What can I do with you, Judah?
Your piety is like a morning cloud,
    like the dew that early passes away.
For this reason I smote them through the prophets,
    I slew them by the words of my mouth;
for it is love that I desire, not sacrifice,
    and knowledge of God rather than holocausts.

Hosea was the only prophet from the northern kingdom of Israel whose writings were preserved in the Bible, and one of only two prophets to the northern kingdom before its fall to Assyria around 720 BCE (the other was Amos, who came from the southern kingdom of Judah). Hosea's prophecies began during a period of political stability at the end of the reign of Jeroboam II (ca. 746 BCE) and ended right before the Assyrian conquest. Most of his prophecies are critiques of Israel, particularly its religious and political institutions. Our reading comes from a divine speech in the heart of the book in which God expresses heartbreak and yearning over Ephraim (another name for Israel) and Judah, whose gestures of penitence are inauthentic and inconstant. God is devoted to the people, yet they do not return the same devotion. Two crucial terms in Hosea's theology are "knowledge" of God, Hebrew *da'at* (2:8; 4:1; 5:4; 6:6), and "loving-kindness," Hebrew *ḥesed* (2:21; 4:1; 6:4, 6; 10:12; 12:6). The term *ḥesed* (pronounced "chesed") encompasses a vast array of terms for love and fidelity. It is one of God's key attributes, and God expects the people to mirror back *ḥesed* in their love for God.

The term appears twice in our reading, once translated as "piety" (v. 4) and once as "love" (v. 6). God is not denying the importance of sacrifice here, only its insignificance if not practiced from this deep, faithful love.

RESPONSORIAL PSALM   PSALM 50:1, 8, 12-13, 14-15

To the upright I will show the saving power of God.

SECOND READING   ROMANS 4:18-25

Brothers and sisters:
Abraham believed, hoping against hope,
   that he would become "the father of many nations,"
   according to what was said, "Thus shall your descendants be."
He did not weaken in faith when he considered his own body
   as already dead—for he was almost a hundred years old—
   and the dead womb of Sarah.
He did not doubt God's promise in unbelief;
   rather, he was strengthened by faith and gave glory to God
   and was fully convinced that what he had promised
   he was also able to do.
That is why *it was credited to him as righteousness.*
But it was not for him alone that it was written
   that *it was credited to him;*
   it was also for us, to whom it will be credited,
   who believe in the one who raised Jesus our Lord from
      the dead,
   who was handed over for our transgressions
   and was raised for our justification.

Abraham exemplifies Paul's argument from last Sunday that a person is justified by faith apart from works (see 3:28). According to Paul, Abraham was chosen by God prior to and apart from any effort on his part. He was made righteous through his fidelity to God and his trust in God's promise that he would have children and become the "father of many nations" (v. 17; also Gen 17:5) despite his and Sarah's old age. Paul quotes from Genesis 15:5-6 ("Thus shall your descendants be"; "credited to him as righteousness") to describe Abraham's righteousness as rooted not in the law but in faith (see also Rom 4:13). In giving "glory to God" (v. 20), Abraham counters humanity's root sin as described in Romans 1:21, which is failing to give glory or thanks to God. Paul then reinterprets the Genesis story to apply it to the present: through Christ, believers are also made righteous or justified through faith.

GOSPEL   MATTHEW 9:9-13

As Jesus passed on from there,
    he saw a man named Matthew sitting at the customs post.
He said to him, "Follow me."
And he got up and followed him.
While he was at table in his house,
    many tax collectors and sinners came
    and sat with Jesus and his disciples.
The Pharisees saw this and said to his disciples,
    "Why does your teacher eat with tax collectors and sinners?"
He heard this and said,
    "Those who are well do not need a physician, but the sick do.
Go and learn the meaning of the words,
    'I desire mercy, not sacrifice.'
I did not come to call the righteous but sinners."

This week, we move from the end of the Sermon on the Mount in chapter 7 to this short account of Matthew's call, skipping over various stories of Jesus healing and performing miracles on the way. This account is paralleled in Mark 2:14-17 and Luke 5:27-32, where Matthew is instead named Levi. It is unclear in this account whether "his house" refers to that of Jesus or Matthew. Sinners (those who violated the well-being of the community and family) were to be avoided, hence the Pharisees' question. Jesus's response implies that the Pharisees were already in good health and standing with God, in contrast to "tax collectors and sinners," who were in need of God's mercy. The word for "mercy" (Greek *eleos*) embraces a wide range of meanings, including "compassion," "pity," or "clemency." Here, in Jesus's quotation of Hosea 6:6, it translates the Hebrew *ḥesed*, or "loving-kindness." Tax collectors were Jews who worked for the Roman government and are a particular focus of Jesus's outreach in Matthew's Gospel (see also 5:46). Jesus quotes again from Hosea 6:6 in Matthew 12:7.

Ponder

In our readings, true sacrifice overflows from deep wellsprings of devotion and praise. Hosea describes these wellsprings as *ḥesed* (love or loving-kindness) and knowledge of God, meaning intimacy and personal relationship. The psalmist and Paul then state that true sacrifice is praise or giving "glory" to God. Quoting from Hosea, Jesus embodies *ḥesed*, or merciful love, in demonstrating that what God desires from us is what God gives to us abundantly. None of our readings denies the importance of sacrifice; instead, they point to the heart of genuine sacrifice. For Judeans, sacrifice was profound worship. We might find a parallel in the eucharistic sacrifice today. As you reflect upon your own religious practice, your "sacrifice," in what is it rooted?

The Gospel should shock us. Let's translate it into our own context: the "sinners" are people on the margins of society because they have put themselves there. They have lied, cheated, or stolen, broken families, or hurt others. They have not acted from "love" or "knowledge of God." The Pharisees are the opposite. They are righteous (see the readings from last Sunday). They protect family, community, and the dignity of human life. They would be in good standing with the church, regular partakers of the eucharistic meal. What is Jesus saying, then? Who would Jesus *not* allow at our table today as a church? As you pray with the passage, imagine him speaking across time to us: "Go and learn the meaning of the words, 'I desire mercy, not sacrifice.'"

Eleventh Sunday in Ordinary Time

FIRST READING   EXODUS 19:2-6a

In those days, the Israelites came to the desert of Sinai and
    pitched camp.
While Israel was encamped here in front of the mountain,
    Moses went up the mountain to God.
Then the LORD called to him and said,
    "Thus shall you say to the house of Jacob;
    tell the Israelites:
    You have seen for yourselves how I treated the Egyptians
    and how I bore you up on eagle wings
    and brought you here to myself.
Therefore, if you hearken to my voice and keep my covenant,
    you shall be my special possession,
    dearer to me than all other people,
    though all the earth is mine.
You shall be to me a kingdom of priests, a holy nation."

The above reading begins the long account of God's revelation to Israel at Mount Sinai (also called Mount Horeb) that extends from Exodus 19:1 to 24:18. During this divine revelation, Israel receives the Decalogue, or Ten Commandments, as well as all the laws, or the "book of the covenant" (24:7). Framing the revelation is God's call into a covenantal relationship, which we read today. It opens with a reminder that God liberated the people from Egypt, enfolding them in "eagle wings" to carry them out and into the desert. Like an eagle parent, who patiently and lovingly pushes the eaglet out of the nest and then catches it while it learns to fly, God catches, encourages, loves, and nourishes all of Israel into a unique and intimate relationship. Their task is to respond; if they listen and "keep" or guard (Hebrew *šāmar*) the covenant, they will be God's "special" or treasured possession (Hebrew *sĕgullâ*).[1] In the Hebrew, the word "hearken" or

---

1. Contemporary readers may be uncomfortable with the language of God claiming "ownership" over us or "possessing" us. We may think of these terms as akin to slavery

hear (v. 5) repeats twice for emphasis, which we lose in our translation (so the Hebrew reads something like "If you really, really hear"). All of Israel is to be a "kingdom of priests, a holy nation," committed to a higher standard of moral and physical purity. According to the arc of the biblical narrative, Israel remains encamped at Sinai until Numbers 10:11-12 while Moses makes continual trips up and down the mountain to converse with God and relay God's words to the Israelites. Mount Sinai is a mystical place, a space where the earth meets the divine realm.

RESPONSORIAL PSALM   PSALM 100:1-2, 3, 5

We are his people: the sheep of his flock.

SECOND READING   ROMANS 5:6-11

Brothers and sisters:
Christ, while we were still helpless,
    yet died at the appointed time for the ungodly.
Indeed, only with difficulty does one die for a just person,
    though perhaps for a good person
    one might even find courage to die.
But God proves his love for us
    in that while we were still sinners Christ died for us.
How much more then, since we are now justified by his blood,
    will we be saved through him from the wrath.
Indeed, if, while we were enemies,
    we were reconciled to God through the death of his Son,
    how much more, once reconciled,
    will we be saved by his life.
Not only that,
    but we also boast of God through our Lord Jesus Christ,
    through whom we have now received reconciliation.

---

or bondage, yet in the ancient context, they meant just the opposite. According to the Hebrew Bible, ancient Israel understood God's "ownership" or "possession" of them in the sense of liberation and a deep, covenantal relationship. This relationship required something of them in return, yet they took on the challenge of covenant living with joy, pride, and free will. Paul uses similar language in Phil 3:12 to describe his intimate relationship with Jesus: "I have . . . been taken possession of by Christ [Jesus]."

In last Sunday's reading, Paul described Abraham as the model of justification by faith. Now, Paul turns to his audience, calling them to "have peace with God" through Christ, through whom they, too, have been justified or have "gained access [by faith]" to grace (5:1-2). Paul describes people as "helpless" or weak, "ungodly," and "sinners," in contrast to one who is "just" and "good," for whom even sinners might sacrifice themselves. Jesus was this truly just and good one, who sacrificed himself "by his blood" to justify all people. The "wrath" refers to God's revelation and final judgment at the end of time. For Paul, this wrath is not a vindictive punishment; instead, it is righteous judgment that stores up over time in response to human actions born from hard and "impenitent" hearts (see 2:5). Paul's closing statements are radical: humans were once true enemies of God through their actions, yet God nonetheless saved them through the Son's sacrifice. If this remarkable statement is true, then now that believers have been truly "reconciled" (a term virtually synonymous with "justified" or "made righteous"), they will *certainly* be saved through the power of the living Christ. Salvation does not simply mean forgiveness of sins but a once-and-for-all liberation from sin and inclusion in God's life-giving kingdom through Christ. The ultimate—and indeed only— human boasting that means anything, then, is to boast of the God who saves through Christ (v. 11; also vv. 2-3).

GOSPEL   MATTHEW 9:36–10:8

At the sight of the crowds, Jesus' heart was moved with pity
    for them
    because they were troubled and abandoned,
    like sheep without a shepherd.
Then he said to his disciples,
    "The harvest is abundant but the laborers are few;
    so ask the master of the harvest
    to send out laborers for his harvest."

Then he summoned his twelve disciples
    and gave them authority over unclean spirits
    to drive them out and to cure every disease and every illness.
The names of the twelve apostles are these:
    first, Simon called Peter, and his brother Andrew;

James, the son of Zebedee, and his brother John;
Philip and Bartholomew, Thomas and Matthew the tax collector;
James, the son of Alphaeus, and Thaddeus;
Simon from Cana, and Judas Iscariot who betrayed him.
Jesus sent out these twelve after instructing them thus,
    "Do not go into pagan territory or enter a Samaritan town.
Go rather to the lost sheep of the house of Israel.
As you go, make this proclamation: 'The kingdom of heaven is at hand.'
Cure the sick, raise the dead, cleanse lepers, drive out demons.
Without cost you have received; without cost you are to give."

Our passage marks a transition in the Gospel. Following the Sermon on the Mount, Jesus has been actively engaged in teaching, healing, and performing miracles. Now, he recognizes that he needs help in his mission, seeing the abundance of people who are "troubled" (Greek *eklyō*, meaning "weary," "fallen," or "harassed") and "abandoned" (Greek *rhiptō*, meaning "scattered," "cast down," or "helpless"). Moved with "pity" or compassion, Jesus calls and sends forth the twelve apostles. They are to be shepherds for the lost sheep or laborers for the harvest, following Jesus's way in all manner but teaching. This is the only time this Gospel writer uses the term "apostle" (meaning "one sent out") rather than "disciple" (meaning "learner") to describe Jesus's followers. The number twelve draws from the twelve tribes of Israel in the Hebrew Bible and represents completeness and unity, the coming together of disparate parts to make something whole. Simon Peter is the most prominent apostle and always comes first in the lists of the apostles, followed by Andrew, James, and John (see Mark 3:16-19; Luke 6:14-16; Acts 1:13). Matthew "the tax collector" was the subject of last Sunday's Gospel, while Simon from "Cana" (linked to the Aramaic *qan 'an*, or "zealot") may have been a Jewish reformer and political rebel (see Luke 6:15). Judas Iscariot is the one "who betray[s]" Jesus or, literally, "who hands him over." The name Iscariot could mean "from Kerioth," a town in southern Judea; or perhaps it is linked to the Latin *sicarius* ("dagger man" or assassin). Though Matthew first delimits the apostles' mission to the people of Israel, this expands throughout the Gospel and beyond. On the relationship between Judeans and Samaritans, see the Gospel notes for the Third Sunday of Lent. In the book of Revelation (which closes the New Testament canon), the author imagines the names of the twelve tribes and twelve apostles inscribed together in the New Jerusalem, which comes down from heaven (21:10-14).

Ponder

Our readings are call stories. In all of them, weakness and dependence are necessary for a relationship with God. In Exodus, it is in the desert, a place of vulnerability and danger, that God calls Israel into relationship, just as an eagle nurtures eaglets into flight. According to Paul, God loves us into union and discipleship *through*, not in spite of, our helplessness. In the Gospel, Jesus's great compassion for the crowds who are "troubled and abandoned" leads to the call of the disciples. Their authority comes not from their own strength and abilities, but in and through Jesus. Society can teach us to conceal our weaknesses, to act independent and strong. Faith teaches us the reverse. What is it like to imagine being called forth today—into relationship, into the world—through weakness and dependence on God?

"We are his people," declares the psalmist. Our readings boast of belonging to God. Israel is God's "special possession" in Exodus, a "kingdom of priests" and a "holy nation." Paul explicitly encourages his community to "boast" loudly of their relationship with God through Christ. And in the Gospel, Jesus exclaims to the disciples that God has given to them "without cost," which is how they are to give to others. Though boasting often has a negative meaning of excessive self-satisfaction, no boasting is too much when it comes to our relationship with God. In fact, we are best able to serve others when our efforts are sustained by an overflowing, inward "boasting" of God, who gives to us without cost. This week, how might you boast of your belonging to God, in your actions, thoughts, and intentions?

Twelfth Sunday in Ordinary Time

FIRST READING   JEREMIAH 20:10-13

Jeremiah said:
"I hear the whisperings of many:
  'Terror on every side!
  Denounce! Let us denounce him!'
All those who were my friends
  are on the watch for any misstep of mine.
'Perhaps he will be trapped; then we can prevail,
  and take our vengeance on him.'
But the Lord is with me, like a mighty champion:[1]
  my persecutors will stumble, they will not triumph.
In their failure they will be put to utter shame,
  to lasting, unforgettable confusion.[2]
O Lord of hosts, you who test the just,
  who probe mind and heart,[3]
let me witness the vengeance you take on them,
  for to you I have entrusted my cause.
Sing to the Lord,
  praise the Lord,
for he has rescued the life of the poor
  from the power of the wicked!"

Jeremiah lived from Judah's golden age during the time of King Josiah (ca. 640–609 BCE) through the Babylonian conquest and destruction of Judah (ca. 597–586 BCE). During this time, many Judeans were dispersed and exiled to Babylon or Egypt, including Jeremiah, who died in Egypt. Jeremiah's prophetic career began while the people were in imminent danger of exile and continued after they were

---

    1. "Mighty champion" translates literally as "awe-inspiring warrior" (Hebrew *gibbôr ʿārîṣ*).

    2. This sentence ("In their failure . . . unforgettable confusion") is difficult to translate from the Hebrew. The Greek translation (LXX) is perhaps the clearest and most compelling option: "They will be greatly shamed, for they did not consider their dishonor, which will never be forgotten."

    3. "Mind and heart": literally "kidneys and heart" in the Hebrew (*kĕlāyôt wālēb*).

exiled from Judah. As a prophet, he was unpopular, for he could not help but speak truth to power, and he often came up against powerful political adversaries. Prior to our reading, Jeremiah comes into conflict with the priest Pashhur, who hears Jeremiah's prophecies against the monarchy and has Jeremiah put in the stocks overnight. After Jeremiah is released the next day, he issues a long, despairing lament, from which our reading draws. He first speaks of being enticed and overpowered by God, who forces him to prophesy against his will (vv. 7-9; see the Twenty-Second Sunday in Ordinary Time). He then praises God with words of thanksgiving, for God champions the poor and the persecuted and will avenge Jeremiah from those who seek "vengeance" against him (vv. 11-13). In the verses following our reading, Jeremiah curses his own life because of his continued sorrow and shame as a prophet (vv. 14-18).

RESPONSORIAL PSALM   PSALM 69:8-10, 14, 17, 33-35

Lord, in your great love, answer me.

SECOND READING   ROMANS 5:12-15

Brothers and sisters:
Through one man sin entered the world,
    and through sin, death,
    and thus death came to all men, inasmuch as all sinned—
    for up to the time of the law, sin was in the world,
    though sin is not accounted when there is no law.
But death reigned from Adam to Moses,
    even over those who did not sin
    after the pattern of the trespass of Adam,
    who is the type of the one who was to come.

But the gift is not like the transgression.
For if by the transgression of the one the many died,
    how much more did the grace of God
    and the gracious gift of the one man Jesus Christ
    overflow for the many.

From last week's discussion of salvation as once-and-for-all liberation from sin and Paul's call to "boast" in God through Jesus Christ, we move to Paul's comparison between Jesus and Adam (see also 1 Cor 15:21-23, 45-49). According to Paul, Adam's "trespass" or "transgression" (similar words that denote a stumbling, deviation, or violation) in Genesis 3 was both a personal and a universal catastrophe. It led to sin, and sin led to death—not just Adam's death but death for all future generations. Here, death connotes not only the reality of human mortality but, more importantly, a separation between God and humans that was not present before Adam's trespass. Sin had dominion or authority until the law came through Moses, the point at which moral conventions were established and thus allowed people to account for sin for the first time. Christ's obedience to God then far surpasses a simple reversal of Adam's transgression. Adam was the "type" or model for Jesus in that he stood at the head of the old creation, while Jesus was the one to come, standing at the head of a new creation. As Paul describes subsequent to our reading, while "death came to reign" through Adam's disobedience, through Christ's obedience and God's "abundance of grace" and "gift of justification," humans "reign in life" through Christ (v. 17).

GOSPEL   MATTHEW 10:26-33

Jesus said to the Twelve:
    "Fear no one.
Nothing is concealed that will not be revealed,
    nor secret that will not be known.
What I say to you in the darkness, speak in the light;
    what you hear whispered, proclaim on the housetops.
And do not be afraid of those who kill the body but cannot kill
    the soul;
    rather, be afraid of the one who can destroy
    both soul and body in Gehenna.
Are not two sparrows sold for a small coin?
Yet not one of them falls to the ground without your Father's
    knowledge.
Even all the hairs of your head are counted.
So do not be afraid; you are worth more than many sparrows.

Everyone who acknowledges me before others
   I will acknowledge before my heavenly Father.
But whoever denies me before others,
   I will deny before my heavenly Father."

After Jesus sends out the twelve disciples (see last Sunday's Gospel), he issues a series of instructions on how they are to travel between towns and villages (10:7-15), warning them to be "shrewd as serpents and simple as doves" in the midst of unavoidable persecution (vv. 16-23). These statements provide the backdrop for our reading, in which Jesus goes on to tell the disciples to "[f]ear no one" (v. 26), likely quoting from God's words in the call narrative of the prophet Jeremiah (see Jer 1:8). The one to fear is not a human adversary but rather God, who can "destroy both soul and body in Gehenna" (or "hell"; v. 28). On fear of God, see also Luke 12:4-5 and Hebrews 10:31. A sparrow is the tiniest, most dispensable, and cheapest creature; therefore, if God cares for the sparrow, how much more will God care for humans? This is a classic "lesser to greater" rabbinic argument (see the Gospel notes for the Eighth Sunday in Ordinary Time). Jesus concludes with a warning to his disciples to be faithful despite persecution.

Surrender

Ponder

What do you fear? According to the Bible, the only thing to fear is "to fall into the hands of the living God" (Heb 10:31). This "fear" is not a literal, paralyzing fear that seeks avoidance, for God is compassionate, overflowing with love and grace (Rom 5:15). Instead, to fear God is to acknowledge and revere what (or who) is real and eternal, which liberates us to follow God fully and fearlessly. In Jeremiah's remarkable speech, he places all of his fears and pain before God as he faces persecution and possible death (Jer 20:7-18). He then continues to follow the path God carves out for him to become one of Israel's greatest prophets. This week, take time to reflect on your fears. Can you name them and place them before God, the one who matters above all else?

Jesus calls his disciples—and us—to proclaim the gospel fearlessly, focusing not on human judgment but on the God who loves and claims us. But what does it mean to proclaim the gospel? Speaking personally as a convert to Christianity, for years wellmeaning evangelization turned me away from, not toward, the gospel. It was when I met people who proclaimed the gospel not with words but through the authenticity and imperfection of their lives that Christianity broke open and claimed me. As you pray with our readings, what does fearless proclamation mean to you? How does it speak truth to people's lives, meeting them where they are in their hopes and fears, inspiring them to turn toward the living God?

Thirteenth Sunday in Ordinary Time

FIRST READING   2 KINGS 4:8-11, 14-16a

One day Elisha came to Shunem,
   where there was a woman of influence, who urged him to dine
      with her.
Afterward, whenever he passed by, he used to stop there to dine.
So she said to her husband, "I know that Elisha is a holy man
      of God.
Since he visits us often, let us arrange a little room on the roof
   and furnish it for him with a bed, table, chair, and lamp,
   so that when he comes to us he can stay there."
Sometime later Elisha arrived and stayed in the room overnight.

Later Elisha asked, "Can something be done for her?"
His servant Gehazi answered, "Yes!
   She has no son, and her husband is getting on in years."
Elisha said, "Call her."
When the woman had been called and stood at the door,
   Elisha promised, "This time next year
   you will be fondling a baby son."

Elisha (whose name means "my god is salvation") was one of Israel's greatest prophets and Elijah's protégé. After Elijah is taken up in a whirlwind in 2 Kings 2, Elisha officially succeeds him by receiving a "double portion" of his spirit (2:9). Our reading is part of a longer story that recounts the miraculous birth, death, and raising of a child that parallels an earlier story about Elijah (see 1 Kgs 17:17-24). Shunem lay at the western end of the Jezreel Valley, north of Jezreel. The description of the "little room" demonstrates the woman's wealth and generosity. The woman never asks Elisha for anything; all she wants is to create a comfortable space for a "holy man of God." We miss key lines in the story (vv. 12-13) when Elisha seeks to repay her generosity, asking what he can do for her and whether he might speak a "good word" on her behalf to the king or the army commander (the highest political offices of Israel). She responds proudly and simply that her own clan and people, who are likely also influential, will take care of her (v. 13). In other words, she wants nothing and seeks no repayment. Elisha's servant Gehazi then suggests that what the woman might need or desire is a son so that she will not remain a childless widow when her husband dies. We do not know whether the woman truly wants a son, but a son she receives. Later, her son dies, and Elisha restores him to life (vv. 32-37). The account of the woman's extravagant generosity and the prophet's subsequent promise of a son to an old, childless woman mirrors the story of the angels' visit to Abraham and Sarah in Genesis 18:1-15.

RESPONSORIAL PSALM   PSALM 89:2-3, 16-17, 18-19

For ever I will sing the goodness of the Lord.

SECOND READING   ROMANS 6:3-4, 8-11

Brothers and sisters:
Are you unaware that we who were baptized into Christ Jesus
    were baptized into his death?
We were indeed buried with him through baptism into death,
    so that, just as Christ was raised from the dead
    by the glory of the Father,
    we too might live in newness of life.

If, then, we have died with Christ,
    we believe that we shall also live with him.
We know that Christ, raised from the dead, dies no more;
    death no longer has power over him.
As to his death, he died to sin once and for all;
    as to his life, he lives for God.
Consequently, you too must think of yourselves as dead to sin
    and living for God in Christ Jesus.

From last week's focus on the almost inconceivable gift of life through Christ, we shift to Paul's reflections on obedience. Christ was obedient to God; thus, obedience is required from those who live in Christ. As Paul describes in this passage, grace is so much more than being liberated from the "trespass" of Adam (see last Sunday's reading). Instead, grace—through baptism—means entry into full participation in Christ's life, death, and resurrection. What this full participation calls for is not a complacent lifestyle but instead a metamorphosis into an entirely new moral life and way of being. Believers have an obligation to live faithfully into this new life, becoming "dead to sin" and "living for God in Christ Jesus." Only then do we fully acknowledge and live into the unimaginable gift that God has given to us through Christ.

GOSPEL   MATTHEW 10:37-42

Jesus said to his apostles:
"Whoever loves father or mother more than me is not worthy
of me,
and whoever loves son or daughter more than me is not
worthy of me;
and whoever does not take up his cross
and follow after me is not worthy of me.
"Whoever finds his life will lose it,
and whoever loses his life for my sake will find it.

Whoever receives you receives me,
and whoever receives me receives the one who sent me.
Whoever receives a prophet because he is a prophet
will receive a prophet's reward,
and whoever receives a righteous man
because he is a righteous man
will receive a righteous man's reward.
And whoever gives only a cup of cold water
to one of these little ones to drink
because the little one is a disciple—
amen, I say to you, he will surely not lose his reward."

This is the first time we find the word "cross" in Matthew's Gospel, on the heels of Jesus's instructions to his disciples in last week's reading. Jesus's words here are a shocking paradox that are meant to put one's priorities in perspective ("paradox" comes from the Greek *para-doxa*, meaning "against common opinion"). For Jesus, discipleship is everything, worth more even than one's family (in the ancient world, family was everything) or one's life on earth. As Jesus says, what truly matters is not one's literal life but one's soul, life in God's kingdom. To be willing to relinquish one's life for the sake of Christ—the sake of the cross—means finding it in God's kingdom (see also Matt 16:24-26). To "take up [one's] cross" refers to a choice of self-surrender and an acceptance of suffering for the sake of the gospel (it does not, however, mean a loss of dignity, a passive allowance of ongoing domination, or abuse in corrupt social systems). Often when Jesus refers to "little ones," he means children (e.g., 19:13-14), but here he is likely referring to wandering disciples who occupy a humble or lowly social position (see also 25:45).

Ponder

The story of Elisha, the Shunammite woman, and her son is worth reading in its entirety (2 Kgs 4:8-37). It is a remarkable story with many twists and turns. In the verses left out of our reading (vv. 12-13), we miss a key detail: the woman's intentions. She seeks nothing from Elisha; her generosity is an end in itself, its own reward. The story tells us something important about intentionality, and it invites us to explore the intentions that underlie our actions. Why do we do what we do, and what reward do we seek?

Life in Christ means death with him, a willingness to turn toward the cross and away from ourselves. Though this can seem daunting, in reality it often looks quite ordinary (especially for those of us whose lives are not in danger simply because we are Christian). Taking up the cross can mean daily, seemingly mundane acts: lending someone our attention, our compassion, a glass of water. Yet in these acts of "death"—turning from self-absorption, self-interest, self-preservation—our lives become that much fuller, richer, more *real*. This, then, is the ultimate paradox of the Christian message: we have to "die" in order to live fully and freely. Augustine famously said that our hearts are "restless" until they rest in God. Another way of putting this is that our hearts are full when they rest in God. And when our hearts are full, our lives become praise, the "joyful shout" of the psalmist.

Fourteenth Sunday in Ordinary Time

FIRST READING   ZECHARIAH 9:9-10

Thus says the LORD:
Rejoice heartily, O daughter Zion,
    shout for joy, O daughter Jerusalem!
See, your king shall come to you;
    a just savior is he,
meek, and riding on an ass,
    on a colt, the foal of an ass.
He shall banish the chariot from Ephraim,
    and the horse from Jerusalem;
the warrior's bow shall be banished,
    and he shall proclaim peace to the nations.
His dominion shall be from sea to sea,
    and from the River to the ends of the earth.

The postexilic book of Zechariah appears only twice in our three-year Sunday cycle (here and on the Twelfth Sunday in Ordinary Time, Year C). Our reading draws from a longer poetic unit in Zechariah (9:1–11:17) that describes God as a divine warrior who liberates Jerusalem/Zion and returns the scattered Judean populations to the Holy City. Jerusalem is sometimes described as God's "daughter" in the Hebrew Bible, a term that reflects intimacy and love (see also Lam 1:6; Zech 2:14; Zeph 3:14). The author prophesies a coming king in the line of David who will arrive humbly yet triumphantly in Jerusalem on a donkey ("ass") or colt, like ancient Middle Eastern royalty (see Gen 49:11; Judg 10:4; 1 Kgs 1:38). The phrase "on an ass, / on a colt, the foal of an ass," uses poetic parallelism to describe one animal with multiple words. Two Gospel accounts recall this text in Jesus's entry into Jerusalem (Matt 21:2-7; John 12:14-15), though the author of Matthew's Gospel does not seem to understand the poetic parallelism and states that Jesus enters Jerusalem riding on two animals simultaneously. Our reading juxtaposes the meekness of a ruler arriving on a donkey with God the divine warrior, whose power sweeps from the Mediterranean to the Euphrates ("sea to sea"), demilitarizing the entire known world, with Israel (Ephraim) and Judah (Jerusalem) at the center.

RESPONSORIAL PSALM   PSALM 145:1-2, 8-9, 10-11, 13-14

I will praise your name for ever, my king and my God.
or: Alleluia.

SECOND READING   ROMANS 8:9, 11-13

Brothers and sisters:
You are not in the flesh;
   on the contrary, you are in the spirit,
   if only the Spirit of God dwells in you.
Whoever does not have the Spirit of Christ does not belong
   to him.
If the Spirit of the one who raised Jesus from the dead dwells
   in you,
   the one who raised Christ from the dead
   will give life to your mortal bodies also,
   through his Spirit that dwells in you.
Consequently, brothers and sisters,
   we are not debtors to the flesh,
   to live according to the flesh.
For if you live according to the flesh, you will die,
   but if by the Spirit you put to death the deeds of the body,
   you will live.

This week, we skip from Romans 6 to 8 and repeat part of the reading from the Fifth Sunday of Lent (Rom 8:8-11). Romans 8 concludes Paul's long explanation of the meaning of God's righteousness (1:18–8:39). In this explanation, Paul first indicts all humanity, stating that no one is righteous (3:9-20). Yet through Christ, God's righteousness repairs the divine-human relationship and justifies all who believe, Jews and Gentiles alike (3:21–5:21). This remarkable gift of (re)unification with God crucifies the old self and sets one free of sin, free to be "slaves" not of sin but of righteousness (6:1-23). To be set free from sin is to be liberated from trying to live in accordance with the law, the highest spiritual standard that no one living "in the flesh" can successfully follow (7:1-25). For Paul, "flesh" is not the body itself, which is a "temple of the holy Spirit" (1 Cor 6:19). Rather, the "flesh" is the person controlled by passions and human weakness. In Romans 8:1-17, Paul then juxtaposes living "in the flesh" with living "in the spirit" through God's indwelling Spirit. Through baptism into Christ's death and resurrection, believers can also "put to death" their passions and human weaknesses and thus be liberated from being bound ("debtors") to the flesh (vv. 12-13). In the verses following our reading, Paul goes on to describe how such liberation leads to spiritual "adoption" (Greek *hyiothesía*) as children of God. Paul uses the same expression in Romans 9:4 to describe Israel as chosen or "adopted" by God. According to Paul, through the Holy Spirit and the presence of Christ within, Gentiles become equal or "joint" heirs to the promises given to Abraham (8:17).

GOSPEL   MATTHEW 11:25-30

At that time Jesus exclaimed:
   "I give praise to you, Father, Lord of heaven and earth,
   for although you have hidden these things
   from the wise and the learned
   you have revealed them to little ones.
Yes, Father, such has been your gracious will.
All things have been handed over to me by my Father.
No one knows the Son except the Father,
   and no one knows the Father except the Son
   and anyone to whom the Son wishes to reveal him.

"Come to me, all you who labor and are burdened,
   and I will give you rest.
Take my yoke upon you and learn from me,
   for I am meek and humble of heart;
   and you will find rest for yourselves.
For my yoke is easy, and my burden light."

In last week's Gospel, Jesus referred to wandering, humble disciples as "little ones," literally those who are "small" (Greek *mikros*; Matt 10:42). Here he describes true knowledge of God's kingdom ("these things") as residing not with the wise and learned according to society's standards, but instead with his followers, whom he describes again as "little ones," literally infants or children (Greek *nēpios*; v. 25). Elsewhere in the Gospel, he states that people will only enter the kingdom of heaven if they "turn and become like children" (18:3). Jesus's expression "Come to me" draws from the language of Wisdom personified in the Hebrew Bible (e.g., Sir 24:19). The "rest" that Jesus promises is the natural result of following God's laws (e.g., Jer 6:16) and is a defining feature of the age to come. A "yoke" was a wooden crosspiece fastened over the necks of two animals and attached to a plow or cart to be pulled. At times in the Hebrew Bible, the "yoke" refers to an oppressive burden or slavery (e.g., Lev 26:13; Isa 47:6). In rabbinic Judaism, the yoke becomes a metaphor for the "light" or joyous study of Torah and obedience to God's laws. Here, perhaps alluding to himself as the Torah personified, Jesus describes his own yoke or teachings as "easy" and "light." Later, teams of disciples will be known as "yokemates," struggling together to pull or promote the gospel (Phil 4:3).

Ponder

Our reading from Zechariah is filled with a sense of liberation, joy, relief, and rest. Speaking to a people who have been living in the shadow of empires for generations—Egypt, Assyria, Babylon, and now Persia—the author envisions the end of foreign rule and the return of the Davidic monarchy to Jerusalem. The God of Israel is a warrior God whose power sweeps across the world, banishing foreign oppressors and their military power. Simultaneously, the Davidic line will return to Israel a just and gentle savior. All will be perfect peace: a demilitarized world, a just political system, a harmonious society. One can feel the yearning that emanates from our reading. As you pray with this text, what peace do you yearn for? What would this peace look like in your life, your community, your world?

Zechariah's promised peace is mirrored in Jesus's offer of rest. But what is this "rest"? It is not necessarily less work, for it is still a "yoke" to bear—one of responsibilities and commitments. Nonetheless, Jesus promises that his yoke feels "easy" and "light." To take on this yoke is simple: all we have to do is take on the qualities of a child (e.g., vulnerability, wonder, trust) and lay all of our burdens on Jesus. When we do this, when we yoke ourselves to Jesus—the one who is meek, gentle, and loving—then this path leads to peace, fulfillment, and the liberation from our lesser selves that Paul describes. It leads to rest. Our Gospel invites us all to ask ourselves: to what, or to whom, are we yoked, and where does the path lead?

Fifteenth Sunday in Ordinary Time

FIRST READING   ISAIAH 55:10-11

Thus says the LORD:
Just as from the heavens
   the rain and snow come down
and do not return there
   till they have watered the earth,
   making it fertile and fruitful,
giving seed to the one who sows
   and bread to the one who eats,
so shall my word be
   that goes forth from my mouth;
my word shall not return to me void,
   but shall do my will,
   achieving the end for which I sent it.

Isaiah 55 closes the second major portion of the book of Isaiah (chaps. 40–55), which was written during the end of Judah's exile to Babylon in the late sixth century BCE (see notes on Isaiah from the First Sunday of Advent). Chapter 55 opens with a call to all "who are thirsty" to come to God's waters and follows with an invitation to repentance and renewal (vv. 1-7). The focus then shifts to a second theme: God's authority and power. Preceding our reading, the author reminds the audience that God's thoughts are not their thoughts, nor are God's ways their ways. "For as the heavens are higher than the earth," he writes, "so are [God's] ways higher than your ways, / [God's] thoughts higher than your thoughts" (v. 9). Our reading then continues this theme in relation to the permanence and effectiveness of God's word. Verses 12-13 close the chapter with a metaphor for Judah's return from Babylon in the imagery of nature flourishing and rejoicing.

RESPONSORIAL PSALM   PSALM 65:10, 11, 12-13, 14

The seed that falls on good ground will yield a fruitful harvest.

Brothers and sisters:
I consider that the sufferings of this present time are as nothing
    compared with the glory to be revealed for us.
For creation awaits with eager expectation
    the revelation of the children of God;
    for creation was made subject to futility,
    not of its own accord but because of the one who subjected it,
    in hope that creation itself
    would be set free from slavery to corruption
    and share in the glorious freedom of the children of God.
We know that all creation is groaning in labor pains even
        until now;
    and not only that, but we ourselves,
    who have the firstfruits of the Spirit,
    we also groan within ourselves
    as we wait for adoption, the redemption of our bodies.

In Romans 5, Paul compares the consequences of Adam's transgression specifically for humans (see the Twelfth Sunday in Ordinary Time). Now Paul offers a wider perspective in terms of the consequences for all creation (the natural world). According to Paul, the current sufferings are nothing compared to the coming "glory" when Christ returns. Paul then draws all of creation into this salvation promise. He describes creation as if it were a person who waits for the coming "revelation" of God, to which the Spirit already bears witness (vv. 16, 23). The "futility" that Paul speaks of is further described as "slavery to corruption," which recalls God's punishments upon the land prior to banishing Adam and Eve from the Garden of Eden (see Gen 3:17-19). According to Paul, these punishments are impermanent and subject to reversal alongside the "glorious freedom" or restoration of human glory when Christ returns (see also Rom 5:2). Paul then draws humans back into the discussion through the metaphor of labor pains, a common eschatological symbol (e.g., Mark 13:8; God also groans as a woman in labor in Isa 42:14). Believers have the "firstfruits" of the Spirit (referring to the first, choice fruits of a harvest), but, like creation, they also "groan" as they await the full realization of their "adoption" or, literally, "sonship" (see also Rom 5:15-17; 9:4). Because human bodies are destined for redemption (v. 23), all of creation will also be redeemed, for the human body is part of creation. In chapters 9–11, Paul will develop a crucial theme that we already see here: God's future plan for human beings (God's "children") is much greater than the circumstances of the "present time."

GOSPEL   MATTHEW 13:1-23 [OR 13:1-9]

On that day, Jesus went out of the house and sat down by
    the sea.
Such large crowds gathered around him
    that he got into a boat and sat down,
    and the whole crowd stood along the shore.
And he spoke to them at length in parables, saying:
    "A sower went out to sow.
And as he sowed, some seed fell on the path,
    and birds came and ate it up.
Some fell on rocky ground, where it had little soil.
It sprang up at once because the soil was not deep,
    and when the sun rose it was scorched,
    and it withered for lack of roots.
Some seed fell among thorns, and the thorns grew up and
    choked it.
But some seed fell on rich soil, and produced fruit,
    a hundred or sixty or thirtyfold.
Whoever has ears ought to hear."

The disciples approached him and said,
    "Why do you speak to them in parables?"
He said to them in reply,
    "Because knowledge of the mysteries of the kingdom
        of heaven
    has been granted to you, but to them it has not been granted.
To anyone who has, more will be given and he will grow rich;
    from anyone who has not, even what he has will be
        taken away.
This is why I speak to them in parables, because
    they look but do not see and hear but do not listen or
    understand.

Isaiah's prophecy is fulfilled in them, which says:
    You shall indeed hear but not understand,
        you shall indeed look but never see.
    Gross is the heart of this people,
        they will hardly hear with their ears,
        they have closed their eyes,
        lest they see with their eyes
        and hear with their ears
    and understand with their hearts and be converted,
        and I heal them.

"But blessed are your eyes, because they see,
    and your ears, because they hear.
Amen, I say to you, many prophets and righteous people
    longed to see what you see but did not see it,
    and to hear what you hear but did not hear it.

"Hear then the parable of the sower.
The seed sown on the path is the one
    who hears the word of the kingdom without understanding it,
    and the evil one comes and steals away
    what was sown in his heart.
The seed sown on rocky ground
    is the one who hears the word and receives it at once with joy.
But he has no root and lasts only for a time.
When some tribulation or persecution comes because of
        the word,
    he immediately falls away.[1]
The seed sown among thorns is the one who hears the word,
    but then worldly anxiety and the lure of riches choke the word
    and it bears no fruit.
But the seed sown on rich soil
    is the one who hears the word and understands it,
    who indeed bears fruit and yields a hundred or sixty or
        thirtyfold."

---

1. The expression "falls away" (Greek *skandalizō*) can also translate as "takes offense" (Matt 11:6), "sins" or "stumbles" (Matt 18:6), or "is shaken" (Matt 26:31).

Our passage is the first of a series of parables (Greek *parabolē*, meaning "comparison") in Matthew 13 (see also Synoptic parallels to this passage in Mark 4:1-20; Luke 8:4-15). This is one of the few parables that includes Jesus's own interpretation. As usual, Jesus draws large crowds to listen to him speak. The sower refers to Jesus, and "sowing" is a common biblical motif for doing God's work (e.g., Jer 31:27-28; Ezek 36:9). As becomes clear later in the passage, the seeds are the "word of the kingdom," and the "fruit" refers to good deeds. In Mark's version of our reading, Jesus speaks in parables to his disciples in order to keep the people in a state of incomprehension (see Mark 4:12). Here, Jesus similarly speaks in parables to the disciples, though it is unclear who is at fault for the people's incomprehension. Jesus explains that knowledge of the "mysteries" (or "secrets") of the kingdom has been hidden from most people. This passive verbal construct ("it has not been granted") suggests that God is responsible for hiding knowledge from the people, as does Jesus's quote from Isaiah 6:9-10 (vv. 14-15). In addition, Jesus states that "many prophets and righteous people longed to see . . . and to hear" what the people are now seeing and hearing, but they could not. Yet the parable itself places responsibility on those who hear God's word to cultivate it and allow it to bear fruit in their lives. Given that the true audience of the parable is Matthew's Jewish-Christian audience after Jesus's death as well as readers across time (including us), the point is to speak to and admonish communities years later to listen to, and follow, Jesus.

Ponder

Isaiah and the Gospel reveal a tension between God's will and human responsiveness. In Isaiah, God's word accomplishes God's will and never returns to God "void." Yet the surrounding verses are a plea to humans to listen and return to God (55:1-7). In the Gospel, while only God can grant knowledge of the "mysteries of the kingdom of heaven," the parable is all about our responsiveness. These readings therefore point to a real tension in faith. Ultimately, faith and knowledge of God are God's gifts, yet we are all responsible for cultivating ourselves in preparation to receive these gifts. How might you practice being open and attentive?

The natural world takes center stage in our readings. In Isaiah, the psalm, and the Gospel, rain, snow, and seeds are metaphors for God's word, promising fruitfulness and abundance in cooperation with human actions. In Romans, what happens in the natural world similarly depends on our actions. According to Paul, our sins—greed, irresponsibility, indifference—have a punishing effect on all creation. In today's climate crisis, Paul's words are far too real. Using Paul's language, we might imagine creation "groaning" to be set free and saved. In Genesis, God loved all of creation into being and commanded Adam to "cultivate and care for it" (2:15). What happens in the natural world, then, is dependent upon our actions. As contemporary people of faith, what is our responsibility in cultivating and caring for creation?

Sixteenth Sunday in Ordinary Time

FIRST READING   WISDOM 12:13, 16-19

There is no god besides you who have the care of all,
    that you need show you have not unjustly condemned.
For your might is the source of justice;
    your mastery over all things makes you lenient to all.
For you show your might when the perfection of your power is
    disbelieved;
    and in those who know you, you rebuke temerity.
But though you are master of might, you judge with clemency,
    and with much lenience you govern us;
    for power, whenever you will, attends you.
And you taught your people, by these deeds,
    that those who are just must be kind;
and you gave your children good ground for hope
    that you would permit repentance for their sins.

Though tradition attributes the book of Wisdom to King Solomon, it was written much later than Solomon's reign (ca. early first century CE), likely in Alexandria, Egypt. It was also originally composed in Greek (not Hebrew) and thus preserved in early Christian, not Jewish, circles. Throughout the book, the text blends Hellenistic philosophy with Jewish understanding. Our reading draws from a broader section (12:3-18) in which the author attempts to justify Israel's conquest of Canaan (see also Josh 1–12 on the conquest itself). Directly preceding these verses, the narrator asks God rhetorically (in relation to the conquest), "For who can say to you, 'What have you done?' / or who can oppose your decree? / Or when peoples perish, who can challenge you, their maker; / or who can come into your presence to vindicate the unrighteous?" (v. 12). The section we read today (and vv. 14-15, which we skip) then describes God's righteousness, power, and tolerance using language that evokes Hellenistic philosophical depictions of the ideal ruler. The expression "no god besides you" draws from elsewhere in the Hebrew Bible (e.g., Deut 32:39). An alternative translation of the phrase "in those who know you, you rebuke temerity" is "you rebuke any insolence among those who know it" (v. 17). In other words, God demonstrates "might" or divine justice specifically toward those who know God yet still choose to defy God's authority. The notion of God rebuking insolence is common in the Hebrew Bible (e.g., Ps 119:21; Isa 13:11).

RESPONSORIAL PSALM   PSALM 86:5-6, 9-10, 15-16

Lord, you are good and forgiving.

SECOND READING   ROMANS 8:26-27

Brothers and sisters:
The Spirit comes to the aid of our weakness;
    for we do not know how to pray as we ought,
    but the Spirit himself intercedes with inexpressible groanings.
And the one who searches hearts
    knows what is the intention of the Spirit,
    because he intercedes for the holy ones
    according to God's will.

Picking up from last week's imagery of creation "groaning" (Rom 8:22-23), Paul links this inward expression of emotion to the work of the Spirit. According to Paul, the Spirit not only speaks to us but intercedes on our behalf. Our "inexpressible groanings" are therefore the Spirit at work within our prayers, articulating our needs better than we can ourselves. God is "the one who searches" the human heart to know the Spirit's intention (v. 27; see also Jer 17:10; Ps 139:1, 23). Later, in verse 34, it is Christ, not the Spirit, who intercedes on our behalf.

GOSPEL   MATTHEW 13:24-43 [OR 13:24-30]

Jesus proposed another parable to the crowds, saying:
"The kingdom of heaven may be likened
    to a man who sowed good seed in his field.
While everyone was asleep his enemy came
    and sowed weeds all through the wheat, and then went off.

When the crop grew and bore fruit, the weeds appeared as well.
The slaves of the householder came to him and said,
   'Master, did you not sow good seed in your field?
Where have the weeds come from?'
He answered, 'An enemy has done this.'
His slaves said to him,
   'Do you want us to go and pull them up?'
He replied, 'No, if you pull up the weeds
   you might uproot the wheat along with them.
Let them grow together until harvest;
    then at harvest time I will say to the harvesters,
    "First collect the weeds and tie them in bundles for burning;
    but gather the wheat into my barn."'"

He proposed another parable to them.
"The kingdom of heaven is like a mustard seed
   that a person took and sowed in a field.
It is the smallest of all the seeds,
   yet when full-grown it is the largest of plants.
It becomes a large bush,
   and the 'birds of the sky come and dwell in its branches.'"

He spoke to them another parable.
"The kingdom of heaven is like yeast
   that a woman took and mixed with three measures of
     wheat flour
   until the whole batch was leavened."

All these things Jesus spoke to the crowds in parables.
He spoke to them only in parables,
   to fulfill what had been said through the prophet:
    I will open my mouth in parables,
     I will announce what has lain hidden from the foundation
      of the world.

Then, dismissing the crowds, he went into the house.
His disciples approached him and said,
   "Explain to us the parable of the weeds in the field."
He said in reply, "He who sows good seed is the Son of Man,
   the field is the world, the good seed the children of the
     kingdom.
The weeds are the children of the evil one,
   and the enemy who sows them is the devil.

> The harvest is the end of the age, and the harvesters are angels.
> Just as weeds are collected and burned up with fire,
>   so will it be at the end of the age.
> The Son of Man will send his angels,
>   and they will collect out of his kingdom
>   all who cause others to sin and all evildoers.
> They will throw them into the fiery furnace,
>   where there will be wailing and grinding of teeth.
> Then the righteous will shine like the sun
>   in the kingdom of their Father.
> Whoever has ears ought to hear."

From last week's parable of the sower, we continue with three additional agricultural parables of growth: the parable of the weeds in the field, including Jesus's explanation of the parable to his disciples (vv. 24-30, 36-43); the parable of the mustard seed (vv. 31-32); and the parable of the yeast (v. 33). The first parable is unique to Matthew, whereas the second and third have parallels in the other Synoptic Gospels (Mark 4:30-32; Luke 13:18-21). When Jesus explains the first parable to his disciples, he identifies the "enemy" as the devil, the "harvest" as the eschaton or "the end of the age," and the "harvesters" as the angels tasked with weeding out those who are unfaithful in the church (the weeds) from those who are faithful (the grain). In the second parable, the mustard seed symbolizes smallness, yet the mustard bush (note: not a tree) can grow between six to twenty feet high. Jesus therefore exaggerates its qualities in stating that it can become "the "largest of plants," quoting from Ezekiel 17:23 and 31:6 ("birds of the sky . . . dwell in its branches"; v. 32). Like the mustard seed, yeast is tiny yet powerful, permeating and expanding. Again, Jesus exaggerates the parable with the detail of "three measures," the equivalent of fifty pounds or more (enough for over one hundred loaves of bread). When Jesus explains the first parable to his disciples, he quotes from Psalm 78:2. The "Son of Man" refers to Jesus, and the furnace represents final judgment. As in last week's reading, it is unclear whether it is up to the people to hear ("Whoever has ears ought to hear"; v. 43) or whether God intentionally hides meaning from the masses through parables ("what has lain hidden from the foundation of the world"; v. 35).

Ponder

The Gospel distinguishes clearly between "wheat" (Greek *sitos*) that produces bread, and "weeds" (Greek *zizania*) that resemble wheat but are worthless. Both grow up together until the "harvest" or eschaton, when angels finally separate the two. This is not great agricultural wisdom (the sooner one separates wheat from weeds, the better), but it is great spiritual wisdom. For us, it means that none of us knows who is "wheat" or "weed," saint or sinner, in our own communities, nor is it for us to judge. Moreover, we are not plant species but imperfect, complex humans. All of us live a wheat-weed reality. The promise, though, is that God cultivates us patiently and lovingly. We can, and will, be transformed into something truly fruitful if we are open to it. Are we?

"[T]hose who are just must be kind." According to Wisdom, God's justice is intrinsically linked with kindness, a patient gentleness that awaits our conversion. God's strength or "might" is exercised never as tyranny but as mercy, which the psalmist corroborates in praising God. This divine justice is rooted in knowledge of the human heart that lies beyond even human comprehension, as depicted in the "groaning" of the Spirit in Romans. Yet human freedom does have consequences—if it did not, God's justice would be meaningless. In the end, as Matthew describes, God will not be mocked, nor will the promise of a just and right world. How do the depictions of God's justice, kindness, and tolerance that flow through all of our readings help you understand the end of today's Gospel?

Seventeenth Sunday in Ordinary Time

FIRST READING   1 KINGS 3:5, 7-12

The LORD appeared to Solomon in a dream at night.
God said, "Ask something of me and I will give it to you."
Solomon answered:
   "O LORD, my God, you have made me, your servant, king
   to succeed my father David;
   but I am a mere youth, not knowing at all how to act.
I serve you in the midst of the people whom you have chosen,
   a people so vast that it cannot be numbered or counted.
Give your servant, therefore, an understanding heart
   to judge your people and to distinguish right from wrong.
For who is able to govern this vast people of yours?"

The LORD was pleased that Solomon made this request.
So God said to him:
   "Because you have asked for this—
   not for a long life for yourself,
   nor for riches,
   nor for the life of your enemies,
   but for understanding so that you may know what is right—
   I do as you requested.
I give you a heart so wise and understanding
   that there has never been anyone like you up to now,
   and after you there will come no one to equal you."

First Kings 1–11 recounts the story of King Solomon, son of David. In the Hebrew Bible, Solomon is often remembered for his wisdom and discernment, and his name is attributed to much later works in the Wisdom tradition of Israel (e.g., see notes for last Sunday's first reading). This remembrance derives from the above reading, in which God appears to Solomon in a dream after David's death and asks the young king what his heart desires. Solomon requests not riches or power but instead "an understanding heart" (literally a "listening" heart in Hebrew, from the verb *šāma ʿ*). We skip verse 6, in which Solomon preempts his request by describing God's steadfast love toward his father David, who had "walked before" God with "fidelity, justice, and an upright heart." God then grants Solomon a wise and understanding heart to "know what is right" or, literally, "to hear what is right" (v. 11). We miss the verse that follows this passage, in which God also grants Solomon riches and honor (v. 13).

RESPONSORIAL PSALM   PSALM 119:57, 72, 76-77, 127-128, 129-130

Lord, I love your commands.

SECOND READING   ROMANS 8:28-30

Brothers and sisters:
We know that all things work for good for those who love God,
    who are called according to his purpose.
For those he foreknew he also predestined
    to be conformed to the image of his Son,
    so that he might be the firstborn
    among many brothers and sisters.
And those he predestined he also called;
    and those he called he also justified;
    and those he justified he also glorified.

Continuing from last week's focus on the Spirit who intercedes for us, Paul moves to the topic of predestination. This is a complicated concept, for in human terms, predestination seems to indicate that those whom God calls have already been chosen, justified, and glorified (note Paul's use of the past tense). However, that which has already been accomplished in eternity remains a future promise for humans to live into. In these verses, Paul describes God's purpose as that which overcomes "all things." In some ancient manuscripts, the clause "We know that all things . . . who love God" is rendered "We know that God makes everything work for good for those who love God." Those who are "called" are primarily the people of Israel (see also 9:4; 11:2), but also Gentiles, whom Paul calls "children of the promise" (9:8; see also 9:23-26). In the creation stories, humans are made in God's image (Gen 1:26-27); through baptism, humans are remade in the divine image through Christ (see also Col 1:15; 3:10). Christ thereby becomes the "firstborn" of all humans, who are his "brothers and sisters" (see also Col 1:18). The word "glorified" refers to the resurrection of the body. Note the movement in the final verse: to be predestined is to be called, to be called is to be justified or made righteous, and to be made righteous is to be glorified or resurrected.

GOSPEL   MATTHEW 13:44-52 [OR 13:44-46]

Jesus said to his disciples:
   "The kingdom of heaven is like a treasure buried in a field,
   which a person finds and hides again,
   and out of joy goes and sells all that he has and buys that field.
Again, the kingdom of heaven is like a merchant
   searching for fine pearls.
When he finds a pearl of great price,
   he goes and sells all that he has and buys it.
Again, the kingdom of heaven is like a net thrown into the sea,
   which collects fish of every kind.
When it is full they haul it ashore
   and sit down to put what is good into buckets.
What is bad they throw away.
Thus it will be at the end of the age.
The angels will go out and separate the wicked from the
      righteous
   and throw them into the fiery furnace,
   where there will be wailing and grinding of teeth.

"Do you understand all these things?"
They answered, "Yes."
And he replied,
   "Then every scribe who has been instructed in the kingdom of
      heaven
   is like the head of a household
   who brings from his storeroom both the new and the old."

This week, we read the final parables in Matthew 13. Like last week, these parables culminate with the "fiery furnace" and the "wailing and grinding of teeth." In the first two parables, the kingdom of heaven is likened to the greatest treasure, for which all else is worth selling in order to buy. In the ancient world, valuables were often buried for safekeeping, and according to rabbinic sources, a person buying property acquired all of its contents. In early Judaism, pearls were metaphors for the study of the Torah and piety. The final parable alludes to the practice of Jewish fishermen who separated kosher ("good") and nonkosher ("bad") fish from their nets. These parables span the economic spectrum: a merchant was a wealthy man, the "person" in the field was likely a tenant farmer or day laborer, and the fishermen were somewhere in between. At the conclusion of this series of parables, Jesus asks the disciples if they have understood "all these things" (v. 51). They reply in the affirmative, perhaps a bit too confidently (see also Mark 4:13, where the disciples do not understand). Jesus then refers to "every scribe," meaning his disciples and all future disciples, all those who have been "instructed" or, literally, "discipled" to become teachers themselves. The "new" and the "old" refer to the "old" Scriptures (the Hebrew Bible) and the "new" revelation in Jesus, both of which are valued. The scribe who is "instructed in the kingdom of heaven" therefore knows Jesus's teachings as well as all the law and the prophets.

Ponder

Our readings invite us to reflect on what is most precious in our lives and on what we would do to protect it. In the first reading and the Gospel, the discovery of the greatest treasure—God's wisdom or the kingdom of God—leads to the utter abandonment of all else in order to pursue it. In 1 Kings, God appears in a dream and tells Solomon to request whatever he wants. What Solomon wants, more than wealth or fame or glory, is God's wisdom or, as the psalmist echoes, God's commandments. In the Gospel, one person finds the greatest treasure by accident, while another finds it in the midst of a patient process of searching. In each of these cases, the method of acquisition is unique, but in all cases, the treasure is easily recognized and joyfully, wholeheartedly claimed. In your own life, what is most precious, and what is it worth to you?

What is God's kingdom, and where is it? The Gospel parables describe it as a great treasure that can be discovered, something outside of ourselves. Yet in 1 Kings, it is an interior gift of wisdom imparted by God. We might name it "faith." In this case, our readings reveal a tension between faith as gift or call and faith as cultivation. In Romans, faith is a call, and when we are called, we are destined to fulfill God's purpose. But 1 Kings and the Gospel place greater emphasis on our own work to cultivate this gift, interiorly and especially through our actions, which in the end have consequences. Yet the end of the Gospel, with its stark imagery of judgment and consequences, is not something to fear. Instead, our readings must be understood in light of last week's readings, where God is described as perfect justice, mercy, and compassion. The promise is that God as Justice is drawing us ever closer in an ongoing process of conversion, encouraging us with priceless treasures along the way.

Eighteenth Sunday in Ordinary Time

FIRST READING   ISAIAH 55:1-3

Thus says the LORD:
All you who are thirsty,
   come to the water!
You who have no money,
   come, receive grain and eat;
come, without paying and without cost,
   drink wine and milk!
Why spend your money for what is not bread;
   your wages for what fails to satisfy?
Heed me, and you shall eat well,
   you shall delight in rich fare.
Come to me heedfully,
   listen, that you may have life.
I will renew with you the everlasting covenant,
   the benefits assured to David.

Isaiah 55 concludes a long message of hope written to exiled Judeans living in Babylon in the late sixth century BCE. We read verses 10-11 on the Fifteenth Sunday in Ordinary Time; consult the notes there for further background on our reading. In these verses, the writer employs metaphors of thirst and hunger to entice the audience to partake in all that God has to offer. The metaphor of a banquet of divine joy represents God's overflowing love and the promise of a continued covenant with Israel. The only conditions for coming to the banquet are an appetite for God and the ability to hear and respond to God. The notion of listening is central to our reading. In verse 2, the phrase "Heed me" translates the Hebrew verb "listen" (*šāmaʿ*), which repeats twice for emphasis, so a literal translation reads something like "*Really* listen to me." In verse 3, "Come to me heedfully, / listen" translates literally as "Bend your ears and come to me, / listen." According to this imagery, God's word is the source of life, and if the people listen, then their covenant with God will be renewed, and they will receive the full benefits of God's original promises to David and his monarchic line.

RESPONSORIAL PSALM   PSALM 145:8-9, 15-16, 17-18

The hand of the Lord feeds us; he answers all our needs.

SECOND READING   ROMANS 8:35, 37-39

Brothers and sisters:
What will separate us from the love of Christ?
Will anguish, or distress, or persecution, or famine,
    or nakedness, or peril, or the sword?
No, in all these things we conquer overwhelmingly
    through him who loved us.
For I am convinced that neither death, nor life,
    nor angels, nor principalities,
    nor present things, nor future things,
    nor powers, nor height, nor depth,
    nor any other creature will be able to separate us
    from the love of God in Christ Jesus our Lord.

Our reading draws from the climactic, triumphal ending not only to Romans 8 but to Paul's argument that he has been developing since Romans 1:18. In these culminating verses, Paul reminds his audience of the power of God's love in and through Christ, which gives believers an unshakable foundation no matter their current circumstances (on the relationship between Christ's love and God's love, see also 5:8). In his list of descriptive nouns ("anguish," "distress," "persecution," etc.), Paul may be alluding to particular difficulties facing the community of believers in Rome. The term "anguish" (Greek *thlipsis*) also translates as "tribulation" or "oppression"; in Romans 5:3, it is rendered "affliction" ("we even boast of our afflictions, knowing that affliction produces endurance"). The "angels" contrast with "principalities" or rulers (Greek *archē*) to represent the fullness of heavenly and earthly powers, good or bad. In Paul's remarkable concluding lines, he sweeps across the entire imagined universe, geographical and temporal, seen and unseen, in an attempt to demonstrate the unimaginable power of God's love that surpasses all potential barriers.

GOSPEL   MATTHEW 14:13-21

When Jesus heard of the death of John the Baptist,
    he withdrew in a boat to a deserted place by himself.
The crowds heard of this and followed him on foot from
        their towns.
When he disembarked and saw the vast crowd,
    his heart was moved with pity for them, and he cured their sick.
When it was evening, the disciples approached him and said,
    "This is a deserted place and it is already late;
    dismiss the crowds so that they can go to the villages
    and buy food for themselves."
Jesus said to them, "There is no need for them to go away;
    give them some food yourselves."
But they said to him,
    "Five loaves and two fish are all we have here."
Then he said, "Bring them here to me,"
    and he ordered the crowds to sit down on the grass.
Taking the five loaves and the two fish, and looking up to heaven,
    he said the blessing, broke the loaves,
    and gave them to the disciples,
    who in turn gave them to the crowds.
They all ate and were satisfied,
    and they picked up the fragments left over—
    twelve wicker baskets full.
Those who ate were about five thousand men,
    not counting women and children.

From the parables in chapter 13, we skip over the story of John the Baptist's death (14:1-12) and move to Jesus's feeding of five thousand men. This is the only miracle that is recounted in all four Gospels (Mark 6:30-44; Luke 9:12-17; John 6:1-15), though Matthew increases the magnitude of those fed by adding the final phrase "not counting women and children." This is the first of two scenes in Matthew's Gospel in which a compassionate Jesus addresses the crowds' physical hunger; the second is in 15:32-39, where Jesus feeds four thousand men (again, besides the women and children). Our reading begins with Jesus disappearing to a deserted place (which he will do again in next week's Gospel), likely to mourn the loss of John the Baptist. Yet he does not remain in isolation for long; instead, he is soon "moved with pity" or "compassion" (Greek *splanchnizomai*) for the crowds. The disciples suggest, quite practically, that he send the crowds away so they might get something to eat. Instead, Jesus insists that the disciples take responsibility for the crowds' hunger. When he says the blessing, breaks the bread, and gives it to the disciples to distribute, the description carries liturgical undertones, anticipating the institution of the Lord's Supper (26:26-29). The miracle also draws from stories in the Hebrew Bible, including the prophetic tales of Elijah and Elisha (see 1 Kgs 17:8-16; 2 Kgs 4:42-44). If we take the account literally, the five loaves and two fish would not be enough to feed even Jesus and the disciples. Yet the numbers five and two are chosen purposefully; they add up to seven, a spiritual number and a symbol of wholeness. The "twelve wicker baskets" of fragments symbolize the twelve tribes of Israel.

Ponder

Suffering and compassion go hand in hand in our readings. Often, the focus is human suffering and God's compassionate love. In Isaiah, God calls a suffering people to satiate themselves at a lavish feast of God's compassion and love. God's compassion is echoed in the psalmist's cries, while Paul claims powerfully that *nothing* separates us from God's love, least of all present sufferings. While in Isaiah God satisfies a deep, metaphoric hunger, in the Gospel the compassionate Jesus satisfies the people's literal hunger. Jesus also demonstrates that compassion and suffering are two integral parts of the human experience. Suffering invites us to lean inward on God, and it can also soften us, leading to greater compassion for others. In the Gospel, compassion emerges as Jesus is grieving, pulling him out of solitude. What is your own experience of suffering like? Does it turn you inward to solitary spaces or outward toward the pain of others?

Our consumerist culture teaches us to acquire and hold tightly, to reach always for the next thing, to pursue what, according to Isaiah, "fails to satisfy." Yet the principle of Christian social doctrine is not to hold tightly but to let go, remembering that the world's goods are meant for all. As Pope John Paul II once said, the gospel's social message is not a "theory" but "a basis and a motivation for action."[1] Jesus's feeding reminds us of this motivation. He forces his disciples to redirect their attention not to what they lack but to what they have, to give rather than to hold, and the result is divine abundance and satisfaction. Imagine Jesus turning to you and saying, "Give them some food yourselves." How do you respond?

1. Pope John Paul II, *Centesimus Annus*, 57.

Nineteenth Sunday in Ordinary Time

FIRST READING   1 KINGS 19:9a, 11-13a

At the mountain of God, Horeb,
    Elijah came to a cave where he took shelter.
Then the LORD said to him,
    "Go outside and stand on the mountain before the LORD;
    the LORD will be passing by."
A strong and heavy wind was rending the mountains
    and crushing rocks before the LORD—
    but the LORD was not in the wind.
After the wind there was an earthquake—
    but the LORD was not in the earthquake.
After the earthquake there was fire—
    but the LORD was not in the fire.
After the fire there was a tiny whispering sound.[1]
When he heard this,
    Elijah hid his face in his cloak
    and went and stood at the entrance of the cave.

First and Second Kings detail the reigns of the kings of Israel and Judah until the two kingdoms fall to Assyria (720 BCE) and Babylon (586 BCE). In the midst of 1 Kings, we find the great prophet Elijah (1 Kgs 17:1–2 Kgs 2:12). Elijah lived during the reign of King Ahab in the north, who married Jezebel and began to promote worship of the Canaanite storm god Baal. Elijah's ministry focused on eradicating Baal worship and promoting devotion to the God of Israel. In 1 Kings 19, Elijah flees from Jezebel, who is trying to kill him. He ends up in the wilderness, where he despairs of his life, is sustained by an angel or divine messenger, then journeys to Mount Horeb (another word for Sinai, the same mountain where God appeared to Moses and the Israelites). We miss key verses around and within the above reading in which God asks Elijah twice, "Why are you here, Elijah?" (vv. 9b, 13b). Elijah responds that he has done everything in

---

1. Literally "a voice of thin silence." This is often translated as "a still, small voice."

his power to serve God, yet the situation seems hopeless in the face of great political corruption (v. 10). God then appears to Elijah in a way that is mysterious and ungraspable, in "a voice of thin silence." The text is also a reminder that God alone controls the natural elements, not Baal (the storm god who would manifest in heavy winds and earthquakes and fires). God then speaks to Elijah mysteriously and intimately, encouraging and sustaining him. Elijah returns to Israel and anoints Elisha as prophet to succeed him.

RESPONSORIAL PSALM   PSALM 85:9, 10, 11-12, 13-14

Lord, let us see your kindness, and grant us your salvation.

SECOND READING   ROMANS 9:1-5

Brothers and sisters:
I speak the truth in Christ, I do not lie;
    my conscience joins with the Holy Spirit in bearing me witness
    that I have great sorrow and constant anguish in my heart.
For I could wish that I myself were accursed and cut off
        from Christ
    for the sake of my own people,
    my kindred according to the flesh.
They are Israelites;
    theirs the adoption, the glory, the covenants,
    the giving of the law, the worship, and the promises;
    theirs the patriarchs, and from them,
    according to the flesh, is the Christ,
    who is over all, God blessed forever. Amen.

In Romans 9–11, Paul addresses the relationship between Judaism and Christ's plan of salvation. His overarching argument is that the failure of some Jews to believe in Christ is part of God's plan to include the Gentiles in Christ's saving message (11:11-12), yet God's promises to Israel remain firm (see 9:6; 11:1). Paul speaks personally to his own people—Jews or "Israelites," the name given to them by God. He states that all the privileges connected with being part of

Israel remain firm: Israel's "adoption" (literally "sonship") as children of God prior to the Gentiles, God's presence or "glory" residing with them in the desert and in the Jerusalem temple, the covenant at Sinai, the law or expression of God's Word given to Moses, the worship of God in the temple, the promises made to the patriarchs and to David, and the ancestral heritage. He concludes with Christ, the Jewish Messiah ("Christ" is the Greek translation of "messiah" or "anointed one" in Hebrew) and true descendant of his people. The final phrase ("Christ, who is over all, God blessed forever") could also translate as "Christ [Messiah], who is God over all, blessed forever." The sentence structure is unclear, but Paul appears to be attributing the title of "God" to Jesus.

GOSPEL   MATTHEW 14:22-33

After he had fed the people, Jesus made the disciples get into
    a boat
  and precede him to the other side,
  while he dismissed the crowds.
After doing so, he went up on the mountain by himself to pray.
When it was evening he was there alone.
Meanwhile the boat, already a few miles offshore,
  was being tossed about by the waves, for the wind was
      against it.
During the fourth watch of the night,
  he came toward them walking on the sea.
When the disciples saw him walking on the sea they were
    terrified.
"It is a ghost," they said, and they cried out in fear.
At once Jesus spoke to them, "Take courage, it is I; do not
  be afraid."
Peter said to him in reply,
  "Lord, if it is you, command me to come to you on the water."
He said, "Come."
Peter got out of the boat and began to walk on the water
    toward Jesus.

But when he saw how strong the wind was he became
   frightened;
   and, beginning to sink, he cried out, "Lord, save me!"
Immediately Jesus stretched out his hand and caught Peter,
   and said to him, "O you of little faith, why did you doubt?"
After they got into the boat, the wind died down.
Those who were in the boat did him homage, saying,
   "Truly, you are the Son of God."

After the feeding of the people, Jesus goes off to pray, the second time in Matthew that he prays alone. The disciples remain in the boat, likely exhausted and afraid—it has been a very full day, and they are soon caught up in a gale. Jesus returns only during the "fourth watch of the night" or early morning, between 3 and 6 a.m. Jesus's power to walk on water means that he, like God, has the power to control the seas (e.g., Gen 1:9-10; Exod 14:21-22). When Jesus says, "[I]t is I," the literal translation is "I AM," which is a reference to the divine name (see Exod 3:14). This is the only Gospel in which Peter walks on water, which perhaps underscores Peter's role as representative of all the disciples. As Peter begins to walk on the water, he enters into the mystery of the reality of who Jesus is. Understandably, he becomes afraid of the large, powerful waves and loses his focus on Jesus. He has faith, yet he has not yet learned perseverance. Some scholars suggest that the story of Jesus walking on water originally takes place after his resurrection. In this case, the disciples represent the early church—which remains connected to Jesus even when he seems far away—and the boat symbolizes the faith journey.

Ponder

On the mountaintop, God asks Elijah twice, "[W]hy are you here?" (vv. 9b, 13b). In this profound question, God invites Elijah to take inventory of his life and its meaning. Why has Elijah sought God out in this silent space? What does Elijah want? Like Elijah, we are invited to choose spaces of silence where we find our own still centers and where we hear God speaking to us. In the quiet, still voice of God within us, we will hear the deepest truths that remind us of what is right, of what matters, and of how we are called. Hearing God speak lifts Elijah out of despair. As you pray with our readings and find the still space, how do you respond to God's question: *Why are you here?*

In our readings, God is both everywhere and in the places we least expect. In 1 Kings, God comes to Elijah not in powerful natural elements but in a "tiny whispering sound." In Matthew, Jesus invites Peter to focus not on the overwhelming gale but on him—a human person standing in the midst of the waves. Invoking imagery from the natural world, our texts push us to look for, listen to, and remain focused on God in the midst of the chaos and overwhelming forces in our own lives. They also remind us that God is present when we are afraid and falter. As you pray with the readings, where is God for you? How are you being called to "take courage" and "not be afraid"?

Twentieth Sunday in Ordinary Time

FIRST READING   ISAIAH 56:1, 6-7

Thus says the LORD:
Observe what is right, do what is just;
   for my salvation is about to come,
   my justice, about to be revealed.

The foreigners who join themselves to the LORD,
   ministering to him,
loving the name of the LORD,
   and becoming his servants—
all who keep the sabbath free from profanation
   and hold to my covenant,
them I will bring to my holy mountain
   and make joyful in my house of prayer;
their burnt offerings and sacrifices
   will be acceptable on my altar,
for my house shall be called
   a house of prayer for all peoples.

Remember that the long prophetic book of Isaiah was written in stages (see notes on Isaiah from the First Sunday of Advent). Our reading marks the beginning of the third section of Isaiah ("Third Isaiah"), which is characterized by the inclusion of all people into the covenant between God and Israel. These "foreigners who join themselves to the LORD" are those who have converted to Judaism and adhere to the Torah laws. In verse 1, one's ability to "[o]bserve what is right" and "do what is just" is based on the laws and covenant. These converts will have access to Jerusalem ("my holy mountain") and the temple, which will be an inclusive "house of prayer" for all those who guard God's commandments.

RESPONSORIAL PSALM   PSALM 67:2-3, 5, 6, 8

O God, let all the nations praise you!

SECOND READING   ROMANS 11:13-15, 29-32

Brothers and sisters:
I am speaking to you Gentiles.
Inasmuch as I am the apostle to the Gentiles,
    I glory in my ministry in order to make my race jealous
    and thus save some of them.
For if their rejection is the reconciliation of the world,
    what will their acceptance be but life from the dead?

For the gifts and the call of God are irrevocable.
Just as you once disobeyed God
    but have now received mercy because of their disobedience,
    so they have now disobeyed in order that,
    by virtue of the mercy shown to you,
    they too may now receive mercy.
For God delivered all to disobedience,
    that he might have mercy upon all.

Our reading draws from Paul's climactic conclusion to chapters 9–11 (11:13-36), which reveals the core purpose of his letter to the Roman Gentile community. Paul explains that while his ministry is to Gentile believers in Christ, his underlying hope and belief is that his "race" (literally his "flesh"; Greek *sarx*), meaning Jews, will come to believe in Christ as their Messiah. Their rejection of Christ was for the sake of the Gentiles (see vv. 11-12) and allowed for the inclusion of non-Jews and hence the "reconciliation" or salvation of the whole world. Yet Paul believes that this rejection is only temporary, for the election of the Jews is "irrevocable" (v. 29). Gentile converts are, therefore, not to be arrogant because they have been "grafted in" to the tree of God's covenant while the Jews have been "broken off" (v. 17); instead, they are to "stand in awe" (v. 20). As Paul powerfully states, God's call and gifts to the Jewish people are irrevocable, and ultimately, it is all part of God's plan to make some "disobedient" (i.e., not believing in Christ) for the longer-term purpose of showing mercy to all, Jews and Gentiles alike.

GOSPEL   MATTHEW 15:21-28

At that time, Jesus withdrew to the region of Tyre and Sidon.
And behold, a Canaanite woman of that district came and
    called out,
  "Have pity on me, Lord, Son of David!
My daughter is tormented by a demon."
But Jesus did not say a word in answer to her.
Jesus' disciples came and asked him,
  "Send her away, for she keeps calling out after us."
He said in reply,
  "I was sent only to the lost sheep of the house of Israel."
But the woman came and did Jesus homage, saying, "Lord,
    help me."
He said in reply,
  "It is not right to take the food of the children
  and throw it to the dogs."
She said, "Please, Lord, for even the dogs eat the scraps
  that fall from the table of their masters."
Then Jesus said to her in reply,
  "O woman, great is your faith!
Let it be done for you as you wish."
And the woman's daughter was healed from that hour.

Our passage depicts one of the more difficult encounters in the Gospels: that between Jesus and a woman from Tyre (see also Mark 7:24-30). In this story, Jesus travels north for reasons the text does not explain, crossing the boundary between Israel into Tyre and Sidon (contemporary Lebanon). There, he encounters an unnamed Canaanite woman ("Canaanite" is a code word for "other" in the Hebrew Bible, hearkening back to the original inhabitants of the land of Israel or Canaan, who were not the Israelite people). His exchange with this woman disorients our understanding of Jesus. She seems to become the teacher, he the student. The woman recognizes Jesus as the Jewish Messiah, or "Son of David," and cries out to Jesus as "Lord." Trusting that he can heal her child, she asks him to have "pity" (or mercy) on her. At first, he does not respond. When she continues to cry out, he calls her a "dog" and states that his mission is to feed the children of Israel. She responds in a way that both recognizes the priority of Israel yet also contends that his mercy can reach all: "even the dogs eat the scraps that fall from the table of their masters." Jesus then acknowledges that her great faith has collapsed boundaries and impelled the healing of her child.

Ponder

In God's kingdom, "election" does not mean the inclusion of some to the exclusion of others. Isaiah demonstrates how God's covenant extends beyond Israel to invite all "foreigners" (non-Jews) to "join themselves" to God. In Paul's letter to the Romans, insiders and outsiders flip, and it is non-Jewish believers who must come to terms with God's irrevocable love for the Jews. In recent history, had the world's Christians taken seriously Paul's unequivocal assertion that "the gifts and the call of God are irrevocable," six million Jews would not have died in the Holocaust. As you pray with these readings, how does this message of inclusivity challenge you, especially with those you consider to be on the "outside" (whether politically, socially, religiously, etc.)?

We often fixate on Jesus's name-calling in this Gospel story, yet the true focus of the passage is the woman: her agency as well as her remarkable expression of faith. If Jesus reminds her of a holy boundary between Israel and outsiders, she tears it down and impels his mercy. When we read this passage, we may relate to the woman, whose role we take on regularly when we say *"Kyrie eleison"* ("Lord, have mercy") in our liturgies. Or maybe we relate to the insiders—Israel or even Jesus—whose ideas of who is "in" seem to be constantly evolving. The human inclination to exclude is as natural as it is boring. What is exciting is the ability to push the boundaries, as the woman does, and to push ourselves beyond the boundaries, as Jesus does, because when human action cooperates with and even compels the divine, the result is a mercy that is truly stunning.

Twenty-First Sunday in Ordinary Time

FIRST READING   ISAIAH 22:19-23

Thus says the LORD to Shebna, master of the palace:
"I will thrust you from your office
 and pull you down from your station.
On that day I will summon my servant
 Eliakim, son of Hilkiah;
I will clothe him with your robe,
 and gird him with your sash,
 and give over to him your authority.
He shall be a father to the inhabitants of Jerusalem,
 and to the house of Judah.
I will place the key of the House of David on Eliakim's shoulder;
 when he opens, no one shall shut;
 when he shuts, no one shall open.
I will fix him like a peg in a sure spot,
 to be a place of honor for his family."

Our reading comes from a long oracle (prophecy) in Isaiah 22 that describes Judah's destruction during the Assyrian siege of the late eighth century BCE. According to Isaiah 36–37, the Assyrians eventually withdrew after God defeated their army, yet Assyrian records suggest a more likely historical scenario: the siege ended when King Hezekiah surrendered to the larger and more powerful foreign army (ca. 701 BCE). Jerusalem was spared, but the land of Judah was left devastated. At the very end of the oracle, Isaiah condemns Shebna, a key administrative official of Hezekiah's royal household. Apparently, Shebna had presumptuously built himself a tomb in Jerusalem, thus attempting to elevate himself in importance despite the fact that his ancestors were not buried there (see vv. 15-16). Isaiah prophesies that God will throw him from his office and replace him with Eliakim, who in Isaiah 36:3 is referred to as "the master of the palace" with Shebna as his "scribe." In the end, however, Eliakim, too, will fall (see 22:25).

RESPONSORIAL PSALM   PSALM 138:1-2, 2-3, 6, 8

Lord, your love is eternal; do not forsake the work of your hands.

SECOND READING   ROMANS 11:33-36

Oh, the depth of the riches and wisdom and knowledge of God!
How inscrutable are his judgments and how unsearchable
    his ways!
  For who has known the mind of the Lord
  or who has been his counselor?
  Or who has given the Lord anything
    that he may be repaid?
For from him and through him and for him are all things.
To him be glory forever. Amen.

Picking up from last Sunday's reading, we reach the climax of Paul's discussion in chapters 9–11 (for further context, see last Sunday's notes). Paul concludes his statements on God's plan for the election and inclusion of all—Jews first and then Gentiles—with this remarkable final acclamation and blessing. Quoting from Isaiah 40:13 ("For who has known the mind of the Lord . . .") and Job 35:7 ("Or who has given the Lord anything . . ."), Paul points to the awesome mystery of the divine plan. In an eschatological sense, human beings have no way of understanding this ultimate plan and how "all things" will be drawn back to the divine source to give glory and honor to God.

GOSPEL   MATTHEW 16:13-20

Jesus went into the region of Caesarea Philippi and
    he asked his disciples,
  "Who do people say that the Son of Man is?"
They replied, "Some say John the Baptist, others Elijah,
    still others Jeremiah or one of the prophets."
He said to them, "But who do you say that I am?"
Simon Peter said in reply,
  "You are the Christ, the Son of the living God."

Jesus said to him in reply,
  "Blessed are you, Simon son of Jonah.
For flesh and blood has not revealed this to you, but my heavenly
    Father.
And so I say to you, you are Peter,
  and upon this rock I will build my church,
  and the gates of the netherworld shall not prevail against it.
I will give you the keys to the kingdom of heaven.
Whatever you bind on earth shall be bound in heaven;
  and whatever you loose on earth shall be loosed in heaven."
Then he strictly ordered his disciples
  to tell no one that he was the Christ.

The setting is Caesarea Philippi, a space of Roman imperial power twenty-five miles north of the Sea of Galilee. Our passage subverts this symbol of Roman power through Jesus's prophecy of the church's ultimate authority. Similar accounts of Peter's confession can be found in Mark 8:27-30 and Luke 9:18-21, though only Matthew includes the subsequent promise to Peter. When Jesus asks the disciples who the crowds say he is, their responses draw from the Hebrew Bible and reflect different Jewish messianic expectations of the first century CE. Jesus refers to himself as "the Son of Man" elsewhere in Matthew's Gospel (see 8:20), a phrase that comes from Daniel 7:13-14. Certain circles believed John the Baptist was the messiah, while others believed that one of Israel's great prophets (such as Elijah or Jeremiah) would return to signal the messianic age. "Christ" is the Greek translation of the Hebrew "messiah," which literally means "God's anointed one." Only in Matthew does Peter call Jesus "Son of the living God" as part of his divinely inspired understanding of Jesus's identity. In Jesus's response, he refers to Simon Peter as "son of Jonah," perhaps remarking on Simon's headstrong ways (see the book of Jonah, about a prophet who sometimes resists God but is ultimately faithful to God's call). Jesus's nickname for Simon was "Peter," which comes from the terms *kepha* (Aramaic) or *petros* (Greek) meaning "rock" or "stone." The only occurrences of the term "church" (Greek *ekklēsia*) in the Gospels are here and in Matthew 18:17 (see the Twenty-Third Sunday in Ordinary Time). The netherworld is literally "Hades" in Greek (Hebrew *sheol*), which is the underworld or realm of the dead for all people. The term "gates of the netherworld" refers to power over death, and Peter's "keys" demonstrate Peter's power and authority (see Isa 22:22). The terms "bind" and "loose" are linked to legal expressions that mean "forbid" and "permit."

Ponder

"I will summon my servant," states God in Isaiah. God summons each one of us to be humble servants. Like Eliakim in Isaiah and Peter in the Gospel, each of us symbolically holds the keys or the responsibility to serve the vision of God's kingdom. In Isaiah, Eliakim becomes the highest official in the Jerusalem palace after the previous official loses the position out of arrogance. Peter's responsibility—and the church's—transcends physical space, reaching to the underworld and the heavens. While Peter has come to symbolize papal authority, each one of us bears the responsibility to serve God's kingdom. Imagine Jesus summoning you and giving you the "keys to the kingdom of heaven." What does this mean to you?

"How inscrutable are his judgments and how unsearchable his ways!" cries Paul. We have been walking through Paul's theological discussion of election, of who is "in" and who is outside of God's salvation. This final acclamation stands as an important juxtaposition to God's granting of authority to human servants in Isaiah and, especially, the Gospel. In contrast, Romans reminds us that no human mind understands God, that God's ways are not our own, and that there is nothing we can do to repay God for the gift of grace. Our job is to praise God, to give God honor and glory, and to remember that God's desire is that "all things" be drawn back to God and into the kingdom of heaven.

Twenty-Second Sunday
in Ordinary Time

FIRST READING   JEREMIAH 20:7-9

You duped me, O LORD, and I let myself be duped;
    you were too strong for me, and you triumphed.
All the day I am an object of laughter;
    everyone mocks me.

Whenever I speak, I must cry out,
    violence and outrage is my message;
the word of the LORD has brought me
    derision and reproach all the day.

I say to myself, I will not mention him,
    I will speak in his name no more.
But then it becomes like fire burning in my heart,
    imprisoned in my bones;
I grow weary holding it in, I cannot endure it.

For further background on Jeremiah, see the Twelfth Sunday in
Ordinary Time, where we read the verses that follow this text (vv.
10-13). Perhaps more than any other biblical prophet, Jeremiah provides his readers with deep insight into the suffering and pain that
can come with being called into a prophetic role by God. In the case
of Jeremiah, such a role led to profound social ostracization and
physical danger, though he had no choice but to follow God's will. A
prophet during Judah's golden age (late 600s BCE), Jeremiah preached
the unpopular message of God's judgment and Jerusalem's impending destruction at the hands of Babylon (ca. 586 BCE). In chapter 20,
the prophet comes into conflict with the priest Pashhur, who hears
Jeremiah's prophecies against the monarchy and has Jeremiah put
in the stocks overnight. After Jeremiah is released the next day, he
issues a long, despairing lament, from which our reading draws. The
language used to describe Jeremiah's relationship with God in these
verses is shocking and vivid. The word "duped" translates literally

as "enticed" (Hebrew *pātâ*) and often denotes deception (e.g., 2 Sam 3:25; Ps 78:36) and seduction (e.g., Exod 22:15; Judg 14:15). The expression "too strong" (more literally, "overpowered"; Hebrew *ḥāzaq*) suggests that God has physically, literally overpowered the prophet. Jeremiah has no choice but to prophesy, for God's words are "like fire" that burns inside of him.

RESPONSORIAL PSALM   PSALM 63:2, 3-4, 5-6, 8-9

My soul is thirsting for you, O Lord my God.

SECOND READING   ROMANS 12:1-2

I urge you, brothers and sisters, by the mercies of God,
    to offer your bodies as a living sacrifice,
    holy and pleasing to God, your spiritual worship.
Do not conform yourselves to this age
    but be transformed by the renewal of your mind,
    that you may discern what is the will of God,
    what is good and pleasing and perfect.

The final section of Paul's letter to the Romans is a call to holy living that extends from chapters 12 through 15. Having formed the basis of his argument on God's salvation in chapters 9–11, he urges the community to faith-filled action as a form of living sacrifice and worship. Through baptism, believers are able to discern God's will and act in accordance with that will. Paul calls them to conform themselves, not to this "age" or world but according to "what is good and pleasing and perfect" to God.

GOSPEL   MATTHEW 16:21-27

Jesus began to show his disciples
    that he must go to Jerusalem and suffer greatly
    from the elders, the chief priests, and the scribes,
    and be killed and on the third day be raised.
Then Peter took Jesus aside and began to rebuke him,
    "God forbid, Lord! No such thing shall ever happen to you."

He turned and said to Peter,
"Get behind me, Satan! You are an obstacle to me.
You are thinking not as God does, but as human beings do."

Then Jesus said to his disciples,
"Whoever wishes to come after me must deny himself,
take up his cross, and follow me.
For whoever wishes to save his life will lose it,
but whoever loses his life for my sake will find it.
What profit would there be for one to gain the whole world
and forfeit his life?
Or what can one give in exchange for his life?
For the Son of Man will come with his angels in his Father's glory,
and then he will repay all according to his conduct."

We now come to this striking exchange and the first prediction of
Jesus's passion directly following Peter's confession last week (see also
Mark 8:31-38; Luke 9:22-27). Peter refuses to accept Jesus's words,
and Jesus responds to him as he responds to the devil in Matthew
4:10, calling Peter an obstacle and an enemy to God's plan. It seems
that, for Peter, it is easier to receive the revelation of Jesus as Messiah
(last week's reading) than the revelation that Jesus must suffer and
die (note that Jesus also predicted his resurrection, but Peter makes
no mention of this). It is hard to blame Peter, though, for the notion
that the coming messiah must suffer and die was a foreign concept
to early Jewish understanding. Jesus then explains the condition for
true discipleship: the willingness to follow Jesus to the point of giving
up one's life. The idea of "denying" oneself connects with statements
elsewhere in the Gospel regarding "denying" Jesus (Matt 10:33; 26:34-
35). One chooses either one path or the other. To deny oneself is to
recognize that the "self" is not the center of one's existence. Instead,
one's true identity and life is found in Jesus. Paul describes the rich
reality of denying one's individual, self-centered existence when he
states, "I live, no longer I, but Christ lives in me" (Gal 2:20). Jesus's
statement in this Gospel also presents a paradox: to hold tightly to
something risks losing it, while letting it go ultimately preserves it.

Ponder

Jeremiah and the psalmist describe their relationships with God using intimate, personal language. For Jeremiah, God "entices" and "overpowers" him, terms that elsewhere in the Bible have sexual undertones. He cries out that God's word is "like fire burning in my heart." Paradoxically, in the responsorial psalm, God is not fire but water for which the psalmist "thirsts" as if he or she were a "parched" and "lifeless" earth. As you pray with these readings, how does this imagery strike you? How do you relate to this language of desire for and intimacy with God?

There is some tension between our first reading and the Gospel. In the book of Jeremiah, we witness a deep interior conflict between the prophet's desires and the divine will. Jeremiah essentially has no choice but to carry out God's will. In the Gospel, Jesus's call to deny oneself is about choice. Moreover, denial of self is not about taking on unnecessary suffering that degrades the dignity of the human person (like staying in an abusive relationship) but about reorienting one's mind and heart. According to our reading from Romans, self-denial means being "transformed by the renewal of [the] mind" to discern God's will. To deny oneself is to take on an expansive identity rooted not in the narrowness of our own minds but in God's love, "to lose oneself entirely in Christ."[1] Think back over the last few days. When have you been invited to turn toward Jesus as the center of your existence at the cost of some other drive or desire you may have had? What did you do with that invitation?

1. Reid, *Abiding Word*, 99.

Twenty-Third Sunday
in Ordinary Time

FIRST READING   EZEKIEL 33:7-9

Thus says the LORD:
   You, son of man, I have appointed watchman for the house
      of Israel;
   when you hear me say anything, you shall warn them for me.
If I tell the wicked, "O wicked one, you shall surely die,"
   and you do not speak out to dissuade the wicked from his way,
   the wicked shall die for his guilt,
   but I will hold you responsible for his death.
But if you warn the wicked,
   trying to turn him from his way,
   and he refuses to turn from his way,
   he shall die for his guilt,
   but you shall save yourself.

For background on the book of Ezekiel, see the Fifth Sunday of Lent. The setting of chapter 33 is Babylon after the exile from Judah (ca. 586 BCE). The central theological question here is the relationship between communal or intergenerational punishment for sins (in other words, the idea that the next generation must pay for the sins of the preceding one) and individual moral autonomy. In context, the above passage stresses that the individual does not need to suffer for communal sins but has the right and the ability to repent and thus live (see v. 11). Toward this aim, God has appointed Ezekiel as a metaphoric watchman or sentinel for the people. The job of the watchman was to stand watch outside a city in case of enemy advance, alerting the people of any impending threat. If the watchman sounded the alarm (normally a horn) and the people did not listen, their blood was on their own hands, yet if the watchman did not do his job and alert the people, he was to blame if anything happened to them. Our reading draws an analogy between the watchman and Ezekiel, who has been similarly commissioned (see 3:16-21). Ultimately, it is the people's responsibility to listen to Ezekiel and turn back to God. Yet if Ezekiel does not do his job and prophesy God's words of judgment honestly, then he will be held responsible for the people's sins.

RESPONSORIAL PSALM   PSALM 95:1-2, 6-7, 8-9

If today you hear his voice, harden not your hearts.

SECOND READING   ROMANS 13:8-10

Brothers and sisters:
Owe nothing to anyone, except to love one another;
    for the one who loves another has fulfilled the law.
The commandments, "You shall not commit adultery;
    you shall not kill; you shall not steal; you shall not covet,"
    and whatever other commandment there may be,
    are summed up in this saying, namely,
    "You shall love your neighbor as yourself."
Love does no evil to the neighbor;
    hence, love is the fulfillment of the law.

A key component of Paul's call to holy living is love, which is the essential character of Christian life and the most "excellent" spiritual gift (see 1 Cor 12:31–13:13). Preceding our reading (13:1-7), Paul exhorts the community to pay to all what is owed to them (taxes to whom taxes are due, respect to whom respect is due, etc.). The community will then owe each other only love (Greek *agapaō*). Citing Exodus 20:13-17 and Deuteronomy 5:17-21, Paul describes all of the commandments as "fulfilled" or carried out in an ideal manner (Greek *plēroō*, which indicates completeness or perfection) by the commandment to love one another (see also Lev 19:18; Gal 5:14; Jas 2:8). Jesus, however, sums up the commandments into two in Matthew 22:34-40 (see also Mark 12:28-34): the "greatest and the first" is to love God with "all your heart, with all your soul, and with all your mind" (see Deut 6:5), and the second is to "love your neighbor as yourself" (see Lev 19:18).

GOSPEL   MATTHEW 18:15-20

Jesus said to his disciples:
   "If your brother sins against you,
   go and tell him his fault between you and him alone.
If he listens to you, you have won over your brother.
If he does not listen,
      take one or two others along with you,
      so that 'every fact may be established
      on the testimony of two or three witnesses.'
If he refuses to listen to them, tell the church.
If he refuses to listen even to the church,
      then treat him as you would a Gentile or a tax collector.
Amen, I say to you,
      whatever you bind on earth shall be bound in heaven,
      and whatever you loose on earth shall be loosed in heaven.
Again, amen, I say to you,
      if two of you agree on earth
      about anything for which they are to pray,
      it shall be granted to them by my heavenly Father.
For where two or three are gathered together in my name,
      there am I in the midst of them."

We last encountered the legal terminology of "binding" and "loosing" (synonymous with "forbidding" and "permitting") on the Twenty-First Sunday in Ordinary Time (Matt 16:13-20). There, Jesus granted the authority to "bind" and "loose" to Peter; here, he grants it to the whole church. Our passage takes place within a long discourse on church relationships and is one of only two attestations of the word "church" (*ekklēsia*) in the Gospels (see also Matt 16:18). The parable of the lost sheep, in which a shepherd goes to the extreme of leaving ninety-nine sheep in search of one that is lost, precedes our reading (vv. 10-14). The parable underscores God's desire that each individual "sheep" be saved and leads directly into this reading, which describes a similar care in reconciling individual community members who have erred. Community members are to do everything possible to bring such a person back to the community skillfully and lovingly. The first step is private discussion so as not to shame the person publicly. If this doesn't work, the second step is correction before two or three witnesses (see Deut 17:6-7; 19:15). If this doesn't work, the issue is brought before the church or community. If this still doesn't work, the "sinner" is to be treated as a "Gentile" or a "tax collector," meaning one who is in particular need of evangelization. The ultimate goal is to draw that person back into right relationship with God and community, as we will see in next week's reading. The final statements remind us of the power and importance of communal prayer and recall important Jewish teachings: "When two or three sit together and words of Torah pass between them, the *Shekinah* [Divine Presence] rests between them" (*Avot* 3:2 in the Mishnah), and "When three sit as judges, the *Shekinah* is with them" (*Berachot* 6a in the Talmud).

Ponder

Sin ruptures our relationships with God and community. Jesus demonstrates the relentless pursuit of reconciliation to heal these ruptures. In Jewish tradition, if a person sins against you, your primary concern should be their repentance so as to mend their relationship with God. You must therefore seek reconciliation tirelessly—not for you or your own woundedness but in order to help the offending party repent and return to God and community. Our Gospel depicts this tradition through the specific steps a community is to take in order to seek reconciliation at all costs. We live in a society where intervention is undervalued and where the notion of "not judging" can become a slippery slope to apathy and the passive allowance of the other's ruin. Our readings this week therefore call us to deep self-reflection. When is judgment appropriate and helpful? How relentlessly do we pursue reconciliation, reparations, and right relationships for the sake of the other?

Ezekiel's watchman metaphor recalls Cain's question to God in Genesis 4:9: "Am I my brother's keeper?" The answer, of course, is yes. We are all responsible for each other. One person's separation from God and community hurts the whole. This is where Paul's call in Romans becomes a linchpin: "You shall love your neighbor as yourself." We can only act as true "watchmen," with care and responsibility toward each other, if we *love* each person as we love ourselves (and vice versa: we can only love each other if we have a healthy sense of self-love and dignity). Right relationships and skillful intervention happen in the context of love. Our readings challenge us to consider whether we are being called to reach out or intervene honestly and lovingly to someone who has gone astray, and whether that person might even be ourselves.

Twenty-Fourth Sunday in Ordinary Time

Wrath and anger are hateful things,
  yet the sinner hugs them tight.
The vengeful will suffer the LORD's vengeance,
  for he remembers their sins in detail.
Forgive your neighbor's injustice;
  then when you pray, your own sins will be forgiven.
Could anyone nourish anger against another
  and expect healing from the LORD?
Could anyone refuse mercy to another like himself,
  can he seek pardon for his own sins?
If one who is but flesh cherishes wrath,
  who will forgive his sins?
Remember your last days, set enmity aside;
  remember death and decay, and cease from sin!
Think of the commandments, hate not your neighbor;
  remember the Most High's covenant, and overlook faults.

We last encountered Sirach on the Sixth Sunday in Ordinary Time. The above collection of sayings focuses on the nature of divine forgiveness. According to Ben Sira (the author), absolution from sins can be earned through pious acts, including honoring one's parents (3:3-4), almsgiving (3:30), and forgiving others (28:2). One of Ben Sira's core beliefs is that God's judgments are just, which helps us to understand God's "vengeance" or God's "remembering," or, according to another translation, God's "keep[ing] a strict account" of a person's sins (NRSV). In other words, divine "vengeance" is not about the desire for revenge but about acting as a mirror for us to see and account for our actions. Ben Sira understands the human condition in exhorting readers to rid themselves of anger and the desire for vengeance, to let go of grudges, and to remember that the ultimate goal is to love one's neighbor as one's very self. Ben Sira also appeals to the inevitability of death as the ultimate motivator to "cease from sin" (meaning to forgive and be reconciled with one's neighbor).

RESPONSORIAL PSALM   PSALM 103:1-2, 3-4, 9-10, 11-12

The Lord is kind and merciful, slow to anger, and rich in
   compassion.

SECOND READING   ROMANS 14:7-9

Brothers and sisters:
None of us lives for oneself, and no one dies for oneself.
For if we live, we live for the Lord,
   and if we die, we die for the Lord;
   so then, whether we live or die, we are the Lord's.
For this is why Christ died and came to life,
   that he might be Lord of both the dead and the living.

This is our final week reading from Romans. Our text draws from a broader discussion on welcoming rather than judging other members of the community in terms of their personal decisions regarding practices of the law. Remember that Paul's letter reflects ongoing tension between Jewish and Gentile believers. Speaking directly to this tension, Paul encourages the community to allow one another to continue to practice Jewish law as each member deems necessary, without judgment and without putting a "stumbling block" in each other's way (see v. 13). The notion of living and dying for Christ reorients one's perspective to place Christ at the center of one's life rather than one's selfish needs or judgments regarding proper religious practices. As in our reading from Sirach, death is the ultimate motivator and wake-up call to right living now. In the verses that follow our reading, Paul exhorts the community not to judge or look down on each other, for "we shall all stand before the judgment seat of God" (v. 10).

Peter approached Jesus and asked him,
  "Lord, if my brother sins against me,
  how often must I forgive?
As many as seven times?"
Jesus answered, "I say to you, not seven times but seventy-seven
    times.
That is why the kingdom of heaven may be likened to a king
  who decided to settle accounts with his servants.
When he began the accounting,
  a debtor was brought before him who owed him a huge
    amount.
Since he had no way of paying it back,
  his master ordered him to be sold,
  along with his wife, his children, and all his property,
  in payment of the debt.
At that, the servant fell down, did him homage, and said,
  'Be patient with me, and I will pay you back in full.'
Moved with compassion the master of that servant
  let him go and forgave him the loan.
When that servant had left, he found one of his fellow servants
  who owed him a much smaller amount.
He seized him and started to choke him, demanding,
  'Pay back what you owe.'
Falling to his knees, his fellow servant begged him,
  'Be patient with me, and I will pay you back.'
But he refused.
Instead, he had the fellow servant put in prison
  until he paid back the debt.
Now when his fellow servants saw what had happened,
  they were deeply disturbed, and went to their master
  and reported the whole affair.
His master summoned him and said to him, 'You wicked servant!
I forgave you your entire debt because you begged me to.
Should you not have had pity on your fellow servant,
  as I had pity on you?'

Then in anger his master handed him over to the torturers
   until he should pay back the whole debt.
So will my heavenly Father do to you,
   unless each of you forgives your brother from your heart."

Last week's discussion on reconciliation continues with a discourse on forgiveness. Our reading describes a capacity for forgiveness that should be limitless. The "seventy-seven times" reverses a depiction of "seventy-seven times," or radical vengeance, in Genesis 4:24 to an equally radical notion of forgiveness. The parable of the unforgiving servant then shifts the discussion slightly to describe the insignificance of human forgiveness relative to God's forgiveness. The servant's promise to pay his master back "in full" is an empty promise, given the ridiculous enormity of the debt: a "huge amount" translates literally as "ten thousand talents" (more than the tribute that Galilee paid to Rome over a fifteen-year period), which would equate to billions of dollars by today's standards. Astonishingly, the master forgives the debt (or "loan") in full. When that servant then demands that a fellow servant pay him back in full, the difference between the two debts is absurd: a "much smaller amount" translates literally as "one hundred denarii" (a denarius was equivalent to a laborer's daily wage). This is not an insignificant amount by human standards (roughly three month's pay), yet it is paltry relative to what the "master" forgives, which is an amount beyond human comprehension. The master hands the unforgiving servant over to torturers, calling him to account for his sins (note the parallel with Sirach). We imagine the punishment will be limitless, for the debt is unpayable. Our own capacity to forgive (which ultimately means to seek reconciliation) should therefore be limitless, for it is insignificant relative to God's forgiveness of us.

Ponder

God's mercy is extravagant and inconceivable by human standards. Both the Gospel and today's psalm underscore this reality. The psalmist describes the greatness of God's mercy using natural imagery, and the Gospel parable depicts the forgiveness of an absurdly high debt to describe God's immeasurable love for us. According to Paul, as people of faith, our call is to live according to God's immeasurable love and grace, placing these gifts at the center of our lives so as to give everything we have—our lives and even our deaths—back to God. This week, our readings invite us to meditate on God's grace and capacity for forgiveness and to pray that our hearts might be broken open to understand this great and unearned gift. Only then will we begin to comprehend—truly—what human forgiveness is about.

According to Sirach and the Gospel, if we do not forgive, God will not forgive us. Why? Because to forgive is to mend relationships, and we cannot be in right relationship with God and with each other when we are broken as a community. God is our exemplar for the process of forgiveness in the Bible, constantly forgiving and reconciling Israel. God always forgives, restores, and heals those who desire it. In the command to forgive "seventy-seven times," we are commanded to follow this same path of forgiveness *always*. Our world is in such need of healing—in our distorted relationships, our deep societal fractures, our wounded earth. Forgiveness is our ultimate act of defiance in the face of disharmony that seems insurmountable, our ultimate challenge to evil, our ultimate act of love. May we all seek to follow this path, which heals all of us and draws us back to God.

Twenty-Fifth Sunday
in Ordinary Time

FIRST READING   ISAIAH 55:6-9

Seek the LORD while he may be found,
  call him while he is near.
Let the scoundrel forsake his way,
  and the wicked his thoughts;
let him turn to the LORD for mercy;
  to our God, who is generous in forgiving.
For my thoughts are not your thoughts,
  nor are your ways my ways, says the LORD.
As high as the heavens are above the earth,
  so high are my ways above your ways
  and my thoughts above your thoughts.

Our reading is part of a broader invitation in Isaiah to seek God (55:1-13). For further notes on this section of Isaiah 55, see the Fifteenth Sunday in Ordinary Time (where we read 55:10-11) and the Eighteenth Sunday in Ordinary Time (where we read 55:1-3). The above verses emphasize the "scoundrel" and the "wicked" as a rhetorical device to motivate the audience to cling to God. The phrase "let him turn to the LORD" also translates as "let him turn back to the LORD," from the Hebrew *šûb* ("turn" or "return"). The notion of turning and returning to God is the deepest meaning of repentance. In the wake of the Babylonian exile and the context of Persian rule in the late sixth century BCE, our passage reveals a theological concern with the meaning of suffering in the context of Israel's restoration and covenant with God. According to Isaiah, suffering is but a small part of God's ultimate plan for Israel's redemption. Humans cannot fully understand this plan, as articulated in the final lines that describe God's "thoughts" and "ways" as beyond human comprehension.

RESPONSORIAL PSALM   PSALM 145:2-3, 8-9, 17-18

The Lord is near to all who call upon him.

SECOND READING   PHILIPPIANS 1:20c-24, 27a

Brothers and sisters:
Christ will be magnified in my body, whether by life or by death.
For to me life is Christ, and death is gain.
If I go on living in the flesh,
    that means fruitful labor for me.
And I do not know which I shall choose.
I am caught between the two.
I long to depart this life and be with Christ,
    for that is far better.
Yet that I remain in the flesh
    is more necessary for your benefit.

Only, conduct yourselves in a way worthy of the gospel of Christ.

This Sunday, we begin reading Paul's letter to the Philippians. Paul may have written this letter while under house arrest in Rome (61–63 CE), though the date and setting are inconclusive. Concerned with the threat of fractures in the community, Paul calls the Philippians to unity throughout his letter. Our reading begins after Paul's opening words of greeting and thanksgiving (1:1-11). He reflects on his own death and the uncertainty that comes from being in prison. Weighing the possibilities of living versus dying, Paul seems to have no real attachment to either option. His only focus is Christ. For Paul, life and death belong to Christ. The point of staying alive is to continue to pour himself out for the gospel, though he also longs to depart this world to be united with Christ. In the meantime, Paul states that no matter the outcome, his life in this world (his "body" and "flesh") will be spent in service to Christ.

GOSPEL   MATTHEW 20:1-16a

Jesus told his disciples this parable:
"The kingdom of heaven is like a landowner
who went out at dawn to hire laborers for his vineyard.
After agreeing with them for the usual daily wage,
he sent them into his vineyard.
Going out about nine o'clock,
the landowner saw others standing idle in the marketplace,
and he said to them, 'You too go into my vineyard,
and I will give you what is just.'
So they went off.
And he went out again around noon,
and around three o'clock, and did likewise.
Going out about five o'clock,
the landowner found others standing around, and said to them,
'Why do you stand here idle all day?'
They answered, 'Because no one has hired us.'
He said to them, 'You too go into my vineyard.'
When it was evening the owner of the vineyard said to his
    foreman,
'Summon the laborers and give them their pay,
beginning with the last and ending with the first.'
When those who had started about five o'clock came,
each received the usual daily wage.
So when the first came, they thought that they would receive
    more,
but each of them also got the usual wage.
And on receiving it they grumbled against the landowner, saying,
'These last ones worked only one hour,
and you have made them equal to us,
who bore the day's burden and the heat.'
He said to one of them in reply,
'My friend, I am not cheating you.
Did you not agree with me for the usual daily wage?
Take what is yours and go.
What if I wish to give this last one the same as you?
Or am I not free to do as I wish with my own money?
Are you envious because I am generous?'
Thus, the last will be first, and the first will be last."

This parable is unique to Matthew's Gospel. Immediately before it, Peter asks Jesus what the disciples will get for leaving everything in order to follow him (19:27-30). Shortly after it, the sons of Zebedee request positions of honor in the kingdom (to the indignation of the other disciples; 20:20-28). For Jesus's disciples, the kingdom of heaven seems to be a competition for the best seats. Our reading flips this perspective on its head, stressing instead that "the last will be first, and the first will be last" in a repeated statement that frames the reading (19:30; 20:16). Matthew's original audience was a Jewish-Christian community struggling with who should be included in the new community of faith. In this context, the parable speaks to the ongoing debate about admitting Gentiles into the community. It suggests that Gentiles are on equal standing with Jewish believers, despite their late inclusion in the covenant. The landowner's generosity in the parable is also a striking contrast to the harsh condition of hired labor in the first-century Roman world. In another sense, the parable also compares the first disciples to those who come after, especially Matthew's audience (remember that Matthew's Gospel is written long after Jesus's death, sometime after 70 CE). The parable assures this later audience that God's kingdom is not the special property of the first disciples. Whenever someone is admitted, that person is admitted to full participation. In this sense, the parable speaks to us as much later disciples. The final question of the landowner (God) is particularly powerful, translated above as "Are you envious because I am generous?" The literal translation is "Is your eye evil [Greek *ponēros*] because I am good [Greek *agathos*]?"

Ponder

Speaking into the hardships and disparities of our world, our readings stress God's justice and mercy. Isaiah promises that God is in control, bending the arc of history toward justice and salvation, beyond what we can see and understand. In this sense, God's ways and thoughts are a mystery. Despite (or because of) this mystery, the prophet calls us to trust and seek God, turning and returning constantly for forgiveness and healing. Our psalm affirms this message in stating that God is near to all who call. God acts with justice, goodness, and mercy for all of us who wait diligently and act faithfully. The promise in these readings—that God is acting in and through our world in ways beyond our comprehension—can be a comfort, a challenge, or even a dare. Within the context of your life right now, how do our readings speak to you?

Our Gospel parable affirms that God is good and generous toward all people. This truth should be a great relief and cause for rejoicing, yet the competitive side of human nature does not always see it this way. We want things to be "fair" and "earned," yet God's ways and thoughts do not function according to human standards (thank God!). As the Gospel tells us, if we seek God honestly and attentively—whether we are the laborers diligently working all day or the laborers diligently waiting all day—we will receive everything God has, a full day's wages. To understand the power of this parable means seeing things from God's perspective and from the perspective of the underdog. As we pray with our readings, what does God's universal goodness, God's indiscriminate justice, God's extravagant mercy, truly mean to us—personally and socially?

Twenty-Sixth Sunday
in Ordinary Time

FIRST READING   EZEKIEL 18:25-28

Thus says the LORD:
You say, "The LORD's way is not fair!"[1]
Hear now, house of Israel:
  Is it my way that is unfair, or rather, are not your ways unfair?
When someone virtuous turns away[2] from virtue to commit
    iniquity, and dies,
  it is because of the iniquity he committed that he must die.
But if he turns from the wickedness he has committed,
  and does what is right and just,
  he shall preserve his life;[3]
  since he has turned away from all the sins that he has
    committed,
  he shall surely live, he shall not die.

For contextual notes on the book of Ezekiel, see the Fifth Sunday
of Lent. The setting for our reading is Babylon during Judah's exile
from Israel (sixth century BCE). The above verses are the final lines
of a long discussion in Ezekiel 18 about personal responsibility for
sins. Ezekiel counters the common, preexilic belief in corporate
responsibility for sins (in other words, a child is responsible for the
sins of a parent and vice versa; similarly, the next generation atones
for the sins of the previous). Ezekiel and other exilic prophets offer
a new perspective to a people who are suffering: every individual
has agency over their own moral life and relationship with God (see

---

1. "Fair" (Hebrew *tākan*) means something measured, regulated, or adjusted to
the standard.
2. "Turns away" (Hebrew *šûb*) means to turn back or return (see notes on Isaiah
from the Twenty-Fifth Sunday in Ordinary Time). When this "turning" is a "return"
to God, it signifies repentance.
3. "Life" (Hebrew *nepeš*) means "life force" or, according to later understanding,
"soul."

also Jer 31:29-30). Ezekiel therefore stresses individual responsibility for one's present circumstances and future. The objection in the first verse demonstrates a fundamental misconception of God, who is by nature fair and thus incapable of acting otherwise.

RESPONSORIAL PSALM   PSALM 25:4-5, 6-7, 8-9

Remember your mercies, O Lord.

SECOND READING   PHILIPPIANS 2:1-11 [OR 2:1-5]

Brothers and sisters:
If there is any encouragement in Christ,
    any solace in love,
    any participation in the Spirit,
    any compassion and mercy,
    complete my joy by being of the same mind, with the same
        love,
    united in heart, thinking one thing.
Do nothing out of selfishness or out of vainglory;
    rather, humbly regard others as more important than
        yourselves,
    each looking out not for his own interests,
    but also for those of others.

Have in you the same attitude
    that is also in Christ Jesus,
    Who, though he was in the form of God,
        did not regard equality with God
        something to be grasped.
    Rather, he emptied himself,
        taking the form of a slave,
        coming in human likeness;
        and found human in appearance,
        he humbled himself,
        becoming obedient to the point of death,
        even death on a cross.

Because of this, God greatly exalted him
    and bestowed on him the name
    which is above every name,
    that at the name of Jesus
    every knee should bend,
    of those in heaven and on earth and under the earth,
    and every tongue confess that
    Jesus Christ is Lord,
    to the glory of God the Father.

The broader context for our reading is Paul's appeal to Christian unity that extends from 1:27 to 4:1. Within this appeal, Paul exhorts the community at Philippi to develop such traits as steadfastness (1:27-30), harmony (2:1-2), humility (2:3-11), obedience, and selflessness (2:12-18). This reading begins with a description of unity and humility and continues with an ancient hymn to Christ. For context on the hymn ("Who, though he was in the form of God . . ."; vv. 6-11), see the notes for the second reading on Palm Sunday.

GOSPEL   MATTHEW 21:28-32

Jesus said to the chief priests and elders of the people:
    "What is your opinion?
A man had two sons.
He came to the first and said,
    'Son, go out and work in the vineyard today.'
He said in reply, 'I will not,'
    but afterwards changed his mind[4] and went.
The man came to the other son and gave the same order.
He said in reply, 'Yes, sir,' but did not go.
Which of the two did his father's will?"
They answered, "The first."
Jesus said to them, "Amen, I say to you,
    tax collectors and prostitutes
    are entering the kingdom of God before you.

---

4. "Changed his mind" (Greek *metamelomai*) means "to feel regret" or "to repent."

When John came to you in the way of righteousness,
   you did not believe him;
   but tax collectors and prostitutes did.
Yet even when you saw that,
   you did not later change your minds and believe him."

During the next few weeks, we read successive Gospel parables in which Jesus speaks to and condemns religious leaders in the Jerusalem temple. This first parable begins after these leaders try to trap Jesus with the questions: "By what authority are you doing these things? And who gave you this authority?" (v. 23). Rather than answering, Jesus turns the following questions back on them: "Where was John's baptism from? Was it of heavenly or of human origin?" (v. 25). The authorities refuse to answer, so Jesus also refuses to answer. Instead, he tells them this parable, which is unique to Matthew. The "tax collectors and prostitutes" represent those judged to have the lowest morals in Jewish society. In the parable, the first son represents all those who repent honestly and sincerely, while the second son represents those whose lives are marked by lies and hypocrisy. The parable stresses that the ultimate test of obedience or faith is action (not words). John's "way" or "road" of righteousness means that he pointed the way toward righteousness.

Ponder

"Is it my way that is unfair, or rather, are not your ways unfair?" Last Sunday, Matthew's parable exposed the human desire for "fairness" (people should be paid according to how long they work). This week, Ezekiel describes "fairness" in terms of moral accumulation of virtue and sin. To the human mind, it's not fair that God would suddenly forgive and liberate a person from their sins or the communal sins they carry. Similarly, it's not fair that God would suddenly condemn someone who has built up cachet by living a model life or by coming from a respectable family. Ezekiel turns the tables on these false ideas of fairness to discomfort the self-righteous and to comfort the afflicted. On the path of faith, no person is ahead, and no person is behind. Each day we begin again. This message should both comfort and discomfort all of us.

Paul urges us to strive to be like Christ, our model of humility who "emptied himself" of his status of divinity out of love for us, a broken and undeserving people. To follow Christ, there is no room for human vanity or self-righteousness. Yet our Gospel parable (directed at religious leaders and authority figures) points out the paradox: in trying to live a virtuous life, in trying to follow Christ, it is so easy to fall into self-righteousness and erroneous ideas about spiritual hierarchy, about who is a "better" or more virtuous person. As you examine your own life, where do you see this temptation to self-righteousness?

Twenty-Seventh Sunday in Ordinary Time

FIRST READING   ISAIAH 5:1-7

Let me now sing of my friend,
    my friend's song concerning his vineyard.
My friend had a vineyard
    on a fertile hillside;
he spaded it, cleared it of stones,
    and planted the choicest vines;
within it he built a watchtower,
    and hewed out a wine press.
Then he looked for the crop of grapes,
    but what it yielded was wild grapes.

Now, inhabitants of Jerusalem and people of Judah,
    judge between me and my vineyard:
What more was there to do for my vineyard
    that I had not done?
Why, when I looked for the crop of grapes,
    did it bring forth wild grapes?
Now, I will let you know
    what I mean to do with my vineyard:
take away its hedge, give it to grazing,
    break through its wall, let it be trampled!
Yes, I will make it a ruin:
    it shall not be pruned or hoed,
    but overgrown with thorns and briers;
I will command the clouds
    not to send rain upon it.
The vineyard of the Lord of hosts is the house of Israel,
    and the people of Judah are his cherished plant;
he looked for judgment, but see, bloodshed!
    for justice, but hark, the outcry!

For introductory notes on Isaiah, see the First Sunday of Advent. In the above allegory, the narrator (Isaiah) portrays God as his "friend" (or, literally, his "beloved"; Hebrew *yādîd*) and a vineyard owner. This friend worked carefully and lovingly to build a productive vineyard, only to be deeply disappointed when it yielded only wild (literally "stinky") grapes that were unfit for eating. Written in the latter half of the eighth century BCE, the allegory targets Judeans, many of whom had an extensive understanding of vineyards because of ancient Judah's climate. Partway through the allegory, the voice shifts from Isaiah to God, and at the end of the allegory, God turns to accuse the audience of being the unproductive vineyard. The final verses play on words in the Hebrew: God looked for "judgment" or justice (*mišpāṭ*) but found only "bloodshed" (*mišpāḥ*); for "justice" or righteousness (*ṣĕdāqâ*) but encountered only an "outcry" (*ṣĕʿāqâ*). These final phrases reveal the underlying concern of the parable as social injustice and misconduct. God accuses Judah, the "choicest vines," of failing to produce fruit or a just society and instead cultivating social inequity.

RESPONSORIAL PSALM   PSALM 80:9, 12, 13-14, 15-16, 19-20

The vineyard of the Lord is the house of Israel.

SECOND READING   PHILIPPIANS 4:6-9

Brothers and sisters:
Have no anxiety at all, but in everything,
  by prayer and petition, with thanksgiving,
  make your requests known to God.
Then the peace of God that surpasses all understanding
  will guard your hearts and minds in Christ Jesus.

Finally, brothers and sisters,
  whatever is true, whatever is honorable,[1]
  whatever is just, whatever is pure,
  whatever is lovely,[2] whatever is gracious,
  if there is any excellence

---

1. "Honorable" (Greek *semnós*) also translates as "holy" or "revered."
2. "Lovely" (Greek *prosphilēs*) translates literally as "dear" or "beloved."

and if there is anything worthy of praise,
    think about[3] these things.
Keep on doing what you have learned and received
    and heard and seen in me.
Then the God of peace will be with you.

At the conclusion of his letter (which we will finish reading next week), Paul issues final appeals to the community to stand firm in the teachings he has passed on to them. He urges them to continue to cultivate inner traits that are the mark of a believer in Christ. In doing so, Paul relies on terminology that comes from Greco-Roman Stoic principles ("true," "honorable," "just," etc.) and reorients these principles toward a Christ-centered outlook on life.

GOSPEL   MATTHEW 21:33-43

Jesus said to the chief priests and the elders of the people:
    "Hear another parable.
There was a landowner who planted a vineyard,
    put a hedge around it, dug a wine press in it, and built a tower.
Then he leased it to tenants and went on a journey.
When vintage time drew near,
    he sent his servants to the tenants to obtain his produce.
But the tenants seized the servants and one they beat,
    another they killed, and a third they stoned.
Again he sent other servants, more numerous than the first ones,
    but they treated them in the same way.
Finally, he sent his son to them, thinking,
    'They will respect my son.'
But when the tenants saw the son, they said to one another,
    'This is the heir.
Come, let us kill him and acquire his inheritance.'
They seized him, threw him out of the vineyard, and killed him.
What will the owner of the vineyard do to those tenants when he
        comes?"

---

3. To "think about" can also mean "calculate" and indicates intentional, careful thinking.

They answered him,
  "He will put those wretched men to a wretched death
  and lease his vineyard to other tenants
  who will give him the produce at the proper times."
Jesus said to them, "Did you never read in the Scriptures:
  The stone that the builders rejected
    has become the cornerstone;
  by the Lord has this been done,
    and it is wonderful in our eyes?
Therefore, I say to you,
  the kingdom of God will be taken away from you
  and given to a people that will produce its fruit."

This is the second of three successive parables that Jesus tells to the religious authorities in the Jerusalem temple (we will read the third next week). It is also the third week in a row that we have read vineyard parables. Clearly, the ancient world was familiar with vineyards! Our parable reflects deep knowledge of Isaiah 5:1-7 (our first reading), in which the vineyard represents Israel. Yet this vineyard could also represent the kingdom of God. The first tenants are the religious authorities to whom Jesus is directing his teachings in the temple, and the servants are Israel's prophets. The son is the messiah. The tenants throw him out of the vineyard to kill him, perhaps alluding to Jesus's crucifixion outside Jerusalem (crucifixions occurred outside of city walls). The quote from Scripture is Psalm 118:22-23. The "people that will produce its fruit" in the last line are faithful followers of Jesus, both Jews and Gentiles. In some sense, the parable is a continuation from last week's parable of the two sons, in which the son who ends up doing the father's will is not the one first expected. Similarly, in this parable, the true servants of God are not the ones first expected (religious leaders and authority figures).

Ponder

In Isaiah, the owner (God) of the vineyard (Israel) works hard to cultivate good grapes yet finally destroys the vineyard. But this is not the end of the story. At the end of Isaiah, God finally restores the vineyard (see Isa 66). Our psalmist trusts that God will eventually "take care of this vine" and "give us new life" so that "we shall be saved." Throughout the Hebrew Bible, God is tenacious and faithful to Israel while also showing a particular concern for the least among us. This is the tension in the vineyard allegory. As God's beloved people, we are called to be God's hands and feet, to "cultivate good grapes," or care for the least among us. And yet, no matter how often we fail or cultivate "wild grapes," God will call us back for another chance. The question is how we respond to God's invitation and whether we are as tenacious and faithful as God in trying again.

None of us owns the vineyard. Sadly, our Gospel parable has often been used to preach and perpetuate supersessionist ideas (i.e., Jews were the original tenants and Christians the new tenants). These ideas are dangerous and demonstrate a fundamental misunderstanding of the parable, which was directed to early communities of believers involved in inner-Jewish debates (think of similar debates about "who's in" and "who's out" happening among Christians today). Like other Gospel readings in recent weeks, this parable targets religious hypocrisy, greed, and self-righteousness. In the final lines, Jesus draws the parable back to Isaiah's vineyard and the concern that those who are entrusted with God's kingdom should care for it faithfully. They must "produce its fruit," or they will lose access to the vineyard. It is so easy to think we have special privileges, that the vineyard belongs to us, yet when we think and act this way, we risk losing it all.

Twenty-Eighth Sunday
in Ordinary Time

FIRST READING   ISAIAH 25:6-10a

On this mountain the LORD of hosts
   will provide for all peoples
a feast of rich food and choice wines,
   juicy, rich food and pure, choice wines.
On this mountain he will destroy
   the veil that veils all peoples,
the web that is woven over all nations;
   he will destroy death forever.
The Lord GOD will wipe away
   the tears from every face;
the reproach of his people he will remove
   from the whole earth; for the LORD has spoken.
   On that day it will be said:
"Behold our God, to whom we looked to save us!
   This is the LORD for whom we looked;
   let us rejoice and be glad that he has saved us!"
For the hand of the LORD will rest on this mountain.

Our reading comes from a long prophecy (often called "the Isaiah apocalypse") that proclaims Zion's restoration and exaltation as God's Holy City (24:1–27:13). The above verses imagine the exaltation of Jerusalem (Zion) as God's holy mountain after God removes the "reproach" of Judah, meaning the humiliation and suffering the people experienced in exile. At this point, all the nations will gather to worship the God of Israel as if coming to a banquet. Feasting calls to mind right worship, for in the Jerusalem temple, sacrificial offerings were understood to be meals or feasts shared between the people and God. Imagery of the richest, choicest foods and drinks describes this feast of pure abundance. The tone is joyful: God has defeated evil (the Babylonian Empire), destroyed death (the "veil" worn in times of mourning), and erased the people's delusions that prevented them from believing in the God of Israel (the "web that is woven over all nations"). Our reading imagines a new world order in which the survivors of all the nations will have intimate access to God from Zion.

RESPONSORIAL PSALM   PSALM 23:1-3a, 3b-4, 5, 6

I shall live in the house of the Lord all the days of my life.

SECOND READING   PHILIPPIANS 4:12-14, 19-20

Brothers and sisters:
I know how to live in humble circumstances;
    I know also how to live with abundance.
In every circumstance and in all things
    I have learned the secret of being well fed and of going hungry,
    of living in abundance and of being in need.
I can do all things in him who strengthens me.
Still, it was kind of you to share in my distress.[1]

My God will fully supply whatever you need,
    in accord with his glorious riches in Christ Jesus.
To our God and Father, glory forever and ever. Amen.

This week, we read the conclusion of Paul's letter to the Philippians. Paul's final words convey the Greco-Roman philosophy of Stoicism or indifference to changing external circumstances. For Paul, this indifference comes specifically through belief in Christ, through whom God grants him and all believers "glorious riches" that reach far deeper than the fleeting vicissitudes of this life. Simultaneously, Paul thanks the community for their monetary support. Though Paul does not need or seek this support (the mark of true discipleship), he is nonetheless appreciative of their aid.

---

1. "Distress" (Greek *thlipsis*) refers to tribulations, trials, or distressing circumstances. See also notes on Romans from the Eighteenth Sunday in Ordinary Time.

GOSPEL   MATTHEW 22:1-14 [OR 22:1-10]

Jesus again in reply spoke to the chief priests and elders of the
    people
    in parables, saying,
    "The kingdom of heaven may be likened to a king
    who gave a wedding feast for his son.
He dispatched his servants
    to summon the invited guests to the feast,
    but they refused to come.
A second time he sent other servants, saying,
    'Tell those invited: "Behold, I have prepared my banquet,
    my calves and fattened cattle are killed,
    and everything is ready; come to the feast." '
Some ignored the invitation and went away,
    one to his farm, another to his business.
The rest laid hold of his servants,
    mistreated them, and killed them.
The king was enraged and sent his troops,
    destroyed those murderers, and burned their city.
Then he said to his servants, 'The feast is ready,
    but those who were invited were not worthy to come.
Go out, therefore, into the main roads
    and invite to the feast whomever you find.'
The servants went out into the streets
    and gathered all they found, bad and good alike,[2]
    and the hall was filled with guests.
But when the king came in to meet the guests,
    he saw a man there not dressed in a wedding garment.
The king said to him, 'My friend, how is it
    that you came in here without a wedding garment?'
But he was reduced to silence.
Then the king said to his attendants, 'Bind his hands and feet,
    and cast him into the darkness outside,
    where there will be wailing and grinding of teeth.'
Many are invited, but few are chosen."

---

2. This reference to the "bad and good alike" contrasts with Luke's account of the
feast, in which those who are called are the beggars, the destitute, the blind, and the
lame (see Luke 14:15-24).

The parable of the wedding banquet is the last of three consecutive parables spoken to religious leaders in the temple. Similar to last Sunday's parable, two groups of servants are sent out, the servants are murdered, the murderers are punished, and the invitation to the wedding feast (the kingdom of heaven) goes out to an entirely new group of people. The parable is meant to shock its audience, for who would refuse an invitation to a lavish feast from their king (God)? Some are distracted by worldly responsibilities, while others are openly hostile to the invitation and murder the king's messengers. Underlying the parable are historical circumstances, for the king's reaction—kill the murderers and burn their city—recalls the destruction of Jerusalem by the Romans in 70 CE. These harsh details are missing from Luke's version of the parable (14:15-24), as are the final verses, when the king comes to meet the guests who are finally gathered, "bad and good alike" (vv. 11-14). This secondary parable warns that one needs to be dressed appropriately, or prepared, when one accepts the invitation. We might view the wedding garment as a symbol of righteousness, preparation, or purity of heart and mind that the man lacked. Others propose that the man signifies someone who apostatizes or rejects God's message.

Ponder

God's abundance is there for us, beckoning to us. Isaiah captures this abundance in the imagery of a rich feast, which our psalm describes as an inner banquet of richness laid out before us each day of our lives. For Catholics, in a tangible way this banquet is the Eucharist. Yet it is also Christ present every moment within and around us, supplying us with "glorious riches," according to Paul, no matter the external circumstances. As you pray with these texts, imagine this banquet. Imagine what it feels like to be there. Imagine what the meal looks and tastes like. According to our Scriptures, this banquet is not merely imagined. It is real, both as a future promise and a present reality within you.

Over the last few weeks, our Gospel parables have tried to probe or even reverse our expectations of who ends up in God's kingdom. The question is not so much who is invited (everyone) but rather who responds. Ultimately, to be chosen by God is an invitation to choose God. This emphasis on choice is subtly distinct from Isaiah's message, in which God physically removes that which prevents people from choosing the God of Israel (the "web that is woven over all nations"). In the Gospel, the banquet is there for all of us, and the question is whether we choose to say "yes" to it each moment of our lives. There is also another, second layer to this message. Coming to the banquet fully prepared is not quite enough. Once there, we are again called to extend ourselves to invite others. Hopefully we do so with open minds and hearts, proclaiming that God's doors are open and welcoming for everyone.

Twenty-Ninth Sunday
in Ordinary Time

FIRST READING   ISAIAH 45:1, 4-6

Thus says the LORD to his anointed, Cyrus,
   whose right hand I grasp,[1]
subduing nations before him,
   and making kings run in his service,
opening doors before him
   and leaving the gates unbarred:
For the sake of Jacob, my servant,
   of Israel, my chosen one,
I have called you by your name,
   giving you a title, though you knew me not.
I am the LORD and there is no other,
   there is no God besides me.
It is I who arm you, though you know me not,
   so that toward the rising and the setting of the sun
   people may know that there is none besides me.
I am the LORD, there is no other.

Our reading comes from the second major division in the book of
Isaiah ("Second Isaiah"), written toward the end of the Babylonian
exile in the second half of the sixth century BCE. In it, God (through
the prophet) announces a plan to use King Cyrus of Persia as a tool
to bring about Judah's return to Israel. God will commission the
Persian king (the king of the most powerful empire in the known
world) to act as God's "anointed one" or, literally, "messiah" (Hebrew *māšîaḥ*) in restoring Judah. Historically, after the fall of the
Babylonian Empire and the rise of the Persians, Cyrus did allow the
Judeans to return home from Babylon and even helped them rebuild
Jerusalem. Yet Isaiah's reference to Cyrus as a "messiah" is a remarkable expression given that King Cyrus did not believe in Israel's God.

---

1. In the ancient Middle East, the king was perceived to be chosen by his god and
was given authority to rule by "grasping" the hand of his god.

This passage therefore makes a powerful theological statement about the one God, Israel's God, whose power extends throughout the entire universe and even manipulates the most powerful of kings, all for the sake of God's beloved Israel. Yet also note how this reading juxtaposes the greatness and expansiveness of God with an intimate love for Israel as God's "chosen one."

RESPONSORIAL PSALM   PSALM 96:1, 3, 4-5, 7-8, 9-10

Give the Lord glory and honor.

SECOND READING   1 THESSALONIANS 1:1-5b

Paul, Silvanus, and Timothy to the church of the Thessalonians
    in God the Father and the Lord Jesus Christ:
    grace to you and peace.
We give thanks to God always for all of you,
    remembering you in our prayers,
    unceasingly calling to mind your work of faith and labor of love
    and endurance in hope of our Lord Jesus Christ,
    before our God and Father,
    knowing, brothers and sisters loved by God,
    how you were chosen.
For our gospel did not come to you in word alone,
    but also in power and in the Holy Spirit and with much
        conviction.

For the next month, we'll be journeying through Paul's first letter to the Thessalonians, which is widely regarded as his earliest existing letter. The letter conveys Paul's affection for the community and is unlike other Pauline letters in the sense that his primary goal is encouragement rather than the correction of behavior or rebuke of bad teaching. In the opening verses, Paul greets the community using the classic style of Greek letters. He first lists the writers of the letter and its recipients, then expresses his thanks for the community's response to the gospel even in the midst of difficulties. The "church" (Greek *ekklēsia*) refers to an assembly or gathering of people (a community), not to a building. The terms "faith," "hope," and "love" are consistently important to Paul (see also 1 Cor 13:13; 1 Thess 5:8).

GOSPEL   MATTHEW 22:15-21

The Pharisees went off
   and plotted how they might entrap Jesus in speech.
They sent their disciples to him, with the Herodians, saying,
   "Teacher, we know that you are a truthful man
   and that you teach the way of God in accordance with
      the truth.
And you are not concerned with anyone's opinion,
   for you do not regard a person's status.
Tell us, then, what is your opinion:
   Is it lawful to pay the census tax to Caesar or not?"
Knowing their malice, Jesus said,
   "Why are you testing me, you hypocrites?
Show me the coin that pays the census tax."
Then they handed him the Roman coin.
He said to them, "Whose image is this and whose inscription?"
They replied, "Caesar's."
At that he said to them,
   "Then repay to Caesar what belongs to Caesar
   and to God what belongs to God."

Picking up from the conclusion of last week's Gospel, Jesus is asked a question that puts him in the middle of a charged debate. The "census tax" was a tax of one denarius (one day's pay) that was imposed on all adults living in Judea and was to be paid in Roman coins. These coins were stamped with an image of the emperor and attributed to the emperor political and divine power. The Herodians were Jewish supporters of this tax; they gained power through loyalty to Rome. The Zealots resisted the tax to the point of armed rebellions, the last of which brought about the destruction of the temple in 70 CE. The Pharisees held the same position as the Zealots, but they did not believe in the use of force to achieve independence. This is, therefore, a debate that Jesus will lose no matter how he responds; he will be pegged either as a Jewish revolutionary or as a Roman sympathizer.

Yet instead of answering the question, Jesus reframes it and rises above it. He draws attention to the hypocrisy of those who question him by asking them to pull out a denarius. Unlike today, very few had access to these coins—they were minted solely by the Romans and were issued carefully with the authority of the Roman government. His final, famous line takes no position on politics, nor does it touch upon Caesar's right to rule. It simply acknowledges that the coin is in the "image" of Caesar, belonging to Caesar. It is Caesar's right to demand it. He leaves it up to the audience (including us) to discern for ourselves the appropriate relationship between politics and religion, the things of this world and the things of God. His response is so remarkable that the people leave "amazed" (v. 22).

Ponder

As Christians, we are called to active political and social engagement, yet the danger is becoming overly caught up in the systems of this world. In our reading from Isaiah, the long-oppressed Judeans see in King Cyrus a savior figure. Isaiah and our psalmist remind their audiences of the right orientation: God is the one true savior. In a slightly different fashion, Jesus tells his interlocutors to give politics the attention it deserves and to give God the attention God deserves. Do not mistake one for the other. Our readings invite us to reflect on this delicate balance and the notion that, ultimately, for people of faith, there is no such thing as divided attention: the focus that we give to the things of this world should always be grounded in and fully attentive to God.

Power corrupts. Honesty and integrity are hard to maintain in positions of power, as highlighted by Jesus's interaction in the Gospel. Those who ask him an impossible question are unconcerned with the truth; they seek only to entrap him. There is nothing Jesus can say that will be "correct" in that setting. If Jesus were a contemporary politician, he would perhaps pivot or try to appease the people in the room by stretching the truth. Yet Jesus seeks truth, not victory. As Paul says in our second reading, his message is grounded not in the power of this world but "in power and in the Holy Spirit and with much conviction." His answer is one that invites the audience to introspection. How does Jesus's response speak to you and challenge you today?

Thirtieth Sunday in Ordinary Time

FIRST READING   EXODUS 22:20-26

Thus says the LORD:
"You shall not molest or oppress an alien,
   for you were once aliens yourselves in the land of Egypt.
You shall not wrong any widow or orphan.
If ever you wrong them and they cry out to me,
   I will surely hear their cry.
My wrath will flare up, and I will kill you with the sword;
    then your own wives will be widows, and your children
       orphans.

"If you lend money to one of your poor neighbors among my
    people,
   you shall not act like an extortioner toward him
   by demanding interest from him.
If you take your neighbor's cloak as a pledge,
   you shall return it to him before sunset;
    for this cloak of his is the only covering he has for his body.
What else has he to sleep in?
If he cries out to me, I will hear him; for I am compassionate."

In the book of Exodus, God claims the Israelites as a treasured possession. The people are therefore to be holy, for God is holy, which they achieve by following a code of conduct that binds them irrevocably to God. Our reading draws from the heart of this code, specifically from a series of community regulations on proper care for each other. The first two verses contain three different words in Hebrew for "oppress" or "wrong" (translated above as "molest," "oppress," and "wrong") to underscore the sacred duty of communal care, especially for the most vulnerable. There is also an underlying threat; no matter how much God loves the Israelites, God is fiercely devoted to the poor and vulnerable, including immigrants or "aliens." The people are also told never to lend with interest. If a neighbor ("friend" or "companion") has only a cloak or outer garment to give as a promise to repay a debt, that cloak must be returned at nightfall so that the person has something to sleep in. These codes regarding proper care and concern for each other, particularly the poor and vulnerable, are at the heart of Israelite law. All of the laws are summed up in the expression "I am compassionate." Those who follow the law are expected to imitate divine compassion.

RESPONSORIAL PSALM PSALM 18:2-3, 3-4, 47, 51

I love you, Lord, my strength.

SECOND READING 1 THESSALONIANS 1:5c-10

Brothers and sisters:
You know what sort of people we were among you for your sake.
And you became imitators of us and of the Lord,
    receiving the word in great affliction, with joy from the
        Holy Spirit,
    so that you became a model for all the believers
    in Macedonia and in Achaia.
For from you the word of the Lord has sounded forth
    not only in Macedonia and in Achaia,
    but in every place your faith in God has gone forth,
    so that we have no need to say anything.
For they themselves openly declare about us
    what sort of reception we had among you,
    and how you turned to God from idols
    to serve the living and true God
    and to await his Son from heaven,
    whom he raised from the dead,
    Jesus, who delivers us from the coming wrath.

We continue where we left off last week in our reading of 1 Thessalonians. Most scholars agree that Paul spent a few months in Thessalonica at the beginning of his ministry, and his statement toward the end of the above reading ("how you turned to God from idols") indicates that his preaching during that time was oriented primarily toward a Gentile audience ("idols" means "statues"). According to this letter, these new converts to Christianity appear to be thriving

in faith, hope, and love despite experiencing "affliction" or persecution. The exact cause of this affliction is unknown, yet it has allowed them to become "imitators" of Christ and the apostles through
their faithful perseverance. For Paul, imitation means solidarity in
Christ through the cross. Faithful and joyful even in their suffering,
the community becomes a "model" for all believers throughout the
Roman provinces in Greece (Macedonia and Achaia).

GOSPEL   MATTHEW 22:34-40

> When the Pharisees heard that Jesus had silenced the
>   Sadducees,
>   they gathered together, and one of them,
>   a scholar of the law, tested him by asking,
>   "Teacher, which commandment in the law is the greatest?"
> He said to him,
>   "You shall love the Lord, your God,
>   with all your heart,
>   with all your soul,
>   and with all your mind.
> This is the greatest and the first commandment.
> The second is like it:
>   You shall love your neighbor as yourself.
> The whole law and the prophets depend on these two
>   commandments."

The question of which laws in the Torah (out of 613!) were most
essential to Judaism was pertinent to Matthew's Jewish-Christian
community, as they were grappling with how to balance Jewish law
with belief in Jesus. In this reading, Jesus quotes from two texts
in answering this question: Deuteronomy 6:5 and Leviticus 19:18.
The first is part of the Jewish profession of faith, called the Shema
(Hebrew for "Hear!") because it begins with the expression "Hear,
O Israel! The LORD is our God, the LORD alone!" (Deut 6:4). Many
Jews of Jesus's time considered this to be the greatest law. Jesus then
adds Leviticus 19:18, giving it equal weight to the Shema. This act of
combining two different laws from the Torah was a common practice
among Jewish scholars at the time (a type of textual interpretation

known as *midrash*). In Luke's version of this dialogue (10:25-28), the scholar/lawyer proceeds to ask Jesus who counts as his "neighbor," and Jesus responds with the story of the Good Samaritan. In Mark's version (12:28-34), which was likely the earliest, a scribe (not a lawyer) is curious (not hostile in any way) when he asks Jesus about the greatest commandment, and the text ends with Jesus praising him as being close to the kingdom of heaven. Mark is the only Gospel writer to include the essential beginning of the Shema in Jesus's response ("Hear, O Israel!"), for the ability to love God fully and completely is dependent upon first acknowledging that this is the true and only God.

Ponder

"I love you, Lord!" cries the psalmist. Love binds together the whole person: the heart, the soul, and the mind, according to the Gospel (or the "whole heart," "whole being," and "whole strength," according to Deut 6:5). All laws and skillful actions hinge on a life lived out of love, a love that has its beginning in God. To love God is to actively love what God loves—all of creation. And when we love God's creation, from our neighbors to the earth to ourselves, we are actively loving God. This week, our readings invite us to ponder this dynamic mystery of love that begins with God and returns to God through us.

We are called to imitate God throughout the Bible, to be holy as God is holy (Lev 11:44) and perfect as God is perfect (Matt 5:48). This week, Paul commends the Thessalonians for their imitation of Christ, while our Exodus reading gives concrete examples of how to imitate God's love or compassion in our care for each other, especially the most vulnerable. What does it mean to be an "imitator of God" in your personal and family life, in your local community, or as a church? What concrete actions are our readings asking of you, or of us, today?

Thirty-First Sunday in Ordinary Time

FIRST READING   MALACHI 1:14b–2:2b, 8-10

A great King am I, says the LORD of hosts,
    and my name will be feared among the nations.
And now, O priests, this commandment is for you:
    If you do not listen,
if you do not lay it to heart,
    to give glory to my name, says the LORD of hosts,
I will send a curse upon you
    and of your blessing I will make a curse.
You have turned aside from the way,
    and have caused many to falter by your instruction;
you have made void the covenant of Levi,
    says the LORD of hosts.
I, therefore, have made you contemptible
    and base before all the people,
since you do not keep my ways,
    but show partiality in your decisions.
Have we not all the one father?
    Has not the one God created us?
Why then do we break faith with one another,
    violating the covenant of our fathers?

Malachi (meaning "my messenger") is a postexilic prophetic text that dates close to the time of the dedication of the Second Temple (ca. 515 BCE). Only four chapters long, it concludes the Hebrew Bible in the Christian canon. The book's primary concern is justice and the problem of evil, which is revealed through a series of arguments between God and various second parties. Our reading draws from the first argument, delivered to the priests, concerning hypocrisy in religious leadership. The prophet alludes consistently to themes found elsewhere in the Bible to make his point. For example, "this commandment" is a phrase used throughout Deuteronomy to express God's commandments or Torah (e.g., Deut 27:1). God threatens to transform the blessing that priests normally give to the people into a curse if they fail to honor God and preserve the commandments (see Num 6:23-27). They have "made void" the special covenant that God made with Levi, the religious priestly lineage descended from Aaron (see Deut 33:8-9; Jer 33:21). The postexilic book of Nehemiah provides further context for the above charges, specifically in the rebuke to religious leaders who "defiled the priesthood and the covenant of the priesthood and the Levites" (Neh 13:29).

RESPONSORIAL PSALM   PSALM 131:1, 2, 3

In you, Lord, I have found my peace.

SECOND READING   1 THESSALONIANS 2:7b-9, 13

Brothers and sisters:
We were gentle among you, as a nursing mother cares for her
    children.
With such affection for you, we were determined to share
    with you
  not only the gospel of God, but our very selves as well,
  so dearly beloved had you become to us.
You recall, brothers and sisters, our toil and drudgery.
Working night and day in order not to burden any of you,
  we proclaimed to you the gospel of God.

And for this reason we too give thanks to God unceasingly,
  that, in receiving the word of God from hearing us,
    you received not a human word but, as it truly is, the word
        of God,
    which is now at work in you who believe.

Paul presents a remarkable image of pastoral care in comparing the affection that he and his fellow missionaries have for the community of faith to that of nursing mothers for their children. Paul and his companions love each member of the community of believers at Thessalonica as their "very selves." In the three verses that we skip in our reading (vv. 10-12), Paul uses a second metaphor to describe his encouragement as that of a father who urges his children to live a life worthy of God. As in other letters, Paul also stresses how important it is for the pastoral team to support themselves ("our toil and drudgery") so as not to "burden" or depend upon the community for monetary support.

GOSPEL   MATTHEW 23:1-12

Jesus spoke to the crowds and to his disciples, saying,
    "The scribes and the Pharisees
    have taken their seat on the chair of Moses.
Therefore, do and observe all things whatsoever they tell you,
    but do not follow their example.
For they preach but they do not practice.
They tie up heavy burdens hard to carry
    and lay them on people's shoulders,
    but they will not lift a finger to move them.
All their works are performed to be seen.
They widen their phylacteries and lengthen their tassels.
They love places of honor at banquets, seats of honor in
    synagogues,
    greetings in marketplaces, and the salutation 'Rabbi.'
As for you, do not be called 'Rabbi.'
You have but one teacher, and you are all brothers.
Call no one on earth your father;
    you have but one Father in heaven.
Do not be called 'Master';
    you have but one master, the Christ.
The greatest among you must be your servant.
Whoever exalts himself will be humbled;
    but whoever humbles himself will be exalted."

The Gospel echoes not only our reading from Malachi but also many texts in the Bible that deal with right worship and, especially, religious leadership. Often, Christians have negative associations with "scribes" and "Pharisees" because we lack the broader context. We do not consider that Gospel polemics against religious leadership reflect painful inner-Jewish conflicts (from a time of tension within the Jewish community before Christianity emerged as a distinct religion), or that many great religious leaders of the time were Pharisees (such as Paul, who was a Pharisee trained by the great rabbi Gamaliel), or that Pharisaic Judaism is considered the ancestor of rabbinic Judaism and what has become normative, mainstream Judaism today. As we enter into this reading, the most sustained and vitriolic attack against scribes and Pharisees in the Gospels, how might we expand our minds and hearts to be shocked by Jesus's words, as if they were spoken to those whom we consider to be the most religious, the most devout, the holiest people *now*? How might Jesus be discomforting *us*? In referring to the "chair of Moses," Jesus acknowledges the authority of the religious leaders and their deep knowledge of Torah. Jesus issues a surprising directive to "do and observe all things" they say but, ironically, not to follow what they do. Jews traditionally look upon Torah as a blessing, not as a "heavy burden." Phylacteries are small boxes containing passages from the Bible worn on the forehead and arm during prayer; they are not meant to impress but to serve as physical reminders to internalize the commandments. "Fringes" (Hebrew *tzitzit*) are similarly worn as reminders of the commandments.

Ponder

Our readings emphasize the unity of all people under God. As Malachi asks, "Has not the one God created us?" And as Jesus reiterates, "You have but one teacher . . . one Father . . . one master," "and you are all brothers [and sisters]." Imagine how different our world would be if we internalized and acted upon this key biblical message: we are all equal under the one God, who unites us all. This is the gospel, or "good news." Yet when our reverence for God becomes warped into self-reverence, we begin to place ourselves at the center rather than God, which ruptures this sense of unity. The way to guard against the pull toward self-centeredness is to return our attention to God through consistent prayer, service, and other tangible, daily reminders. What are your tangible, daily reminders of this good news?

True service comes from a deep and intimate sense of the one God who made us. The responsorial psalm describes this intimate sense as a soul that is "stilled" and "weaned" rather than "proud" and "haughty." Paul's pastoral service is an example of this humble, intimate sense of God that overflows into care for others. His commitment to the community at Thessalonica is grounded in the gospel message, which frees him and his pastoral team to care for others as their "very selves." Our readings this week invite us to ponder how we, too, ground ourselves in the good news of God, which leads us to love and serve each other freely, humbly, and with gratitude for the one God who made us and loves us.

Thirty-Second Sunday
in Ordinary Time

FIRST READING   WISDOM 6:12-16

Resplendent and unfading is wisdom,
   and she is readily perceived by those who love her,
   and found by those who seek her.
She hastens to make herself known in anticipation of their desire;
   whoever watches for her at dawn shall not be disappointed,
   for he shall find her sitting by his gate.
For taking thought of wisdom is the perfection of prudence,
   and whoever for her sake keeps vigil
   shall quickly be free from care;
because she makes her own rounds, seeking those worthy of her,
   and graciously appears to them in the ways,
   and meets them with all solicitude.

For information on the book of Wisdom, see the Sixteenth Sunday in Ordinary Time. According to the Wisdom tradition of ancient Israel, wisdom is intimately connected to God and draws one closer to God. To seek wisdom is to seek God, and to desire wisdom is to desire God. This form of "wisdom" is not intellectual wisdom but rather wisdom of God and God's commandments. In the Hebrew Bible and in later Jewish literature, Wisdom is personified as a woman. Over time, she comes to be equated with the Torah itself. In the above reading, she is "[r]esplendent" (Greek *lampros*), or bright and radiant like the sun and stars. To be "readily perceived" (Greek *theōreō*) means that she is easily contemplated, and this contemplation or "taking thought" of her leads to perfect understanding or "perfection of prudence." To follow her teachings is to channel one's desire and follow the right path that leads to God and life. In contrast, following other forms of worldly desire leads one down the path to death. Wisdom is easily found by those who pursue her, for she also pursues them. The final word, "solicitude" (Greek *epinoia*), means "thought" or "intent" (in other words, Wisdom meets them with "full intention" or "every thought").

RESPONSORIAL PSALM   PSALM 63:2, 3-4, 5-6, 7-8

My soul is thirsting for you, O Lord my God.

SECOND READING   1 THESSALONIANS 4:13-18 [OR 4:13-14]

We do not want you to be unaware, brothers and sisters,
    about those who have fallen asleep,
    so that you may not grieve like the rest, who have no hope.
For if we believe that Jesus died and rose,
    so too will God, through Jesus,
    bring with him those who have fallen asleep.
Indeed, we tell you this, on the word of the Lord,
    that we who are alive,
    who are left until the coming of the Lord,
    will surely not precede those who have fallen asleep.
For the Lord himself, with a word of command,
    with the voice of an archangel and with the trumpet of God,
    will come down from heaven,
    and the dead in Christ will rise first.
Then we who are alive, who are left,
    will be caught up together with them in the clouds
    to meet the Lord in the air.
Thus we shall always be with the Lord.
Therefore, console one another with these words.

Toward the conclusion of his letter, Paul encourages the Thessalonians by describing Christ's imminent return and the fate of all believers, beginning with those who have already died ("fallen asleep"). He states that the dead will rise to new life when Christ returns (see also his discussion in 1 Cor 15:12-22). The imagery of clouds, angels, trumpets, and the thief in the night draws from themes found throughout the Hebrew Bible (e.g., Isa 27:13; Zeph 1:16). For Paul and the early disciples, Christ's return is imminent and is expected to happen before their generation dies. The expression "caught up . . . in the air" is the basis for belief today among some Christians in what is called the "Rapture" or "Assumption" of all believers into heaven when Christ returns. Paul's goal is to comfort and reassure his audience that the living and the dead will rise together to be with Christ.

GOSPEL   MATTHEW 25:1-13

Jesus told his disciples this parable:
  "The kingdom of heaven will be like ten virgins
  who took their lamps and went out to meet the bridegroom.
Five of them were foolish and five were wise.
The foolish ones, when taking their lamps,
  brought no oil with them,
  but the wise brought flasks of oil with their lamps.
Since the bridegroom was long delayed,
  they all became drowsy and fell asleep.
At midnight, there was a cry,
  'Behold, the bridegroom! Come out to meet him!'
Then all those virgins got up and trimmed their lamps.
The foolish ones said to the wise,
  'Give us some of your oil,
  for our lamps are going out.'
But the wise ones replied,
  'No, for there may not be enough for us and you.
Go instead to the merchants and buy some for yourselves.'
While they went off to buy it,
  the bridegroom came
  and those who were ready went into the wedding feast
    with him.
Then the door was locked.
Afterwards the other virgins came and said,
  'Lord, Lord, open the door for us!'
But he said in reply,
  'Amen, I say to you, I do not know you.'
Therefore, stay awake,
  for you know neither the day nor the hour."

At the beginning and end of each liturgical season, we turn to readings focused on the return of Christ (or the *Parousia,* a Greek term meaning "arrival," "visit," or "presence"). Our reading is the first of three parables in Matthew 25 with this focus (we'll read the second parable next Sunday). In this parable, heaven and Christ's return are likened to a marriage celebration in which Jesus is the bridegroom. The term "virgins" (Greek *parthenoi*) also translates as "bridesmaids"; their task is to escort the bridegroom to the bride's house, then escort both to the wedding. "Lamps" in the ancient world were made from rags that were wrapped around the end of a pole and soaked in olive oil. Throughout the Bible, oil, light, and lamps are metaphors for God's word or teachings, wisdom, and good deeds (e.g., Ps 119:105; Prov 6:23; Matt 5:14-16). These are qualities to be cultivated individually; one cannot share them like physical possessions. To "trim" a lamp means to trim off the charred cloth and add more oil. Elsewhere, Matthew describes the wise as those who listen to and act upon Jesus's word, while the foolish listen but fail to act (7:24-27). This is not the first time that Matthew exhorts believers to "stay awake"; for the early followers of Jesus, the Second Coming could happen at any moment (see also Matt 24:42 as well as our second reading from 1 Thess). For Matthew's community (80s CE), this coming has taken longer than expected (the "bridegroom" has been "long delayed"). Parables often have a single, simple focus. Ours is preparation and alertness for the coming of Christ.

Ponder

The reading from Wisdom and our responsorial psalm are saturated with longing for God. According to ancient tradition, true wisdom is a manifestation of God and is connected to God. Notice the words used to describe those who long for this divine Wisdom: they "love," "seek," and "[keep] vigil" for her; they "desire" and "[watch] for her." Similarly, the psalmist experiences longing for God as thirst and physical pining. In our readings, the promise is that Wisdom—the embodiment of the path that leads to God—also longs for us. So long as we seek her, she will seek us and guide us into all understanding, grounding us in a life of faith, hope, and love. Take time this week to contemplate these readings, allowing yourself to open up to and experience this deep and holy desire for God and knowledge of God.

Do we have oil in our lamps? This is the question Matthew invites us to ponder. As we near the end of the liturgical year, our readings turn to the promise of Christ's return. This promise is not a cause for fear but for hope, as we hear in 1 Thessalonians. To be "prepared" for this return does not mean to be *fully* prepared, meaning to reach some state of spiritual perfection. Preparation means only to desire Christ, or at least to *desire* to desire Christ. It is this desire that puts us on the right path, and on this path, we do the best we can in our thoughts, words, and actions, one step at a time. The practice of doing our best gives us oil for the journey, and the desire for God gives us Wisdom as our gentle and persistent guide. If we are doing our best, one small step at a time, then God will take our hand and do the rest.

Thirty-Third Sunday in Ordinary Time

FIRST READING   PROVERBS 31:10-13, 19-20, 30-31

When one finds a worthy wife,[1]
   her value is far beyond pearls.
Her husband, entrusting his heart to her,
   has an unfailing prize.
She brings him good, and not evil,
   all the days of her life.
She obtains wool and flax
   and works with loving hands.
She puts her hands to the distaff,
   and her fingers ply the spindle.
She reaches out her hands to the poor,
   and extends her arms to the needy.
Charm is deceptive and beauty fleeting;
   the woman who fears the LORD is to be praised.
Give her a reward for her labors,
   and let her works praise her at the city gates.

Like last week's reading from the book of Wisdom, this reading from Proverbs is part of the Wisdom tradition of Israel. Wisdom sayings comprise the majority of the book of Proverbs, while the first nine chapters introduce the book with instructions from a parent to a young man on virtuous living. These chapters describe two clear paths: the path to God (the path of life) and the path to death. Both paths are characterized by women: the path of life is Lady Wisdom and one's own wife, while the path of death is the wife of another man (literally the "strange" or "foreign woman"; see Prov 2:16). The nar-

---

1. Alternative translations of the phrase "worthy wife" (Hebrew *'ešet*, "wife" or "woman," and *ḥayil*, "strength" or "wealth") include "capable wife" (NRSV; JPS), "virtuous woman" (KJV), and "valiant woman" (Douay-Rheims). Ruth is also depicted as a "worthy woman" in Ruth 3:11 (NABRE). When the word *ḥayil* is associated with a man, it has traditionally been translated as wealth, substance, or power (e.g., Boaz in Ruth 2:1) or physical strength (e.g., Jephthah in Judg 11:1). Searching for contemporary colloquial language, my friend Keith Maczkiewicz, SJ, translated the phrase as "fierce woman" for students at the College of the Holy Cross.

rator or parent exhorts the young man to channel his desire toward the path of life. We return to these characterizations at the end of the book with this final description of the worthy wife (literally "wife [or woman] of strength") from the perspective of her husband and children. She acts in accord with "fear" (awe/reverence) of God and becomes the human embodiment of Lady Wisdom. We miss key verses (vv. 14-18, 21-29) that detail the woman's business expertise outside the home and describe her husband and children praising her excellent work and resourcefulness.

RESPONSORIAL PSALM   PSALM 128:1-2, 3, 4-5

Blessed are those who fear the Lord.

SECOND READING   1 THESSALONIANS 5:1-6

Concerning times and seasons, brothers and sisters,
    you have no need for anything to be written to you.
For you yourselves know very well that the day of the Lord
        will come
    like a thief at night.
When people are saying, "Peace and security,"
    then sudden disaster comes upon them,
    like labor pains upon a pregnant woman,
    and they will not escape.

But you, brothers and sisters, are not in darkness,
    for that day to overtake you like a thief.
For all of you are children of the light
    and children of the day.
We are not of the night or of darkness.
Therefore, let us not sleep as the rest do,
    but let us stay alert and sober.

Continuing from last week's text about the return of Christ, Paul reminds the community to "stay alert and sober" as one would during the day, expecting Christ to return at any moment. The "day of the Lord" is a common expression in prophetic writing, where it refers to divine action that includes vindication of the oppressed, the reestablishment of Israel, and God's glory (e.g., Isa 13:6-9; Ezek 30:3; Amos 5:18-20). "Peace and security" likely refer to the Roman Empire and suggest that it will eventually come to "disaster." Light and darkness commonly represent good and evil in early Judaism, as demonstrated by the Dead Sea Scrolls and in New Testament texts such as the Gospel of John. Romans 13:11-13 contains a similar call to stay awake and "put on the armor of light."

GOSPEL   MATTHEW 25:14-30 [OR 25:14-15, 19-21]

Jesus told his disciples this parable:
   "A man going on a journey
   called in his servants and entrusted his possessions to them.
To one he gave five talents;[2] to another, two; to a third, one—
   to each according to his ability.
Then he went away.
Immediately the one who received five talents went and traded
      with them,
   and made another five.
Likewise, the one who received two made another two.
But the man who received one went off and dug a hole in the
      ground
   and buried his master's money.

"After a long time
   the master of those servants came back
   and settled accounts with them.
The one who had received five talents came forward
   bringing the additional five.
He said, 'Master, you gave me five talents.
See, I have made five more.'
His master said to him, 'Well done, my good and faithful servant.
Since you were faithful in small matters,
   I will give you great responsibilities.
Come, share your master's joy.'

2. A talent (Greek *talenton*) was a monetary unit worth more than fifteen years' wages for a laborer.

Then the one who had received two talents also came forward
   and said,
 'Master, you gave me two talents.
See, I have made two more.'
His master said to him, 'Well done, my good and faithful servant.
Since you were faithful in small matters,
   I will give you great responsibilities.
Come, share your master's joy.'
Then the one who had received the one talent came forward
   and said,
 'Master, I knew you were a demanding person,
 harvesting where you did not plant
 and gathering where you did not scatter;
   so out of fear I went off and buried your talent in the ground.
Here it is back.'
His master said to him in reply, 'You wicked, lazy servant!
So you knew that I harvest where I did not plant
   and gather where I did not scatter?
Should you not then have put my money in the bank
   so that I could have got it back with interest on my return?
Now then! Take the talent from him and give it to the one
      with ten.
For to everyone who has,
   more will be given and he will grow rich;
   but from the one who has not,
   even what he has will be taken away.
And throw this useless servant into the darkness outside,
   where there will be wailing and grinding of teeth.'"

This is no simple parable. In the context of Matthew 25, it is the
second of three parables about the Second Coming (for an alternative context, see Luke 19:11-27). Traditionally, the parable is read
allegorically. The man or master (Christ) "entrust[s] his possessions"
to his servants, leaving them a sum of money beyond imagining (the
remarkable gift of God's grace, the gospel message, or the kingdom
of God). When he returns (the Second Coming), the master holds
the servants accountable for their actions while he was gone. In our
modern, capitalistic context, the actions of the first two servants
make complete sense. However, in an ancient, communal context

that frowns upon excessive personal savings (e.g., the story of Ananias and Sapphira in Acts 5:1-11), the actions of the third servant are a normal, good way to safeguard money (as a comparison, see the parable of the buried treasure in Matt 13:44). Therefore, some read this parable nontraditionally as making a literal point about money and economic growth: the third servant is ultimately in the right, while the first two servants are aiding a system that helps the rich get richer. In this interpretation, the master is not Christ but one who abuses power, "harvesting" where he does not "plant" and "gathering" where he does not "scatter." In a series of parables about the end times, however, one cannot entirely disregard the allegorical reading, which makes a powerful point not about economic growth but about faith that is productive and active. The first two servants receive the master's "money" and transform it into more. The third servant wraps up the gift and hoards or preserves it out of fear of the master. The "wailing and grinding of teeth" is an exaggerated expression commonly employed by Matthew. The point of the parable is that God's gifts are treasures not to hoard but to use toward productive, transformative ends.

Ponder

"Fear" (Hebrew *yārē'*) runs through our readings, but with very different meanings. In the ancient world, fear of God means awe and reverence. Reverence motivates the woman in Proverbs to live selflessly and resourcefully. Our psalmist similarly describes the blessings that come from "fear" or a life of reverence. Reverence may also underlie the active attention and alertness described in 1 Thessalonians. Yet the "fear" that motivates the third servant in the Gospel is totally different. His is not reverence and awe but a paralyzing, preservationist fear (that ultimately leads him to be thrown "into the darkness"!). Our readings call us to examine the motivations that underpin our actions. To what extent are they rooted in self-preservation that paralyzes us versus reverence that opens us to live meaningful lives?

Grace and belief are treasures. The question, according to Matthew, is what we choose to do with these treasures. We might ask a similar question about the church and its traditions. Do we take a preservationist stance, metaphorically burying the faith in order to hold on to what we believe is its essential "core"? Or do we release it into the world, trusting both the strength of this core and its malleability to transform and be transformed with the times? Jesus is continually beckoning us toward the second path, telling us to be not afraid, to have a firm foot in God's kingdom while embracing this world, and to use God's gifts for productive ends that transform our lives and our communities.

Our Lord Jesus Christ, King of the Universe

Thus says the Lord GOD:
  I myself will look after and tend my sheep.
As a shepherd tends his flock
  when he finds himself among his scattered sheep,
  so will I tend my sheep.
I will rescue them from every place where they were scattered
  when it was cloudy and dark.
I myself will pasture my sheep;
  I myself will give them rest, says the Lord GOD.
The lost I will seek out,
  the strayed I will bring back,
  the injured I will bind up,
  the sick I will heal,
  but the sleek and the strong I will destroy,
  shepherding them rightly.

As for you, my sheep, says the Lord GOD,
  I will judge between one sheep and another,
  between rams and goats.

Set within the context of the Babylonian exile (ca. 586–536 BCE), our reading draws from an extended indictment of the rulers of Judah in Ezekiel 34. Using the common ancient Middle Eastern metaphor of sheep (the people) and their shepherds (rulers), the prophet describes Judah's kings as bad shepherds who are responsible for the scattering (exile) of their sheep, the people of Judah. God as the Good Shepherd is the ultimate contrast to human leadership (for more on the metaphor of God as a shepherd, see, e.g., Isa 40:11; Jer 31:10; our responsorial psalm). God promises to gather all the dispersed or exiled flock and bring them home to Judah. Halfway through our reading, the metaphor shifts from God's judgment of the rulers (shepherds) to the people (sheep, rams, goats). God does not judge between sheep versus goats (as in our Gospel passage) but between each individual animal. God will "destroy" the greedy animals (the "sleek and the strong") while caring for the lost, injured, and sick animals.

RESPONSORIAL PSALM   PSALM 23:1-2, 2-3, 5-6

The Lord is my shepherd; there is nothing I shall want.

SECOND READING   1 CORINTHIANS 15:20-26, 28

Brothers and sisters:
Christ has been raised from the dead,
    the firstfruits of those who have fallen asleep.
For since death came through man,
    the resurrection of the dead came also through man.
For just as in Adam all die,
    so too in Christ shall all be brought to life,
    but each one in proper order:
    Christ the firstfruits;
    then, at his coming, those who belong to Christ;
    then comes the end,
    when he hands over the kingdom to his God and Father,
    when he has destroyed every sovereignty
    and every authority and power.
For he must reign until he has put all his enemies under his feet.
The last enemy to be destroyed is death.
When everything is subjected to him,
    then the Son himself will also be subjected
    to the one who subjected everything to him,
    so that God may be all in all.

First Corinthians 15 is Paul's carefully reasoned argument for the resurrection of the dead. Some members of the Corinthian community were skeptical of this theological claim, in particular the resurrection of the body (see Acts 17:32 for similar skepticism or "scoffing"). A more common Greco-Roman belief was the immortality of the soul and its separation from the body in death. Paul therefore draws from these philosophical proofs regarding the soul's immortality to make a similar claim about physical resurrection. In our reading, Paul describes a particular order to the resurrection in the end times. The "firstfruits" is an agricultural expression that describes the coming harvest; in this case, Christ's resurrection signals the resurrection of all believers. In early Judaism, the coming messiah was understood to be an antitype to Adam (see also Rom 5:14-15). Just as Adam introduced mortality or death, so the messiah will introduce fullness of life. Another early Jewish concept, which comes in part from the Hebrew Bible (e.g., Isa 24:21-22), is that the messiah will destroy all earthly forces ("every sovereignty and every authority and power"; 1 Cor 15:24) and demonic forces ("enemies"; 15:25). The messiah's ultimate victory will be over death itself, after which God will assume total sovereignty.

GOSPEL   MATTHEW 25:31-46

Jesus said to his disciples:
  "When the Son of Man comes in his glory,
  and all the angels with him,
  he will sit upon his glorious throne,
  and all the nations will be assembled before him.
And he will separate them one from another,
  as a shepherd separates the sheep from the goats.
He will place the sheep on his right and the goats on his left.
Then the king will say to those on his right,
  'Come, you who are blessed by my Father.
Inherit the kingdom prepared for you from the foundation of
      the world.
For I was hungry and you gave me food,
  I was thirsty and you gave me drink,
  a stranger and you welcomed me,
  naked and you clothed me,
  ill and you cared for me,
  in prison and you visited me.'
Then the righteous will answer him and say,
  'Lord, when did we see you hungry and feed you,
  or thirsty and give you drink?
When did we see you a stranger and welcome you,
  or naked and clothe you?
When did we see you ill or in prison, and visit you?'

And the king will say to them in reply,
  'Amen, I say to you, whatever you did
  for one of the least brothers of mine, you did for me.'
Then he will say to those on his left,
  'Depart from me, you accursed,
  into the eternal fire prepared for the devil and his angels.
For I was hungry and you gave me no food,
  I was thirsty and you gave me no drink,
  a stranger and you gave me no welcome,
  naked and you gave me no clothing,
  ill and in prison, and you did not care for me.'
Then they will answer and say,
  'Lord, when did we see you hungry or thirsty
  or a stranger or naked or ill or in prison,
  and not minister to your needs?'
He will answer them, 'Amen, I say to you,
  what you did not do for one of these least ones,
  you did not do for me.'
And these will go off to eternal punishment,
  but the righteous to eternal life."

We reach the last of our three parables on Christ's return in Matthew 25, a fitting conclusion to the liturgical year. The separation of the "sheep from the goats" draws in part from our first reading, in which God judges between all animals, yet here Jesus judges between all peoples (not just the Jews). The sheep are destined for "eternal life," while the goats are destined for "eternal punishment." It's unclear why goats are designated as "bad," as they provide milk, need little land for grazing, and have good dispositions (they're also clean and cute!). Some scholars propose that the designation has to do with the fabric these animals produce: in the ancient world, sheep wool was a sign of prosperity (allegorically, prosperity equals eternal life), while goat hair was used for sackcloth (a form of clothing worn in times of mourning). At any rate, the parable is not meant to be a literal claim about how ancient people viewed all goats versus sheep. Instead, the parable is meant to shock in how it completely upends human notions of power. It also upends religious claims on who is "Christian" and what "belief" truly means. According to Matthew, belief is not a statement (the "goats" certainly profess belief in Jesus!)

but an action. In our actions, how we treat the "least ones" becomes a direct reflection of our belief in Jesus.

Ponder

Our readings present us with the ultimate paradox about God. On the one hand, God is a gentle and loving shepherd who guides each one of us, who disdains human greed, and who is attentive to the "strayed," "injured," and "sick" (Ezekiel). Therefore, our belief in God manifests in how well we care for the least among us (Matthew). Our readings are clear that in the end, when Christ "hands over the kingdom to his God and Father" (1 Corinthians), we will be held accountable for how we are acting *now* and the extent to which our lives mirror God's fierce commitment to those on the margins. Together, our readings and this feast day urge us to consider the long view. How do our actions and the choices we make demonstrate where our true loyalties lie and in what, or in whom, we really believe?

Today we end the liturgical year and move toward Advent, in preparation for Christmas, or Christ-with-us. Moving from one season to another, one liturgical year to the next, our Gospel is a fitting call to ponder how well we have lived this past year, not only in anticipation of Christ coming, but of Christ always with us. How have we "seen" Christ in our daily lives and in the people around us, especially those who often go unseen? How have we served them? Reflecting on the Gospel, John Shea once envisioned asking the "sheep" in God's kingdom how they got there, and they said, "We just cared for every person we met, immediately, without calculation." The sheep then added, "It was no big deal," an indication of how habitual, how natural, this attitude is in the kingdom of God.[1] How well have you prepared for God's kingdom?

---

1. Shea, *Spiritual Wisdom of the Gospels*, 329.